Lost to the Sea

Also by Lisa Woollett

Rag and Bone: A History of What We've Thrown Away

Sea Journal

Sea and Shore Cornwall: Common and Curious Findings

FOR CHILDREN

Treasure from the Sea

Lost to the Sea

A Journey Round the Edges of Britain and Ireland

LISA WOOLLETT

JOHN MURRAY

First published in Great Britain in 2024 by John Murray (Publishers)

1

Maps drawn by Tracy Watts

Extract from 'Casualty' from *Opened Ground* by Seamus Heaney reproduced by kind permission of Faber & Faber Ltd.

Extract from 'Lyonesse' from *Collected Poems* by Sylvia Plath reproduced by kind permission of Faber & Faber Ltd.

A CIP catalogue record for this title is available from the British Library

Hardback ISBN 9781529373653
ebook ISBN 9781529373677

Typeset in Bembo MT by Hewer Text UK Ltd, Edinburgh
Printed and bound in Great Britain by Clays Ltd, Elcograf S.p.A.

John Murray policy is to use papers that are natural, renewable and recyclable products and made from wood grown in sustainable forests. The logging and manufacturing processes are expected to conform to the environmental regulations of the country of origin.

Carmelite House
50 Victoria Embankment
London EC4Y 0DZ

www.johnmurraypress.co.uk

John Murray Press, part of Hodder & Stoughton Limited
An Hachette UK company

For Saan

and in memory of Alfie

Contents

There rolls the deep where grew the tree

Alfred Lord Tennyson, 'In Memoriam'

Barony of Culbin
Sands of Forvie
Medieval Forvie
SCOTLAND
Waddum Thorpe
Kilgrimol
Singleton
Thorpe
Hyde
Cleeton
Rungholt
Frisia
Old Kilnsea
Ravenser Odd
Blackpool
Llys Helig
Spurn Head
Doggerland
Kilstifeen
Eccles
Mutton Island
IRELAND
Happisburg
Isle of
Fitha
Borth
ENGLAND
Dunwich
WALES
Old Dunwich
Cantre'r
Gwaelod
Isle of Sheppey
Kenfig
Isle of Lomea
Langarroc
Isle of Wight
Isles of Scilly
Hallsands
Bouldnor
Cliff
Lyonesse
Old
Hallsands
Kêr Ys
Brittany
Places visted
Places lost to the sea
and drifting sand,
real and in legend

Goodwin Sands, legendary site of the Isle of Lomea

Introduction

Isle of Lomea

Isle of Sheppey, Kent

In the stillness a faint mist hung over the cliff. Rising from damp London clay, it left each crumbling ridge more spectral than the last. In the past, their profiles have suggested beasts or faces: a brow, perhaps, or the slope of a nose. Yet the speed of erosion here means the likeness can be fleeting. For some time, one of the more striking features was known as the 'Side of Beef', although little remains today. Above it now, thin, leafless trees crowded close to the edge, with one leaning out partway down, its branches flung like the arms of someone falling.

Once again, I was back below the cliffs where I grew up. I'd set out early, with the scattered light casting the familiar stranger than usual. The only sound was a gentle shuffling of pebbles at the water's edge. It was good to be back. I left the Isle of Sheppey at the age of nineteen, but again and again I've been drawn back to this same stretch of coast: in reality, in my work and in my sleep. In dreams, it never looks as it does in life. Instead, it appears in wildly different guises. There might be sandflats or steep, craggy cliffs, grassy hilltops, deep mud or smooth standing stones in the sea. Yet in the dream, I always know I am here.

Through the last century, the island's north-facing cliffs have retreated by an average of some five feet a year. Yet that rate isn't steady. Sometimes, after decades with barely any change, acres of land can be lost at once. Geologists know this, hauntingly, as a 'deep failure'; following one here, a farmer found nine of his sheep grazing unhurt on half an acre of pasture a hundred feet below the cliff-top. Between here and Warden some four miles east, the losses have included farms and houses, two pubs – although one ended its days as a post office – and Warden Church. This pre-sixteenth-century church, with its tower rebuilt using stones from the old London Bridge, was the source of the stories I heard as a child.

'On a still night,' my nan would say, 'if you stand out on the cliffs you can hear church bells toll beneath the sea.' It was a tradition passed down the generations. More than a century and a half ago, the church stood at the edge of the cliff, with records claiming that a century earlier it lay a quarter of a mile inland. Already damaged by storms and the shifting ground, the building gradually became derelict, with locals eventually taking the pews and the pulpit for firewood. By 1887 the ruin was demolished, with the foundations and graveyard left to go over the edge. Today, given the speed of erosion, any remains lie some distance offshore.

Passing what remained of the Side of Beef, I was now below Royal Oak Point. No longer a point, it takes its name from a pub that once stood at the top of the cliff. Back in the 1860s this had 'extensive pleasure gardens' on its seaward side. In the 1940s and early '50s my nan played piano there, but by then the gardens had gone, leaving the pub dangerously close to the edge. Later that decade it closed down, and by the time we went there as children in the 1970s it was known as The Pub With No Beer. The building was derelict, with the ruined piano still in the bar and the gents already partway to the beach. High above the shore in empty air were once its beer gardens, along with an orchard (that as a boy my dad was chased from by a shotgun-wielding farmer for scrumping). Today, skeletal trees stood out in the shallows, draped with seaweed and fishing line.

As I walked, the ebb tide slid from the shore like silk. Here and there, dark shapes had begun to break the surface. At first no more than glimpses of solidity, they were soon laid bare. Along with fifty-million-year-old fossils that erode from the clay, human traces also wash from the toe of the cliff and are left stranded on shore. Before me now were several sea-worn kerbstones, a drain hole and a few concrete steps.

This sense of tidal concealment and revelation has intrigued me for decades. It began in childhood when we combed the shingle below our house for sharks' teeth, or headed out beyond the sandbanks on low spring tides to search for old bottles. Since leaving the island, I'd always been drawn to eroding coasts. Walking their shores, especially after storms, I have no idea what I might find – or what clues it might offer to the near or distant past. For this book, I eventually settled on ten locations at the edges of England, Ireland, Scotland and Wales. At each of the places I visit, at some point in history or prehistory, human settlements have been lost to the sea. In many, the greatest losses came with violent gales and storm surges. And today, similar scouring storms can reveal traces of those earlier losses: eroding from cliffs, entombed on the foreshore, uncovered in the dunes by shifting sands.

Some places proved harder to reach than others, with many of the natural or man-made remains only occasionally exposed. Sometimes I waited months for the appropriate weather, season or sea conditions: for light winds or a scouring winter storm, often a low spring tide. Given many alternatives, I chose a variety of coastal landscapes. They ranged from sheer chalk and bare granite cliffs to mudflats, dunes and the odd concrete promenade. Over two years, I visited exposed Atlantic islands and fragile shifting spits, wide-open sandflats, submerged forests and the soft cliffs of the crumbling east coast. At these tidal thresholds between land and sea, I picked up peaty chunks of drowned Doggerland, and off the Welsh coast saw ancient oaks still rooted in the forest floor. Off other coasts lay submerged Mesolithic hearths, Iron Age field walls, carved stone from medieval church towers.

With erosion ongoing, many of these landscapes also revealed more recent layers of loss. In places this lent an air of transience reminiscent of cliff-top Sheppey, and a very literal sense of reaching the end of the road. Walking above the island's fast-eroding cliffs in the past, many of the roads remained unmade (as they do today). There were light-construction bungalows, lean-tos and mobile homes, the remains of The Song of the Sea caravan park: a narrow strip of cliff-top field where brambles and nettles choked the concrete of abandoned hardstandings. On other coasts I would find relics of fallen campsites, a retreating amusement park, even a nudist camp partway down a landslide.

Often, a rich tradition of stories had grown up at these eroding edges. From folktales to myths and legends, they told of fine cities, rolling fields and palaces lost beneath the waves; islands shrouded in a magical mist; the tolling of drowned church bells (it was with some disappointment that I first learned how common my nan's tradition was, not just in Britain but across northern Europe). At the edges of Britain and Ireland, entire towns, villages and islands were said to have been lost to great storms and tidal waves, floods and rages of sand. They were catastrophes raised by curses, witchcraft or the Devil. Or they were vengeance from God, for sins ranging from neglected duties to drunkenness and promiscuity.

Despite growing up on the island, it was only after casting my net for stories that I learned of a legendary 'lost Isle of Sheppey'. This was the Isle of Lomea, which tradition claims lies several miles off the Kent coast beneath the notoriously treacherous Goodwin Sands. In *A Perambulation of Kent* (1576), the antiquarian William Lambarde described how in the eleventh century, following 'a soddaine and mightie inundation of the Sea', the island was 'violently overwhelmed' with sand. Other sixteenth-century accounts describe Lomea as fertile and low-lying – 'very fruitful and abounding in pasture' – until it 'sonke sodainly into the Sea'.

There are a number of versions of the legend, with the island said to have once been owned by the Anglo-Saxon Earl Godwin. In some, its loss is blamed on the Earl, with Lomea submerged as vengeance from God for his disloyalty and deceit. Sometimes Earl Godwin is 'a vacillating believer' who breaks a vow to the Blessed Virgin; alternatively, his betrayal leads to the death of the son of Ethelred the Unready. In other versions, the island is lost when its sea walls are neglected, with the funds needed to rebuild them – sometimes the stones themselves – diverted to build a steeple at Tenterden Church.

Through the centuries, the Isle of Lomea has appeared in everything from folktales and antiquarian local histories to sermons and tall tales at the pub. By the eighteenth century, John Lewis, 'Vicar of Mynstre, and Minister of Mergate', knew a landlord in Broadstairs who claimed his 'Oaken Shuffleboard . . . was made from a Tree that grew on this Island, which is now Sand'.

Lomea was first likened to Sheppey in the nineteenth century. Until then, there was no evidence of the island's existence, and no mention of it in Domesday or other medieval records. Yet when leading geologist Charles Lyell surveyed the Goodwin Sands in 1817 as a potential site for a lighthouse, he described finding London clay fifteen feet beneath the sand. This clay, he proposed, could be the eroded remains of an island similar to the Isle of Sheppey, which may well have flooded within historical memory. For more than a century, his findings were considered evidence of the Isle of Lomea's existence. Later surveys, though, have found only chalk beneath the sands (the eroded remains of a land bridge that in prehistory connected Britain to continental Europe). Today, the general consensus among geologists is that the Isle of Lomea probably never existed.

Yet the storm said to have claimed it does appear to have taken place, on 11 November 1099. Its impact was recorded in the *Anglo-Saxon Chronicle*, with Cornwall's legendary Lyonesse often said to have been lost that same night. 'On the festival of St Martin', wrote the scribe in elegant Old English, 'the sea flood sprung up to such a height and did so much harm as no man remembered before'. Other records suggest that in Britain and the Netherlands, some 100,000 people may have lost their lives, many as floodwaters surged up the Thames.

Following violent storms, people have long sought cause for such destruction and loss of life. In 1703, six centuries after the legendary loss of Lomea, another great storm saw more than a thousand sailors drown when their ships were wrecked on the Goodwin Sands. In the aftermath, most Britons had little doubt that the storm was punishment from God: 'the dreadest and most universal judgment that ever almighty power thought fit to bring upon this part of the world'. The government at the time declared that the catastrophe 'loudly calls for the deepest and most solemn humiliation of our people'. As atonement, and in recognition of the 'crying sins of this nation', a National Day of Fasting was announced. Archbishops wrote prayers for the occasion, and throughout Britain sermons addressed 'God's Empire over the Winds'.

Unsurprisingly, there was some disagreement over the nature of the transgressions that might provoke such wrath. Some, including Daniel Defoe, considered the storm punishment for Protestant Britain's poor performance against the Catholic armies of France and Spain. Others blamed more wide-ranging sins, everything from debauchery, sloth and 'idolatrous paganism' to foppery and the rising popularity of theatre and science. 'If any of you are stain'd with scandalous Crimes,' thundered Reverend Thomas Bradbury from his pulpit on the day of the fast, 'take your last farewell of 'em. The Winds are gather'd into His Fists.' The message was clear. To prevent anything like this from happening again, everyone must observe the Church's moral code. Like the loss of the Isle of Lomea, the Great Storm of 1703 would feature in sermons for centuries to come.

In many places around the British coast – as across the world – major submergences date back to prehistoric times, in particular the Mesolithic with its fast-rising seas. And recent research from other countries suggests some stories – including flood myths – may be an extraordinary survival of folk memory over thousands of years. So might our own flood stories have roots in actual inundations? At submerged British sites where the science and storytelling converge, this opens up the fascinating if murky territory of geomythology.

In recent decades, research into submerged landscapes has benefitted from advances in science and technology, from genetics and palaeobiology to sonar and digital modelling. Together, the findings allow researchers to read a scientific story archived in the sediments of the drowned landscapes themselves. While submerged sites pose many challenges, one benefit is how the waterlogged peats and anaerobic silts can preserve fragile organic traces and materials. Wonderfully, geneticists can now analyse DNA shed into the soil and water of those prehistoric landscapes, to find molecular traces of particular species of mammal, insect and bird, flowers, grasses and trees. In these modern, more secular attempts to understand how and when a landscape drowned, species of plankton can reveal changing salinity, or a grain of sand the last time it was exposed to sunlight. As well as dating floods, laboratory analysis can also reveal whether marine incursions were gradual or catastrophic, or caused by storms or tsunamis. Increasingly, this allows researchers to reconstruct those drowning landscapes, bringing them – almost – to life.

That morning, though, as I stood beneath the island's shrouded cliffs – with the ebb tide revealing everything from fossil palm fruits to sea-worn brick walls – I had no idea what lay ahead. Here, the dead trees were now ankle-deep in the sea. But I didn't know what I would find – or not – on other coasts, or what traces of lost lives and landscapes still lay beneath the waves and sand. I was yet to learn how doggedly people had clung on at the edges of this fragmented kingdom through the centuries, in the face of relentless erosion and storm-lashed seas. Yet the strangeness of this childhood shore had long suggested those places would be steeped in story.

Failed sea defences, Happisburgh

I

Doggerland

Happisburgh, Norfolk

I drove out to the Norfolk coast at the end of a spring Bank Holiday, with everyone headed in the opposite direction. My first glimpse of Happisburgh (pronounced Hazeborough) was a mown field edged with saplings: the relocated caravan site where I'd booked a pitch for several nights. Now, after a prolonged planning battle, it lay inland on the outskirts of the village, as the old cliff-top site crumbled into the sea. Driving on through a cluster of flint and red-brick houses, I headed first for Beach Road, which I'd read so much about.

Having driven as far as I could, I left the van in a car park designed to be 'rolled back' as the sea advanced, and walked out to the end of Beach Road. Only the last of its houses looked abandoned: a brick bungalow with broken fencing, an empty living room and bushes grown up against windows. Not far beyond its woody hedge, the lane came to an end, at ragged tarmac jutting out over the cliff. Below was just sand and sea. Ahead was a metal barrier and a red 'ROAD CLOSED' sign, where someone had written regularly in black felt pen.

13th Dec 2021 8.
13th Feb 2022 6.6 m
28th Feb 2022 4.35 m
29th March 4.18
20th April 4.00 m

Presumably, this was the distance between the barrier and the end of the road, with the last of the dates twelve days ago. It was hard to tell if any tarmac had been lost since then.

I took out my phone to take a photograph, and minutes later learned something fantastical about Google Maps. On the aerial views of these fast-eroding coastlines, ghost roads sometimes continued out beyond the edge of the land, over beaches and the sea. This was something I'd noticed before, and the ghost of Happisburgh's notorious Beach Road was longer than most. Yet it was only now – as I clicked into Street View – that I understood what the overlaid routes represented. Street View allows a virtual street-level wander, and the realisation came as I navigated to where I stood. On my phone screen, the view was not the truncated tarmac ahead of me now. Instead, the virtual lane still stretched off towards a distant sea, lined with houses I'd seen in news reports – as they were bulldozed or hung out over a cliff. Yet inside Street View, everything was fine. It was still June 2009, when so much of what I knew of Beach Road lay ahead.

It turned out Google's ghost roads were more magical than I'd imagined: a discrepancy in time that allowed streets to live on after they'd been lost to the sea – and me to pass through a portal. On-screen, the June sun still cast shadows on the road ahead, of hedgerows and tall verge grasses, of power cables looping off to distant bungalows. I could almost feel the warmth off the tarmac. While some of the sunlit houses had the look of second homes – drawn curtains, plain lawns, empty flower beds – others were obviously lived in. So I set off down this virtual road, inside technology that invited me to linger, to turn and peer over fences, or wander back and take another look. First, I stopped at a small retirement bungalow, with bird feeders hung among sweet peas and foxgloves. Further along the lane stood the more imposing Cliff House. A pair of Edwardian villas in a row of four, they were built amid rumours that the railway was coming to Happisburgh, which it never did. This was the place I remembered most from the news reports. Zooming in for a closer look, I found faded aubergine paint still peeling from window frames, missing roof tiles and the lawn grown a little wild. Still propped on its side by the bins was a sign saying 'Tea Shop'.

Diana Wrightson, a schoolteacher taking early retirement, had bought the two houses in 1980, and for twenty-six years ran Cliff House as a tea shop and guest house. To begin with, it was forty metres – and a row of bungalows – away from the sea, and she was told it would last a hundred years. But that estimate was revised as Happisburgh's sea defences began to fail. Already, this stretch of coast had a long history of loss. More than a thousand years ago, the village of Happisburgh and its Norman church stood some distance inland. Yet since the mid-nineteenth century a local farmhouse and barn had been lost to erosion, along with the row of bungalows, the old coastguard cottages and lifeboat house, a twelve-acre wheat field that disappeared overnight, and what was once a candle-powered lighthouse. Throughout that century, various attempts were made to buy time. There were wooden breakwaters and a dune embankment, boats sunk offshore by local landowners, and eventually – in 1959 – a three-metre timber and steel revetment that ran parallel to shore.

Over the next two decades, erosion slowed to an average of no more than half a metre a year. But by the 1980s, after Diana had opened her tea shop, Happisburgh's revetments reached the end of their lifespan. Through the 1990s, various schemes were proposed, but rejected as not cost-effective; meanwhile, the old defences were left to deteriorate. By then, a bay had begun to form at the end of Beach Road, with the sea advancing at an alarming seven metres a year.

As a quintessential English tea shop on a coast eroding so fast, Cliff House became a national and international story. In the years before it closed, British, German, Dutch, French and Japanese journalists came to stay with Diana. They described her warm hospitality, her Churchill teacups and lighthouse-shaped biscuits, and said she preferred not to give her age. They described her as calm and resigned, and asked her to pose for photographs drinking tea at the end of her retreating garden. Usually, they also noted the current distance between the tea shop and the cliff: twenty metres, sixteen yards, ten metres.

'She smiles a lot,' wrote one, 'but her eyes are sad.'

'We didn't realise there was a problem until 1999,' Diana told another, 'when we saw the bungalows disappearing. Even then we thought someone would stop it before it got to us.'

Yet in Street View, Cliff House still stood in June sunshine under a china-blue sky. Reaching the end of the virtual lane, where the sandy ground dropped away to the shore, I pivoted to look back at the two seaward bungalows. Built in the 1930s, one had a lean-to conservatory crowded with plants, and at the time was home to Bryony Nierop-Reading and her four cats. Within three years of the photograph, though, she would be the only one left on this stretch of Beach Road. She would refuse the compensation her neighbours accepted, and see all nine of the homes around her demolished. Once the bulldozers left, Bryony stayed on alone in the house she called Felicity: happiness. With surprising speed, grass grew over the footprints of her neighbours' vanished homes. Later, as the edge of the cliff drew nearer, different newspapers would describe her as 'a feisty pensioner' (*Sun*), 'Granny Canute' (*Daily Mail*) and 'a slightly gruff woman' (*Guardian*).

Then in December 2013, with a severe storm surge forecast overnight, Bryony and her cats took refuge in a caravan on the far side of Beach Road. 'In the morning,' she said later, 'I looked across at the bungalow and I thought: "It's still there – I'm safe." But when I went towards it, I could see that the whole of the cliff and a third of the bungalow had just vanished.' Now, several rooms hung out over the edge. So photographers came, and from down on shore looked up through what was once her bathroom floor. Although the bath had plummeted to the shore – leaving a plughole and severed copper pipe – the bungalow's flimsy-looking walls remained intact. A few toiletries stood on the shelf, and a towel still hung behind the bathroom door.

Today, if I walked any further, I'd step off into air. On the shore below, there was no trace of any debris or foundations. Beyond smooth low-tide sand, only the posts of failed revetments stood out in the sea: some at drunken angles, others claimed by a watchful gull. Google Maps' aerial view from 2009 showed the sand dotted with people on beach towels, but today – as there was no way down – the shore was deserted. With the rate of retreat so fast, temporary beach ramps were simply cut into the sandy cliff near the roll-back car park – and two years ago the most recent was washed away in a storm. This clearly discouraged the tourists, as had the replacement of Happisburgh's cliff-top caravan site. Later that day, I would arrive at its inland replacement after reception had closed. A neat grey-haired man materialised and came over to the van, and when I told him my name he said, 'I know who you are.' Leading me over to a gap in the saplings, he looked from me to the empty field and said: 'Park where you like.'

The same stormy year Bryony's house hung over the cliff, the erosion revealed something far more extraordinary on Happisburgh beach. Within days, it brought archaeologists flocking from London museums, in search of traces left in a landscape lost almost a million years ago.

The story had really begun a decade earlier, with a chance find by a man out walking his dog. 'It was damn cold, I remember that', recalled Mike Chambers in a later interview for Norfolk Museums. An ex-policeman and keen beachcomber, he was a regular on Happisburgh beach, and often brought something home. Along with ironwood from disturbed shipwrecks, he'd previously found amber and fool's gold, old belt buckles, relics of downed warplanes, the fossil bones of elephants and mammoths.

On an icy day in February 2000, Chambers' walk coincided with a big low tide, after winter storms had scoured sand from the foreshore. Out at the water's edge, a familiar layer of peaty clay was again exposed. Embedded with wood and perfectly preserved pine cones, it was a place he'd been drawn to search before (sometimes he'd taken pine cones home and left them in water to open, as if they'd only just fallen from the tree).

That day, as always on his beach walk with the dog, he kept an eye out for anything unusual. And this time what caught his attention was a 'virtually straight line . . . and straight lines, as far as I'm concerned, are unusual in nature'. From the ancient, compacted sediment, the dark edge protruded 'about an eighth of an inch'. The only tool he had on him was a knife, so he used that to chip away at hardened clay and reveal a flint axe. 'It had a beauty all of its own,' he said. So he took it home, cleaned it up and put it on the mantelpiece. Later, his wife suggested they take it to the local museum.

How long, asked the interviewer, did it spend on the mantelpiece?

'A month,' Chambers said, maybe two. 'Four,' came his wife's voice from the back of the room. It was only later, after he was asked to mark on a diagram where the axe was found, that 'everything went ballistic'. Embedded at the lowest point of low tide, it suggested the Cromer Forest Bed Formation, which is at least half a million years old.

'The phone started to ring,' Chambers said. 'Everybody came rushing down . . . the British Museum, the Natural History Museum . . . wanting to be shown exactly where on the beach it had been found.'

Returning to the same spot with experts, he then found a flint knife and a piece of bone embedded in the clay – and the bone had cut marks made by the knife. This was all a first. Unlike other flint tools found on this coast, they were still *in situ*. It meant surrounding sediments could be securely dated. And as hoped, they turned out to be 500,000 years old. This meant the 'Happisburgh Hand Axe' had been struck by a species that predated not only modern humans but also the Neanderthals.

From then on, Happisburgh beach was monitored more closely. This was often by locals, especially after storms had scoured away sand and eroded the cliff. And thirteen years after Chambers' extraordinary find, it led to a discovery that would rewrite the story of early humans – not just in Britain but also northern Europe.

This time a research team was on-site within days, with the notoriously inclement 'rescue dig' captured on film for the Natural History Museum. In the video, raindrops mist the lens as it pans across ebb sand below the old caravan site, to settle on freshly exposed mudstone. Archaeologists are scattered across the shore. Some are shovelling away sand, while others slosh buckets of seawater like cold tea: clearing slick surfaces to reveal a confusion of undulations and depressions. Beside Happisburgh's failed sea defences, one man kneels in the wet, hands pink with cold as he scoops sand from elongated hollows that just might be human footprints. Many are filled with water that trembles with raindrops, and archaeologists come to sponge it away. Pressed by the incoming tide, a couple speak briefly to camera. They peer through streaming glasses, hair plastered to wet heads, pointing out particular hollows. One, Dr Nick Ashton, traces what could be the imprint of a heel and the curve of an arch, then he shrugs in the rain, cautious, not yet sure if this will prove to be momentous.

Afterwards, a few stayed on at the local pub and returned at each low tide, though every day the impressions grew less distinct. And within less than a fortnight they were gone. The official announcement was made the following year. Although only one of the fifty Happisburgh footprints was lifted in time, the rest were cast, measured with lasers, and photographed to create digital models. To build a picture of the day the footprints were made, the results were then combined with other findings from the same geological layer. Among them were ancient pollen and insect remains, a mammoth tooth, the bones of rhino and the fossil dung of a hyena the size of a lion.

In time, the layer was dated to either 850,000 or 950,000 years ago, putting humans in Britain at least 350,000 years earlier than previously thought. At the cooling end of a warm interglacial period, the climate in Norfolk would have been similar to that in southern Scandinavia today. These earliest known Britons are likely to have been *Homo antecessor*, or Pioneer Man, as they already lived in warmer southern Europe. Given the colder climate, global sea levels were considerably lower at the time. So Britain wasn't yet an island, and it was possible to walk through a shallow valley from the Netherlands to England.

That day almost a million years ago, a small group of about five were making their way upstream along the shore of a wide, slow-flowing river close to its estuary. Around them lay a rich and varied landscape. Beyond a floodplain of pools, marshes and reed beds, grasslands were edged with darker coniferous forest (the sediments of this new 'Hill House Formation' – named after Happisburgh's pub – also contained pine cones so exquisitely preserved they look carved from ebony). As some of the footprints were made by children, it's thought to have been a family group rather than a hunting party, suggesting year-round occupation not seasonal migration. The way the footprints meander also suggests the group paused at the river's muddy edge to potter about, perhaps collecting food such as roots, seaweed or shellfish.

There is no evidence that Pioneer Man ever used fire. Until the discovery of the footprints, the climate in northern Europe was considered too cold for such early humans to survive. So perhaps this small group had thick body hair, or used simple flint tools to make rudimentary clothes from the skins of animals. We don't know if they were hunters or scavengers, or how they competed with the lion-sized hyenas and sabre-toothed cats out here at the cold north-westerly fringe of Europe. We know so little of this enigmatic species that left barely a trace: here, just cut bones and a few flint flakes, and something as fleeting and evocative as the weight of a foot pressed briefly into mud.

Before the visit, I'd pinned photographs of the Happisburgh Hand Axe to my wall. Struck from local black flint, it looked weighty and still sharp, its teardrop shape more beautifully crafted than experts consider necessary for the job (the oldest of multi-tools, hand axes were used for everything from hammering and digging to cutting, scraping and butchering meat). Museum photographs show the axe suspended iconically in the air, with each struck facet catching the light differently.

In the Mike Chambers interview, there is a compelling moment after the sound of something being lifted from the table. 'It starts the imagination, doesn't it?' the interviewer says with quiet awe. 'As soon as I touched it . . .' Chambers laughs, and reminds him that what he's holding is only a replica. He then describes how everyone wants to hold the real thing. 'Professors pick it up and I've seen their eyes glaze.'

'You just want to touch it,' Chambers says, 'and think of it.'

Having learned it was on display at Norwich Castle Museum, I'd made an appointment to meet the curator. Rashly, after a couple of drinks before leaving for Norfolk, I'd told friends I was hoping to touch the Happisburgh Hand Axe.

A couple of days later, introduced by a mutual friend, I met Colin in a car park a mile south along the coast from Happisburgh. Unassuming and softly spoken, he said he'd been beachcombing this stretch of coast for thirty years. It was low tide, and I was hoping we could walk along the beach to Happisburgh. First, though, he said he'd brought along a few of his earlier finds – 'if you want a look' – which of course I did. Opening the boot of his old grey car, he handed me the weighty molar of a mammoth, complete with enormous root. The worn grinding surface was wonderfully sculptural, and I learned later that the number of ridges indicates both species and climate (more ridges imply the tougher shrubs and lichens of an ice age). He then passed me a length of mammoth tusk, pointing out the cross-hatch texture that distinguished it from bone.

Next, he lifted out a crate filled with padded brown envelopes. They were the kind used to post something ordinary, and I watched as he opened the first. Inside was a ziplock bag. And from inside that, he slid a heavy flint hand axe. It was black and shaped like a teardrop. I stared. While less sharp, it was almost exactly like the one I'd looked at on my wall for weeks: the one that was half a million years old. Yes, Colin said when I asked, this would be of a similar age. He held it out and I took its cold weight in my hand. As Chambers had said in the interview, it was an extraordinary sense of connection, to a human species that lived here so long before us.

We sat on the grass beside the crate as Colin opened more bags. And inside every one was a hand axe. I couldn't believe it. No one, including Colin, had mentioned a hand axe. (Later, looking at the Happisburgh Hand Axe behind glass at the museum, the curator would hand me only the worn, well-handled plastic replica.) Now, Colin laid hand axes out on the ground around us with care, each on its padded envelope with neatly written number, location and date. It was here in the car park, he said, that he would meet the man from the British Museum; each time, Colin handed over new finds and those previously recorded were returned.

By the time the crate was empty, at least fifteen axes lay spread on the ground around us. They varied in shape and colour, from pale greys to ochres and black. While some were still relatively sharp – presumably washing free just before they were found – others had long been rolled by the waves. One or two were as carefully crafted as the first. Others, though, had been more quickly and roughly made. The last was a simple 'pebble chopper' with a rounded top, the stone selected to fit the palm of a hand. I noticed how many were dated 2019. That was a good year for finds, Colin said, as it followed the 2018 storm that became known as the 'Beast from the East'.

Today the weather was quiet as we set off from the car park towards Happisburgh. Low on shore, the ebb tide was exposing the remains of failed sea defences. Wooden posts were studded with barnacles, and the iron sheet piling was now curved and holed by the waves, reduced to striking but ineffectual rust-orange sculpture. Although I'd walked here the previous day, alongside Colin and his well-worn rucksack I half expected the shore to be strewn with hand axes.

It wasn't long before he handed me a branch the size of an arm bone. Still brown but heavy as iron, it had small pebbles wedged into the open grain. It had likely eroded from the Cromer Forest Bed – which includes the Hill House Formation – so could be up to two million years old.

By this point, my own finds had been mainly washed-up 'pebbles' of what is known here as moorlog. Those I'd pocketed were smooth and damp, although others on the strandline had dried to the fibrous texture of peat. More than a century ago, these remnants of ancient drowned landscapes were investigated by the geologist Clement Reid, in a first study of what he called North Sea Land. In *Submerged Forests* (1913) he described how for the past fifty years, Norfolk fishermen had been unintentionally trawling up moorlog. This was often out on the Dogger Bank, a North Sea sandbank more than sixty miles from the nearest land. Usually, the fishermen simply threw the peaty slabs overboard. But as research for the book, Reid collected some of those brought to shore. Back home in their kitchen, he and his wife boiled the tough chunks for several days. After sieving what remained of the fibrous peat, he identified mainly 'swamp-species': mosses and ferns, willow leaves, birch and hazel wood, and seeds of the bogbean.

Given the lack of brackish species in his samples, Reid concluded the moorlog was eroding from what was once 'the middle of a vast fen', which now lay beneath the North Sea. 'Nothing,' he concluded, 'but a change of sea level will account for its present position.' By the end of the century, that vanished landscape would be known as Doggerland.

Doggerland was first named in 1998, in a paper by the prehistoric archaeologist Bryony Coles. The name was from Dogger Bank, a sandbank that in turn took its name from the Dutch fishing boats – *dogges* – that once worked its rich, shallow waters. Until then, the submerged landscape was seen as little more than a land bridge that once allowed migration between Britain and Europe.

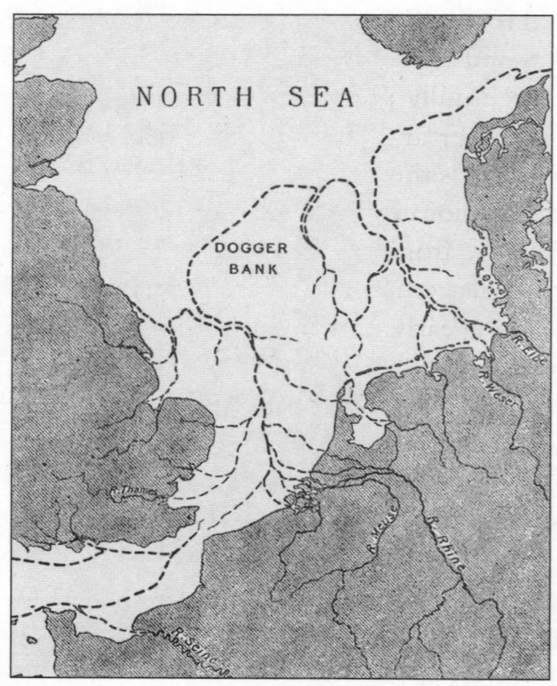

Map from *Submerged Forests* by Clement Reid (1913) envisaging what would later become known as Doggerland

Murky and inhospitable, the North Sea floor remained largely a mystery throughout the twentieth century. Yet all the while, along with the moorlog and remains of ancient marine mammals – walrus tusks, the ribs of manatee – the fishermen also trawled up the bones of terrestrial animals. From miles offshore and many fathoms deep, both Dutch and British fishermen regularly landed the bones of wolves and bears, reindeer, rhino and elephants. Sometimes, among the writhing mass of fish that slithered out on deck were also the bones of creatures that no longer existed: 'stone-heavy skulls', enormous leg bones, impossibly long curling tusks.

The first trace of humans in Doggerland was recovered in 1931, between the Leman and Owen sandbanks twenty-five miles off the Norfolk coast, after a fishing boat trawled up a slab of moorlog. Before throwing it back, one of the fishermen broke it up with a shovel and hit something hard. Inside, entombed in the peat, was a beautifully preserved barbed point, carved from the antler of a red deer and likely to have been used as a spear or harpoon. Known as the Colinda Point (after the fishing boat), it would later be radiocarbon-dated to 14,000 years old.

More recently, from the growing collection of North Sea finds, a picture has emerged of several phases of occupation of Doggerland, with early humans gaining temporary footholds as the climate warmed. To the surprise of Happisburgh locals, their dry riverbed with its ancient footprints turned out to be an ancestral course of the Thames. Later, that river would be forced south, in the same dramatic Ice Age melt that some 450,000 years ago breached the last chalk land bridge between Britain and France. In time, small, hardy bands of Neanderthals would begin following the herds of reindeer, mammoths and steppe wisents (extinct bison) that migrated across Doggerland, spending summers at this icy fringe of habitable Europe.

Later, though, they would be driven south by increasing cold, leaving long periods when Neanderthals were entirely absent from both Britain and Doggerland. It is a pattern that continued until the Neanderthals eventually died out in Europe some 40,000 years ago. Only a few thousand years after the arrival of *Homo sapiens*, this is unlikely to have been a coincidence. By then, though, temperatures were dropping, and the numbers of modern humans remained small as the world headed for the most recent Ice Age.

As Colin and I crossed the bay at the end of Beach Road, he said how much more sand there was now than in the past. Some was from a vast 'sandscaping' project a few miles further north at Bacton and Walcott (unlike at Happisburgh, money was found for sea defences there as they protect the Bacton gas terminal). In the years since, he said, the sand had shifted south through longshore drift.

Colin worked in Walcott, at a centre for adults with learning difficulties, and often spent his lunch hour fossicking on the nearby beach. And once the sandscaping was completed in 2019, quite different things had begun turning up on shore.

The project was the third of its kind. The first was an experimental scheme known as the *Zandmotor* or 'Sand Engine', near the Dutch town of Monster. It was completed in 2011, with millions of tons of sand sprayed onto an existing beach to protect the low-lying coast from rising seas. By chance, the sand turned out to have been dredged from an area of Doggerland that was occupied by humans. So along with sand, the Dutch beach was sprayed with ancient bones and artefacts. Inevitably, as word spread, the *Zandmotor* became a magnet for beachcombers, archaeologists and amateur fossil hunters. Among the most common finds have been Mesolithic barbed points: more than 2,000 carved from antler and bone. Other artefacts include stone axes, arrowheads and bone fish hooks, a decorated bone adze and Neanderthal tools made from river cobbles. Earlier, the brow ridge from a young male Neanderthal skull had also turned up, among dredged shells destined to be turned into cat litter.

Perhaps the most striking of the *Zandmotor* finds, though, is a simple flint flake with a handle-like coating of birch tar. Analysis of this Neanderthal 'glue' dated the tool to 50,000 years ago, when Doggerland was mammoth steppe. It also showed its manufacture involved a complex process with a number of steps, probably involving some kind of oven – further evidence that we have seriously underestimated Neanderthals.

Earlier at the car park, Colin had also shown me a crate of his lunch break finds from the beach at Walcott. These were also flints, but quite different: oranges and creamy yellows, knapped using more sophisticated techniques than the older hand axes. Developed by European Neanderthals, these tools were shaped from a domed 'tortoise' core, for use as knives, axes and scrapers, a technique that would later be used by modern humans.

The Walcott sand, Colin recalled, was dredged from perhaps twelve miles off the Great Yarmouth coast. But the sand at neighbouring Bacton was from another location, and finds from there were different again. They included flints of a similar Neanderthal age, but were a different style produced using a different technique. Later, I learned of another sandscaping project at Clacton in Essex, and there too Neanderthal tools were turning up on the artificial beach. Together, it gave the impression of a prehistoric Doggerland teeming with people: quite different to the earlier idea of a land bridge used mainly for migration between Britain and the continent.

This last decade and a half have seen striking advances in our understanding of the land that was submerged. Much comes from seismic surveys of the North Sea bed, originally undertaken by oil and gas companies and later shared with scientists and academics. Prohibitive costs mean the information would otherwise have remained unavailable to scientists researching the effects of rising sea levels in the past (an irony not lost on some, as the data's primary purpose was to search for new reserves of fossil fuels).

From ships at the sea's surface, pulses of sound penetrate the sea-floor sediments and sandbanks to deeper, more ancient layers that were once dry land. Reflecting off boundaries between different types of rock, the data can reveal features of that prehistoric landscape: sinuous riverbeds and retreating coastlines, rolling hills, valleys and lakes. For the research project 'Europe's Lost Frontiers', these findings were combined with the work of archaeologists, geophysicists and molecular biologists.

As well as sediment 'grabs' made with metal claws, core samples were drawn up from deep beneath the seabed. Within dateable layers of peat and silt, researchers have found everything from fossil wood, pollen and insects to fish, algae and plankton that indicate whether an environment was freshwater, brackish or marine. The cores also contain 'sedimentary DNA'. These invisible traces are genetic material shed into soil and water thousands of years ago by living organisms: from buttercups and oak trees to eels, spiders and bears. Together, they conjure life in those sonar hills, rivers and lagoons. Brought together with the mapping and computer modelling, it tells a story of the vanished Doggerland first glimpsed a century earlier by Clement Reid at home boiling moorlog.

Gradually, around 11,500 years ago at the end of the last Ice Age, Doggerland began to emerge from the weight of the ice. Although in winter it remained a freezing desert, in summer the permafrost now held a shallow covering of water. In time this supported mosses, marsh grass and reeds. Later, as dwarf shrubs of the tundra took hold, melt-water carved rivers and streams. Woolly mammoths returned, along with reindeer, bison and aurochs (a giant ancestor of modern cattle). On their trail – as with the earlier Neanderthals – came pioneering bands of hunter-gatherers.

As the climate continued to warm, forests and grasslands grew. All the while, Britain remained a peninsula of continental Europe.

To the north of Doggerland lay the Dogger Hills (now the Dogger Bank), which drained into a freshwater lake known today as the Outer Silver Pit (a depression between sandbanks). South of this vast Mesolithic lake lay wooded valleys and open grasslands, with braided streams and rivers that meandered through fertile lowlands.

As the ice continued to melt, water increasingly dominated the landscape. With its wetlands, estuaries and lagoons, Doggerland was rich in year-round resources for the hunter-gatherers. Along with deer and wild boar, it provided timber and reeds for weaving, plentiful fish like trout, pike and eel, along with woodcock and ducks with their nutritious eggs. By the mid Mesolithic, these were the richest hunting and fishing grounds in north-west Europe.

Today, Doggerland remains largely inaccessible beneath seabed sediments and many metres of a murky and often rough North Sea. Yet in recent years, sonar maps and digital 3D reconstructions have allowed archaeologists to target sites that would have been attractive to hunter-gatherers: close to estuaries, and on higher ground near watercourses, lakes and fens. In 2019, this led to sampling of the banks of the ancient Southern River system: a sonar shadow on the seabed, twenty-five miles off the Norfolk coast. 'It was terrible weather and we didn't have long to do our survey,' said Professor Vince Gaffney, one of the project leaders. 'But straight away we found a hammerstone – a 10,000-year-old flint core used to make other flint tools.'

It's possible that at its height, Doggerland was home to tens of thousands of hunter-gathers. By then, modern humans, *Homo sapiens*, had outcompeted all other hominids and the Neanderthals were long gone. Yet much of Mesolithic life remains a mystery. One reason is that sea levels were rising worldwide. With human populations often concentrated along low-lying coastlines, much of the world's Mesolithic archaeology has either been lost to the sea or remains inaccessible underwater. So anything that hints at a Mesolithic worldview is intriguing: a glimpse perhaps of those living in Doggerland as it began to drown.

Further north near the Yorkshire coast, the Mesolithic site of Star Carr lies on high ground west of the Dogger Bank. Often described as 'England's oldest house', it includes remnants of a teepee-like structure with a reed and moss floor. This stood by what was then a lake, with a timber 'dock' at the water's edge. From around 9300 BC, the site appears to have been used for more than two centuries, possibly as a seasonal hunting camp. If so, those who stayed there may have overwintered at lower-lying grounds in Doggerland.

Among the smaller Star Carr finds were almost 200 barbed points like those dredged from the North Sea floor. Used to make arrows, spears and harpoons, these were key to the livelihoods of Europe's hunter-gathers, and were usually crafted from the bone or antler of various species. Yet those from Star Carr were all from red deer, with an interesting echo in a later analysis of barbed points found on the *Zandmotor* sands. Of those in the study, all were carved from the bone of red deer apart from two made from human bone. This intrigued researchers, as other materials were readily available, more durable and in tests performed just as well, which suggests a choice made for cultural reasons. Perhaps the bones had symbolic value related to social or spiritual beliefs. Was the red deer sacred in Doggerland? Were the human bones from a venerated ancestor or particularly skilled hunter?

Most striking of the Star Carr finds were thirty-three antler 'frontlets' or headdresses made from the skulls of red deer. These are eerie, resonant objects. Each has had the antlers trimmed back and the nose bone removed. The insides have been carefully smoothed, with two holes carved into the back of the skull. While they may have been used to tie the headdress on, it's these 'eyeholes' that give the skulls their haunting presence.

From comparison with more recent hunter-gather societies, the Star Carr skullcaps may have been part of a costume worn during some ritual or ceremonial practice. In other deer and reindeer-hunting societies – including Siberian tribal cultures – similar antler headdresses are worn during shamanic rituals. Along with fire, trance, dancing and sometimes hallucinogens, the costumes and deer-like movements enable the shaman to 'become deer', crossing over to the other world to mediate with spirits. Often part of a hunting rite, the rituals are to ensure deer fertility and the success of the hunt; in some societies, they also legitimise the killing of an animal. Such ceremonies are expressions of animism, a belief system common to indigenous societies around the world – and the oldest trait of religion. Often seen as the foundation of human spirituality, its central belief is that a soul or spirit resides not just in humans, but also in animals, plants and trees, in the wind and moon, in mountains, rivers and rocks.

Gathering around a Doggerland campfire for such rituals would have strengthened social bonds. It is also likely to have been a place to tell stories, encouraging language and communication. On a practical level, stories were a memorable way of passing on knowledge crucial to the survival of a younger generation. Yet as today, it also enhanced cooperation within groups, not least through sharing social norms and taboos. At the same time, it also helped people make sense of what was happening in the world around them.

In Doggerland, as in other low-lying parts of the world, it was certainly a time of significant change. As glaciers continued to melt with the warming climate, some of Europe's richest hunting grounds had begun to drown. Isotope research on human teeth and bones shows diets were changing, with a shift away from hunted game to wetland species like waterfowl, otters and freshwater fish. Where their grandparents hunted deer, people were now setting fish traps.

No stories survive of the inundation of Doggerland. But on the other side of the world, rising seas were also encroaching on coastal Australia. In *The Edge of Memory* (2018), Patrick Nunn lays out geological evidence suggesting many indigenous Australian stories retain folk memories of submergences that took place thousands of years ago (in Arnhem Land, for example, one estimate is of land lost to the sea at an extraordinary three miles a year).

These inundation myths tell of ancestral homelands 'over the sea', some including place names and intimate knowledge of islands and landscapes that have long been submerged. They involve forbidden fish and magical land bridges, a seagull woman, a Creation Shark and angered spirits that cause the sea to rise up in punishment. Unlike many stories influenced by the Biblical flood, though, the ocean surges over the land and never retreats.

Through comparison with geological findings, Nunn concludes that elements of many of Australia's indigenous flood myths appear to have survived for more than 7,000 years. If so, they have endured with an extraordinary degree of fidelity over more than 300 generations. Isolation and the harsh landscape were certainly factors. Also, great cultural importance is attached to telling a story properly, and to who has the authority to tell certain stories. Formalised processes then ensure that when these pass down the generations, they are not only accurate but also complete (one example is a system of cross-checking across three generations of a male line, with the grandfather required to check a grandson's version against that of an uncle).

But things were very different in temperate and populous north-western Europe. In the usual pattern of human migration, Doggerland's population would have concentrated along coasts, estuaries and waterways – the very places most affected by rising sea levels. Sometimes these rises were driven by pulses in glacial melt, with the largest deepening seas by up to two metres a century. In low-lying parts of Doggerland, this could mean coastlines shifting miles inland in a single generation. Although no stories survive, it seems likely they would have been told to explain such dramatic change.

Fortunately, drowning land creates its own archive of the changing landscape. So today, scientists and scholars piece together the story of Doggerland's submergence from core samples. Cut into one-metre lengths, they reach back in time through the sandy sea floor to fine-grained silts and dark bands of peat. Brown Bank, for example, is a twenty-five-mile under-sea ridge midway between Norfolk and the Netherlands, where fishermen have long trawled up mammoth and elk bones, flint tools, worked bone and arrowheads.

Cores from Brown Bank show a Mesolithic woodland that grew around 10,000 years ago, with the peat rich in traces of roots and bark, insects and terrestrial snails, and the sedimentary DNA of mammals such as bears and boars. Moving upwards through time, the colours of the core sediments lighten, through the muddy browns of increasingly wet ground. Within these are fossil remnants of bog plants and reeds, and genetic traces left by wildfowl, otters and beavers. Later came mosquitoes and the species of marshes and wetlands, thriving as the land became part of a seasonal floodplain. Higher still, it shows how the ground became increasingly waterlogged, as old ecosystems collapsed and new species moved in. From then on, the salinity increases, showing salt marsh taking hold as the land began to flood more frequently. By then, the core silts are the colour of sealskin.

As the sea rose, Doggerland became increasingly fragmented. Coastlines retreated and river deltas began to flood, carving islands from the land. Freshwater lakes breached to form marine inlets, and groundwater sources turned briny. For the hunter-gatherers, this would have been an increasingly unpredictable, disorienting landscape. Sources of timber and food were being lost, along with access to traditional hunting and fishing grounds. One result would have been large population shifts, with people forced to move to higher ground and change the way they lived. In *The Remembered Land*, archaeologist Jim Leary suggests they would have lost not just homes and familiar landscapes to the sea, but also a 'storehouse of memories and ideas . . . where a community's legends were created and identities forged – a landscape that had a past, both mythical and historical, and was inscribed with paths and places that were meaningful.'

At its height, Doggerland was a major part of Europe's land mass. But by 6200 BC, much had already slipped beneath the sea. Yet the changes to come – in fairly quick succession – would be far more dramatic. The first was when melting ice sheets caused a dam to give way near what is now the Canadian–North American border. The result was the sudden and catastrophic draining of the vast Lake Agassiz into the North Atlantic. Global sea levels jumped by several feet. The Dogger Bank – once the Dogger Hills – was already an island, but the wider landscape was now an archipelago of scattered islands. Coastlines were also in rapid retreat: on some parts of the low-lying Dutch coast, this would reach a hundred metres a year.

For those still living in Doggerland, such rapid and unforeseen change would no doubt have intensified a sense of vulnerability in the face of unpredictable seas. At several archaeological sites in Europe, objects appear to have been buried – perhaps ritualistically – along inundating Mesolithic shorelines. They include axes and mace heads in Norway, and in the Netherlands worked flints and aurochs' skulls at one site, and 500 barbed points at another.

'One response to sea-level rise,' suggests Leary, 'may have been to intensify ceremonial and ritual practice.' There is plenty of evidence of ritual deposition in watery locations in later Bronze and Iron Age Britain. So it's quite possible that one response of Doggerland's remaining communities was to make offerings to local gods or spirits at the advancing shoreline. 'One could envisage this,' says Leary, 'as a way of placating the waters or water spirits that were transgressing onto the land – a cry to the gods to make it stop.'

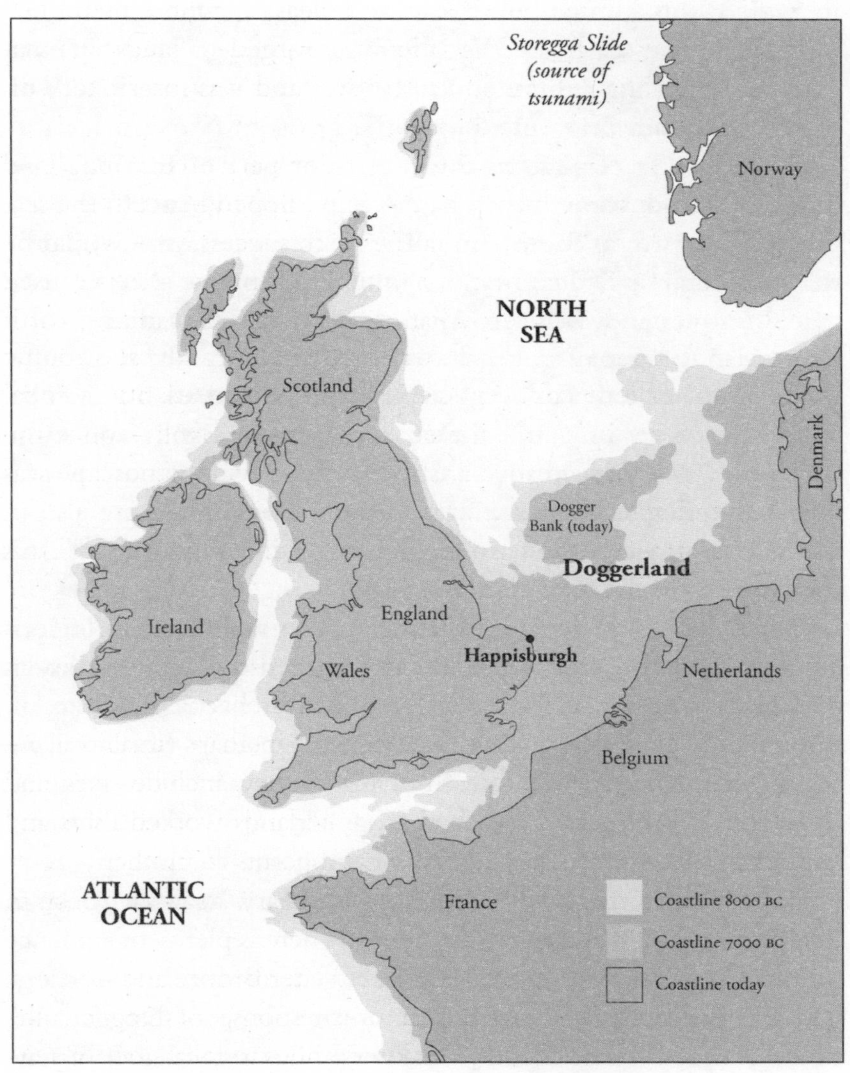

Reconstruction showing Doggerland coastlines in 8000 BC and 7000 BC

Yet there was worse to come. Around 6150 BC, a tsunami – actually a rare 'megatsunami' – swept across the last of Doggerland. The cause was the Storegga Slide, a massive underwater landslide, in which 200 kilometres of the Norwegian continental shelf plunged to the sea floor (the Norwegian *Storegga* means 'Great Edge'). Displacing vast amounts of water, this sent waves tens of metres high radiating out towards the coasts of Norway, Iceland and Britain. Traces left in the rock show waves reaching the Shetland Islands were twenty metres high, and five metres as they entered the Firth of Forth. Sweeping up to eighteen miles inland, the sea surged up Scottish valleys, funnelling its power to the very places people tended to live. At some sites, eroding Scottish cliffs also reveal the geological signature of a tsunami: 'chaotic' sandy layers of pulverised plankton, shellfish and fish bones. Some even show the layers in pairs, the first containing shells and sand (deposited as a wave rushed in) while the second is fibrous and land-based (left as the surge withdrew).

Analysis suggests there were three major waves. And at one terrestrial site, a species of moss shows the tsunami struck in autumn. As hunter-gatherers, many of Doggerland's inhabitants are likely to have returned to spend winter at the coast – already a vulnerable landscape of low-lying islands. The first sign of impending catastrophe would have been the sea's withdrawal, in a way no one had seen before. Soon afterwards came the surge of its return. By the time it reached Doggerland, the wall of brown water was some ten metres high. Sweeping away everything in its path, including the sandy soil, the tsunami is thought to have killed thousands of people.

In the past, this was understood to have been the final submergence of the land. Yet more recent research suggests that after the surges receded, some islands remained above sea level. In a few places, above the telltale sandy line of pulverised shells, core samples show a layer of new plant growth and faunal remains. So while altered, some high ground appears to have recovered, making it possible that despite dwindling resources some people may have returned. But with Canadian melt-water continuing to pour into the sea, it was the beginning of the end. Within centuries, by 5500 BC, the last of the Dogger Hills had slipped beneath the sea.

Still heading for Happisburgh with Colin, I'd now picked up several more pieces of moorlog. Inevitably, I'd checked each for anything of interest: fragments of prehistoric bone, say, an exquisite pine cone or carved bone point . . . and predictably found nothing. A few days later, though, I did find a more impressive specimen – at least until it broke. Stranded high on shore, it was the size of a shoe sole, dried a fibrous black and dusted with crystals of salt. Best of all, it was pierced with the finger-sized holes of piddocks. Usually, these marine bivalves live embedded in soft seabed rock. Yet here they had burrowed into a fen beneath the sea.

Occasionally, woody remnants of Doggerland are glimpsed *in situ* on the seabed. One striking discovery was made by chance in 2014, revealed by the same scouring storms that took Bryony's house. Following a marine survey, amateur diver Dawn Watson was almost out of air some 300 metres off the Norfolk village of Cley next the Sea (twenty-five miles up the coast from Happisburgh). Before heading back to shore, she was finning over rippled sand when a dark ridge loomed up ahead, 'like a standing wave'. She thought first of a shipwrecked hull. Instead, it turned out to be a mass of compressed peat and wood uncovered by the storms. An outcrop of drowned forest floor, it was complete with fallen oak trunks that would prove to be 10,000 years old.

This was the same age as the woodland that drowned out at Brown Bank, halfway between Britain and the Netherlands. It was also contemporary with the hammerstone dredged from the banks of the lost Southern River, which at the time would have been a day or two's walk away.

By 2014, at eight metres deep, the exposed trees offered a rare stability out on the shifting seabed sands. So they were soon colonised by sea life. Later, when Dawn and her partner Rob returned to the site with plenty of air, they found an extraordinary reef garden. The ancient oak trunks were flushed pink with sponges and softened by delicate tentacles. In the yellowy under-sea light, feathery hydroids swayed with the currents as if in a breeze. Fat-armed starfish crept along trunks and crabs lurked in knot-holes. Great lobster claws withdrew into the dark, beneath trees that fell thousands of years ago. It was a magical sight, as if the mossy floor of the ancient forest had returned to life.

Yet it was only a brief re-emergence. Throughout the summer, this dark fragment of Doggerland was reburied in sand.

When Colin and I reached the shore at the end of Beach Road, there was little but smooth golden sand. Any last trace of Bryony's bungalow or the Cliff House tea shop was now buried deep (what had I expected, I wondered: wave-worn cup handles, a protruding bath?). From there, my gaze slid up the face of the cliff. At the toe, the darker, more ancient boulder clays had been smoothed by the sea. Above, the sandy till was younger: left by retreating glaciers as Doggerland emerged from the ice.

Now, the till was topped by a thin layer of darker topsoil, gripped by the exposed roots of leafless bushes. Near the fractured tarmac end of Beach Road, the roof of the abandoned end bungalow peeked over the edge. Where its garden fell away, a cylindrical brickwork structure was exposed in the face of the cliff. Walking this way yesterday, I'd presumed it was a well – romantically, it turned out, as Colin seemed sure it was a cesspit.

From my pocket, I pulled out a flint I'd found nearby on that walk. I'd picked up several, but this was the one I hoped might be worked. The flint was slender and grey; held up to the light, its edges were glassily translucent. Colin took it between roughened fossiler's fingers, angling it so the light caught its ripples.

'Yep,' he said. 'Looks worked to me.'

I tried not to look as pleased as I felt. Later, I was told – from its fineness – that it was probably a Neolithic waste flake (struck from a core that became the tool). As it remained relatively sharp, and not battered by the tide, it may have only recently washed free of the cliff. I returned it safely to my pocket.

By the time my own flint was struck, Doggerland had drowned. Its nomadic bands of hunter-gatherers had moved to higher ground: Britain, the Netherlands, Germany, Denmark. *Homo sapiens* had settled and begun to farm. And with the loss of Doggerland, Britain was now an island.

As we reached the beach below the abandoned campsite, Colin pointed out where Happisburgh's famous footprints were found. Here the cliff was relatively high, and close to the top, traces of more recent humans protruded from its face. Plastic terracotta drainpipes were exposed like trace fossil burrows, along with water pipes and the brickwork of the campsite's old septic tank. Mid-shore, there were also two huge concrete blocks. On the deserted shore they were ugly and angular, the tops green with weed and the sides dark with wrack. The day before I'd presumed – mistakenly – they must be remnants of failed sea defences, or some wartime defensive structure (with fallen concrete pillboxes common on this coast).

Colin, though, had witnessed their story through his decades of beachcombing. By the turn of the century, erosion meant the caravan site and this end of the village no longer had access to the shore. So in 2003, a metal tower was constructed on the beach, with four flights of stairs linked to the cliff-top by a railed metal walkway. Early photographs show families walking along it above the crumbling cliff-face, carrying beach bags down to the sand. Behind them, caravans line up along the grassy cliff-edge.

Later, as the cliff retreated, the aerial walkway was extended. In less than a decade, though, the distance was too great to be safe.

So the walkway was removed, and for a time the tall metal tower stood marooned in the middle of the beach. With its four flights of stairs leading nowhere, it was a gaunt and incongruous monument to erosion. Today, all that remains are the two concrete blocks: the stairs' foundations, originally buried in the sand. Now low on the shore, they have become markers of the cliff's retreat.

On my last evening in Happisburgh I had a drink at the Hill House Inn. An alehouse since the seventeenth century, it was now a dimly lit pub with dark beams and pictures of ruins and rough seas. In one corner, above a painting of prehistoric Happisburgh, was a sign saying 'Happisburgh-on-Thames'. I bought a beer and took a seat in the near-empty bar. Given the predicted rate of erosion, it had perhaps no more than thirty years. It was the same for Happisburgh's remaining lighthouse, its Arts and Crafts manor house and medieval church. By the end of the century, the rest of the village was also expected to have gone.

By a quarter to nine I was the only customer left, so I stepped out into the dusk. It was that cusp of the light, with crows still cawing in the churchyard but also the flitter of bats. I wasn't ready to go back to the van. So, as the pub backed on to the abandoned caravan site, I made my way out there. Out on the cliff, I wandered along grassy aisles between the old hardstandings, where nettles and dock flourished over concrete slabs, gravel and weed-control membranes. Inland, the thin blade of a new moon hung above wind-bent trees huddled around the church tower. Below, for now, high tide washed placidly at the toe of the cliff. As I made my way back towards the road, the last outline of a static caravan was edged with the papery petals of last year's hydrangeas. In the stillness, it was like looking out over a giants' graveyard.

Ten minutes later, heading back through the deserted village, I felt like the only person in Happisburgh (perhaps, as in Cornwall, the darkened rooms and lack of cats were a sign of second homes). It was so quiet I was walking in the main road when a creature stepped out from someone's garden. Halfway across the street it stopped. As it turned to look in my direction, both of us froze. We stared, and for a long moment – perhaps due to the beer – I had no idea what it was. It didn't look like a dog, a deer or a pig, but all three. Like some mythical hybrid or shamanic conjuring, it was no taller than a Labrador, with a hog's body, short horns and goatish legs. I let out a breath and it broke the spell. The creature started and trotted away, and it was only then I saw it was a muntjac.

A 'barking' deer. I laughed in the half-light. It seemed so appropriate in strange, liminal Happisburgh. This was a place of portals, where anything might happen, where a million years could exist at once – at least until the sea washed it all away.

Looking out over submerged Mesolithic Bouldnor Cliff

2

Bouldnor Cliff

Isle of Wight

Above a seven-mile landslip at the 'Back of the Wight', I looked out over Britain's oldest amusement park. At the top of the cliff, a skeletal rust-coloured roller coaster towered over the car park, like something from 1970s *Scooby-Doo.* Long famous for its whimsical creepiness, the family-run Blackgang Chine has been in retreat from the eroding cliff-edge since it opened in 1843.

A chine is a deep coastal ravine, cut through soft rock by water, a term fallen out of use beyond the island and adjacent mainland (except in butchery, where it is still a cut through the backbone). Today the gorge has almost entirely eroded away, but even before the park opened, Blackgang attracted wealthy Georgian travellers. They came in search of the picturesque and sublime: the grandeur of an untouched wilderness and the destructive forces of nature. Paintings and engravings show the chine deep in shadow, sliced into unstable cliffs that tower 400 feet above the sea. In 1799, one visitor described a recent landslide leaving 'a Druid scene of wildness and ruin'.

Aimed at a new breed of Victorian tourist, Blackgang Chine opened first as a pathway that zigzagged its way to the shore, past a series of scenic viewpoints. It was the brainchild of entrepreneurial Alexander Dabell, who'd moved to the Isle of Wight at the age of fifteen. Following a series of jobs that ranged from selling lace and souvenirs to hair oil, he had the idea after speaking to the owner of a newly opened hotel. Ignoring a bathing guide's description of Blackgång as 'a vast and horrible opening', Dabell duly took out a lease on the chasm and surrounding land, with its extent determined by how far he could throw a stone. He soon began work on his creative vision: a landscape of romantic gardens, walkways and seating areas, down a 'ravine of savage magnificence'.

Blackgang Chine

As the work was being completed, another opportunity arose on the island. Just off the Needles, an 'enormous whale had been discovered, scarcely dead, and floating'. Later, when the decomposing fin whale was auctioned – drawing quite a crowd – Dabell was the highest bidder, as he'd had an idea. With the carcass stripped and the blubber sold, he arranged for the bones to be bleached and rearticulated at the top of his path. Soon, the ninety-foot skeleton was covered by what one visitor described 'a species of tent'. Inside, in the belly of the whale, was the Blackgang Chine Bazaar.

Essentially a gift shop, it was inspired by cabinets of curiosities or *Wunderkammer*, 'rooms of wonder' long popular among the wealthy in Europe. A precursor to museums, these private collections showed off their owner's wealth and travels, often entertaining guests after dinner. Celebrating the glory and variety of God's creation, specimens included everything from skulls, minerals and 'antiquities' to dried seahorses, taxidermy dodos, fossils and celestial globes. There were 'divine monstrosities' like jars of deformed foetuses, and also fabrications: 'Fiji mermaids', for example, with the tails of fish stitched to the torsos of monkeys.

At Blackgang, inside the ribcage of the whale, the Dabells laid out their wares: bone china plates and teacups, natural history prints, Victorian shell art, fossils found on local beaches. Another Isle of Wight speciality – still sold today – was souvenir glass filled with bands of the island's striking-coloured sands. As today, much of the island's popularity with visitors rested on its spectacular views of eroding cliffs such as Alum Bay and the Needles. Like Blackgang, they took the brunt of the island's prevailing south-westerlies (more recently, England's highest-ever wind speed was recorded at the Needles).

On my way out to Blackgang, I'd stopped briefly at Compton Bay, one of several island viewpoints where the car park is steadily being lost to the sea. On the shore below, novice fossilers – like myself – are said to sometimes mistake sea-rolled chunks of the tarmac for dinosaur bone. Today, we know the island's eroding cliffs and bright sands tell an almost unbroken story of rising and falling sea levels spanning more than a hundred million years, in strokes of sweeping, impressionistic colour.

Out beyond the crumbling edge of the car park, the ochre cliffs were laid down beneath shallow coastal seas. Low tide there reveals the huge, three-toed footprints of dinosaurs. With the bones and teeth of more than twenty species found on the island – from iguanodons and pterosaurs to armoured ankylosauria and long-necked sauropods – it is marketed today as Dinosaur Island. Curving north-west from the car park, the ochre cliffs merge with the white chalk of deep seas far from land, tapering to the narrowest of points at the Needles. Around the headland, rust-oranges bleed into the yellows and reds of the Alum Bay sands, indicating a return to shallower tropical seas.

Further still, where the island faces the mainland, the cliffs are brown clays and mudstones, laid down as the climate cooled and the sea once again retreated. While less spectacular, these younger northern cliffs – that I would visit the next day – were also rich in fossils. A closing chapter in the island's sweeping geological and evolutionary story, they were from ancient reptiles and strange, extinct mammals that followed the dinosaurs.

When Blackgang opened, the word dinosaur – 'terrible lizard' – had only just been coined. It would, though, be another decade and a half before the publication of Charles Darwin's *On the Origin of Species* (1859), which challenged the idea of divine creation. By then, iguanodon bones had already been found on the island, with fossil hunting and collecting becoming increasingly popular. In the coming decades, one local vicar, Reverend William D. Fox, referred to his scouring of the island's beaches and chines as 'hunting for old dragons', and went on to have more dinosaurs named after him than any other Englishman. 'Always bones first and the parish next,' his wife would complain. Yet despite being a second cousin to Darwin (the 'D' in Fox's name), the fossil-hunting curate would never fully accept his cousin's theory of evolution.

This reflected great upheavals in the understanding of geology, as science came into conflict with the accepted religious world-view. A relatively young discipline, geology began as an early scientific interpretation of the Bible story, with many landforms and geological features attributed to the destructive forces of the

Flood. With the Earth believed to be no more than 6,000 years old, rocks and minerals were classified accordingly. Older 'Pre-Adamic' rock was created before Adam – so in the first five days of Genesis – while younger Adamic rock was laid down between the creation of humans and the Flood. Yet increasingly, geologists would challenge the constraints of having to fit scientific discoveries to a literal interpretation of the Bible. Contentiously, some also argued that science and religion should separate (and against the involvement of clergy in science, which was common at the time). The Earth, the new geologists claimed, was far more ancient than previously thought. And fossil 'curiosities' told a very different story to Genesis.

Still owned by the Dabell family today, the Blackgang Chine amusement park has been in an ongoing process of retreat and reinvention for more than 180 years. By the 1970s, the paths down the chine had eroded away and there was no longer any access to the beach. Instead, those who came as children recall with nostalgia the Hall of Mirrors and Electric Shock Chair, the Mouth of Hell and the famous life-size dinosaurs (which in 1972 featured on an episode of *Blue Peter*, when they were flown in dangling from a helicopter). Since then, the cliff has continued to lose an average of more than ten feet a year. As a result, with each major landslip Blackgang attractions have been dismantled and moved inland, including the fibreglass dinosaurs.

Out of sight at the edge of the cliff, Adventureland is now little more than a rusted roundabout. It is part of a broad cliff-top area abandoned in 1994, when heavy rainfall triggered massive landslides and the 'upper tier' of the Undercliff dropped fifty feet. While the ground surface remained relatively intact, it also took sections of the Old Blackgang Road, along with caravans, chalets and cars. The fall also undermined two cottages at the top of the cliff; later, Alexander Dabell's great-grandson described how his floorboards had begun to lift as he sat down to dinner, and the wallpaper tore as cracks opened up in the walls. Over the next week, as the land continued to shift and settle, the cottage walls collapsed. (Later, the park's ever-evolving attractions would include a moving platform to simulate the experience of a Blackgang landslip.)

In the park's early days, the chine reached almost three-quarters of a mile inland; today it has almost entirely eroded away. Beyond the 'Cliffhanger' roller coaster, the top of the vast Blackgang landslip slumps to form a series of scrubby tiers or 'benches' that can remain relatively stable for years. Given recent weeks of torrential rain, I wasn't going down there. But in drier times others had, and their photos and shaky phone videos form a striking archive of what has been lost.

It was a journey through the strangest of lost settlements. Close to the top were ruptured sections of the Old Blackgang Road, with faded double-yellow lines and garden steps leading nowhere. From there, paths were worn through rough grass and patches of bramble, leading down through more stable parts of the landslip. Beyond the carcasses of several caravans were the last huts of the South View Sun Club. This ended its days as a nudist camp, and nearby – in the junk-filled clubhouse – a peeling mural showed life-size naked parents smiling strangely beside naked children. Some of the huts, though, appeared to have been lived in more recently. Here and there, ivy trailed elegantly down from a ceiling, and makeshift curtains hung at broken windows with stunning sea views. There was a sleeping bag, rancid milk, a newspaper with a year-old date. Outside, torn vinyl car seats had been ripped out and angled for the view.

A more solid relic stood further along the 'lost road': the elegant, honey-coloured stone of a coach house built in the years after the whale arrived at Blackgang. This was once part of the Southview estate, a Victorian villa boasting wine cellars and servants' quarters, with an early estate agent's ad extolling the Italianate tower and surrounding scenery 'where nature sports in sublime grandeur'. The main Southview house was lost in the 1970s, with road access first affected by a landslide in 1928. But a decade ago, against the odds, its gutted coach house remained intact, with glassless windows and the doors of the Aga hanging off.

On an active landslip, this was of course a temporary reprieve. From where I stood this was all out of sight, and in recent years they may well have resumed their journey to the shore. Lower down, where the scarps become steeper, the 'blue slipper' clay speeds its descent. Eventually, at the foot of these cliffs, storms and high tides would wash everything free of the mud. One day, as on Sheppey, the last of the concrete steps and Aga doors would lie among pebbles, muddled with fossils and the bones of dinosaurs. Here, though, there was also an unsettling horror soundtrack: intermittent screams from the 'Cliffhanger' roller coaster, and the groaning roar of new animatronic dinosaurs.

The next morning I set off early to catch the tide at Bouldnor Forest, where a submerged Mesolithic settlement now lies several hundred yards offshore. The woodland runs down to the sea between Cowes and Yarmouth, harbour towns facing the mainland on the island's leafy and more affluent north coast. In Victorian times, there were ambitions to take advantage of Bouldnor's position. A railway and hotel were proposed, along with a pier to attract passing cruise ships. But the clay ground proved far too unstable, and in time the plans were shelved and quietly forgotten, although the pier's abandoned foundations are still exposed at low tide. Yet the cliffs are lower on this coast, and the waters more sheltered, so there are no dramatic landslides like those at Blackgang. Instead, the northern edge of Bouldnor Forest slips gradually – almost gracefully – into the sea. This time, I fully intended to make it down to the shore.

I pulled up at a patch of ground exactly as described in directions I'd found on a fossiling website. The route didn't sound the easiest – there was a warning of extreme mud after rain – and the notes were also several years out of date. Hoping for the best, though, I pulled on wellies and set off down the track in a steady drizzle.

The mud soon worsened. As the previous boot-prints became fewer and deeper, I presumed others had already turned back. In places the path was now a watercourse, hollowed out where recent rains had poured off the land. I slid along the firmer edges, grabbing branches and the trunks of whippy trees. Before long, there was just a single set of oversized boot-prints – left I hoped by someone who knew what they were doing.

I stopped, holding an overhead branch to peer down at the drop ahead. Knowing no other route to the beach, I didn't want to turn back. It was only then that I saw the rope hung off to one side. After a trial tug I slid my way down, glad of its regular, neatly tied knots. From there on, the big boot-prints were deep holes filled with water. And while I could still see nothing but trees, I could hear the sea. So I kept on, making slow progress, until again I came to a standstill.

Ahead was another sharp drop, but steeper and longer. I looked around for a rope and there it was, dangling from a solid-looking branch. This time there were also knotted loops for feet. I half slipped and half swung my way down, before coming again to a halt. Ahead, water lay pooled in the clay. And while two possible routes branched off to either side, there were no longer any reassuring boot holes. Had the man (I guessed from the boot size) come all this way and decided to turn back? For a while I stood staring at the still surface of clay-coloured water, where broad-leafed plants crowded close to the edge. Familiar from the cliffs where I grew up, they were the places we were told to avoid.

I considered turning back myself. But the sea was loud on the shore now, glinting through woodland that was beginning to thin. I was almost there. So I stepped out gingerly, keeping well away from the pool, reaching for trees that seemed to lean towards the sea. Then at last I was down, scrambling over fallen trunks and stumbling out onto the shore with relief. Unsurprisingly, the beach was deserted.

Down at the water's edge I washed the platforms of clay from my boots. Up at the top of the shore, the tangle of half-dead trees stretched off in both directions as far as I could see. Already, I could barely make out where I'd emerged onto the beach. I took a photograph in case I returned and couldn't find the path. The rain had stopped, though, and I might find fossils. I'd worry later about the route back.

Bouldnor Forest shore

As the island's youngest rocks, Bouldnor's clays were laid down around thirty-three million years ago, before the sea withdrew from the Hampshire Basin. Towards the end of the Eocene, what is now the Isle of Wight was part of a subtropical coastal plain, with palms and sequoias rising above wetlands, lakes and sluggish rivers. Every few hundred thousand years, the sea would encroach on the land, forming brackish lagoons and drowned estuaries, and at one time a shallow sea. Then as the climate cooled, it again retreated, leaving swamps and wetland floodplains.

I sloshed my way back to shore, with Eocene or Oligocene mud swirling away from my boots – much as it does from the toe of the cliff during storms and high tides. It is then that many of the fossils emerge, bringing those vanished landscapes to life. While the island's older rocks retain traces of theropods and iguanodons, by the warm, swampy Eocene dinosaurs were extinct. Instead, Bouldnor's wetlands were home to ancient reptiles like turtles and crocodiles, and an array of what seem to us bizarre hybrid mammals. The local bear-dogs – Amphicyon or 'ambiguous dog' – were bear-like but with the teeth of wolves. There were predatory hyaenodons, hornless rhino, and striking entelodonts: 'hell pigs' with slender legs, spinal humps and huge pig-like heads, yet more closely related to whales.

Sometimes, often after scouring winter storms, Bouldnor's 'Log Bed' is uncovered on shore. This is a remarkable geological layer, marking an extinction event that occurred when sea levels fell low enough to uncover a land bridge between Europe and Asia. Containing the fossilised trunks of fallen pines and redwoods (some up to five metres long), it was once a logjam in a river.

The extinction event was the *Grand Coupure* or 'Great Break' in continuity: the boundary between the tropical Eocene and cooler Oligocene. In Bouldnor's low cliff there is a clear change in the fossil species found above and below the Log Bed. As at other European sites of a similar age, it indicates the extinction of many endemic European mammals, and their replacement by migrant species from Asia. This was the first time a land bridge allowed migration between Asia and the European continent, which until then had been isolated from the rest of the world. With the new route open, the bear-dogs and hell pigs could make their way to Britain.

As I set off along the shore at a stoop, I was lulled by birdsong and the sea, by the idea of solitude, an ebb tide and plenty of time. Even the drizzle had almost stopped. For some time, courting disappointment I knew, there had been something I wanted to find here: a 'scute', a plate from the armoured skin of a crocodile.

Soon, though, I was distracted by the ironstone, which was new to me and wonderfully sculptural. It was often holed with what looked like trace-fossil burrows, and – tantalisingly – some of the shapes echoed life. As I inched my way along the shore, I dropped some in the bag: one that curved like the grasp of a bird's foot, another like the fossil ear bone of a whale. One had grooves like a turtle shell, and several were crazed like reptilian skin. It was only later that I learned such patterns in ironstone are common, and nothing to do with reptiles. Instead, wonderfully, they are mud-cracks that formed as a pool or puddle dried out under a prehistoric sun.

An hour and a half in, my novice enthusiasm had begun to wane. While the ironstones evoked such creaturely traces, I was fairly sure this was merely resemblance and they weren't the fossils their forms suggested. It meant my only real find was a piece of what sea-glass collectors call 'television glass'. Shaped like a frosted chandelier drop, it had a thin yellow band sandwiched between layers of clear and grey glass. Perhaps from an early colour set, it was considerably younger than what I'd been hoping for. Then just as I was thinking of calling it a day, I saw the scute, resting edge-on between stones at my feet. This time I felt sure as I picked it up, as it looked exactly like those I'd seen in photographs: a dark bony plate pocked with irregular divots. Mine was small and sea-worn, and I smoothed my thumb across its dimpled surface with delight.

Ten minutes later I looked up to see a group of white-haired people in the distance, close to where I'd struggled down onto the shore. Four or five of them were meandering slowly my way, heads bent in the familiar posture of people searching for fossils (on Sheppey, the occasional holidaymaker will shout, 'Oi! Lost your car keys, mate?'). Given the state of the path I was astonished, imagining them clutching trees and swinging down ropes.

'Any luck?' one asked as we crossed paths, a common fossil hunter's greeting.

I slipped the scute from my pocket and held it out. He looked closely before handing it back.

'Crocodilian scute,' he said.

It sounded a knowledgeable opinion and as we chatted, I learned it was. One of them, it turned out, was Alan Morton, a local fossil hunter with an extensive Eocene and Oligocene collection. The other was down from London: Dr Adrian Rundle, palaeontologist and Curator of Learning at the Natural History Museum.

I couldn't help but mention my surprise at seeing them down on the beach, given the state of the path. There was a brief pause before Adrian raised his eyebrows.

'The old path?' he said, and shook his head. 'No one uses that. Haven't done for years.' He described the way they'd come today: a gently sloping path through woodland, that emerged further east along the beach. He mentioned butterflies, the fresh spring green of the leaves.

The pair headed off then, as the tide had already turned and they were keen to reach the headland. I stood watching as they walked away, delighted on two counts now. Not only did I not have to worry about treacherous mud-pools, but my scute was definitely a scute: the skin of a thirty-million-year-old crocodile.

Later, I learned the crocodilian species was probably Diplocynodon, 'double dog tooth', named for its fang-like teeth. One reason I'd been so keen to find a scute was that for me it was crocodiles and alligators that best evoke the swamps and sluggish rivers of Bouldnor's Oligocene floodplains. Running a finger over the surface of armoured skin, it was easy to imagine the creature's splayed legs and belly crawl, the muscular tail flex as it slipped into murky prehistoric waters not far from where I stood.

Later that afternoon, I took the easy route up off the shore, and followed dappled inland paths towards the drowned Mesolithic site at the far western edge of the forest. By the time I re-emerged on shore, it was warm and unusually humid. Across the water, rain veiled the mainland beneath an indigo sky. Behind me, as before, dead and dying trees lined the top of the shore. Here, the most striking jutted at odd angles, stripped of bark and starkly white against the dark of the sky. Others lay out in the shallows, the flood tide rising quietly around them, refloating seaweed and rags that hung from their branches. I'd arrived with the sun behind cloud, with the Solent silver and the light unexceptional. Yet as the sun emerged, everything transformed. Offshore, the sea turned a milky turquoise. Nearer shore, though, the shallows were yolky with suspended silt. The shift was extraordinary. Here, midweek on the Isle of Wight, the humidity and colours of a tropical mangrove swamp.

Today, the submerged Bouldnor Cliff settlement lies 250 metres offshore, beneath eleven metres of water. This is out where the silty shallows give way to deeper water, which unfortunately for divers combines poor visibility with the Solent's complex tides.

Maritime archaeologists began diving off Bouldnor after the discovery of a submerged forest in the 1980s. In 1999, as two divers swam above remnants of ancient fallen oaks, one saw worked flints ejected from a lobster's burrow. On investigation, it turned out the lobster had tunnelled down beneath seabed mud to an ancient land surface, at the foot of a submarine cliff. Further surveys revealed the site of a Mesolithic settlement, still *in situ* and exquisitely preserved by the waterlogged peat for more than 8,000 years. It was what the Doggerland researchers dreamed of finding.

For over a decade, divers returned to the site every year (a place so extraordinary that some archaeologists – including at least one television presenter – have learned to dive in order to see it). Over the years, many have finned down through the murky Solent following a shot line, carrying shovels, metal boxes and saws. Conditions are good only for a couple of hours around slack water, which allows researchers to gather seabed samples to take back to the lab. The boxes are for slabs cut from the forest-floor peat, brought by divers to the surface with slow-motion under-sea care. Others take saws to cut samples from the Mesolithic trees. To a dendrologist, each tree ring holds an archive of a year the tree grew, helping researchers reconstruct both the landscape and climate.

In Rikke Houd's radio documentary *Under the Water*, archaeologist Professor Nigel Nayling describes the difficulty of collecting samples of wood from Bouldnor. 'It's very hard work sawing underwater,' he says. 'You have no real leverage. Sometimes the saw just stays where it is, and *you* move up and down.'

Gradually, as the work of archaeologists, dendrologists, geophysicists, palaeobotanists and geneticists was drawn together, the lost Mesolithic landscape began to emerge. Around 8,200 years ago, the Isle of Wight remained part of the mainland, with the sheltered settlement perhaps a day or two's walk from the sea. Beside a stream, it was also close to a lake or wetland fringed with deciduous woodland including oak, hazel and apple trees. Back at the lab, geneticists also found the molecular ghosts of deer, aurochs, grouse, rodents and wolves – or possibly dogs.

Radiocarbon dating suggests the site was inhabited for around two centuries, between 8,200 and 8,000 years ago. This was the period of accelerated sea-level rise that saw Doggerland slip beneath the sea. At Bouldnor, the artefacts recovered by divers are extraordinary, not only for their age and remarkable degree of preservation, but because so many remained *in situ*. Over the past two decades, finds have included flint tools, oak timbers and wood shavings, and wooden platforms perhaps used to cross an increasingly boggy landscape. There was also what is thought to be part of a log boat. If so, this makes Bouldnor Cliff the oldest boatbuilding site in the world.

Of particular interest was evidence of sophisticated craftsmanship at such an early site. Some of the woodworking techniques, along with a beautifully made flint axe, were not thought to have been used in Britain until the Neolithic, 2,000 years later. Another striking find was the DNA of wheat, which proved controversial due to the extraordinary degree of preservation – leading some to dispute its age. Its importance was that wheat is a marker of the agricultural revolution: the shift from Mesolithic hunter-gathering to the Neolithic's more settled farming communities (which allowed human populations to explode). For some, though, Bouldnor's most evocative find was a simple coil of twisted fibres: Britain's oldest piece of string.

Scoured by the Solent currents, the site continues to erode, and every year the divers returned to find it changed. On one dive, the face of the submerged cliff had eroded enough to reveal a hearth in cross section, perhaps under the floor of a living space. Beneath a wooden covering, the fire-pit contained charcoal, burnt clay and hazelnuts. There were also crazed superheated flints; often known as 'pot boilers', these are thought to have been used to heat water and carbonise wood. If the gaps between dives had been longer, the strong Solent currents are likely to have washed it all away. This remains the challenge of these submerged coastal sites, where rare, precious glimpses of our past are so beautifully preserved, but so fragile once exposed to the waves.

The story of Bouldnor's gradual inundation can be read in the glassy, microscopic skeletons of diatoms. Preserved within dateable layers of core sediments, different species of the plankton live specifically in environments that are freshwater, brackish or marine. Cores from Bouldnor show that over a century and a half – when the settlement was inhabited – there were profound changes to the surrounding landscape. As well as the submergence of Doggerland, low-lying coasts were drowning worldwide. At Bouldnor, as in so many coastal locations, freshwater supplies were turning brackish. The surrounding woodland first became waterlogged, before transitioning to salt marsh and then mudflats, as sediments turned estuarine about 8,000 years ago. It was around then that the settlement was abandoned, after remaining in use for maybe eight generations. Closing up the hearth, and leaving behind timber and a few stone tools, those who'd lived and worked here never returned.

In *Under the Water*, a wider question emerges repeatedly of these fast-rising Mesolithic seas. Is this the flood all stories derived from? Along with so much else, this encompasses the hypothesis that the Genesis flood story has origins in folk memory from around that time; perhaps devastating floods that occurred when the rising Mediterranean finally broke through into the Black Sea.

On my last evening on the Isle of Wight, I headed out from Tennyson Down to the Needles: the western end of the chalk ridge that forms the island's crooked spine. These striking white pinnacles are the remains of a land bridge that once connected the island to the mainland. In the past, the Isle of Wight was thought to have separated from mainland Britain around 7,000 years ago. Yet unexpectedly, core samples brought up from Bouldnor also held what appears to be a record of the breach. They revealed a marked change around 4,500 years ago, with a switch from the deposition of sediment to erosion (which eventually exposed the Bouldnor Cliff site). The findings imply a major change in the Solent currents, which would result from the breaching of a final land bridge. The Isle of Wight, then, appears to have become an island several thousand years after Britain had separated from mainland Europe, as the Neolithic was giving way to the Bronze Age.

Along their length, the island's high, whalebacked downs are dotted with both Neolithic and Bronze Age burial grounds. I'd passed a couple of the barrows already: roughly circular mounds, long grassed over at the brow of the hill. Further east at Ashey Down, the excavation of a series of Bronze Age barrows found charred human bones in five of them, with four of those also containing a single fossil sea urchin.

Over the past few days, I'd been fossiling on several of the island's beaches, and a favourite find was a heart-shaped fossil sea urchin. These erode from the chalk, which formed from the calcium-rich skeletons of marine creatures – mainly planktonic coccolithophores – that drifted to the sea floor in what is known as 'marine snow'. Eventually, the resultant ooze then hardened to form chalk. My fossil was the internal flint mould of a sea urchin that once burrowed through the white seabed mud. Its harder flint formed from the glassy skeletons of sponges and plankton, which on the sea floor formed opaline silica. Molecule by molecule, this then replaced the chalk within seabed burrows, inside shells and the tests of sea urchins. In essence, though over vast amounts of time, the opal-filled seabed hollows like molten metal poured into casts. So my fossil was a perfect flint replica of the sea urchin, etched with a five-pointed star.

The inclusion of fossil urchins – echinoids – as grave goods appears to have been fairly widespread, not just in England but also in continental Europe. At Neolithic Whitehawk, for example, beneath Brighton Racecourse, a woman and young child were found buried with a sea urchin. The fossils have also been found in the graves of newborns. Most extraordinary is the Bronze Age grave of 'Maud'; buried in the chalk of the Chilterns cradling a young child, they are wreathed in hundreds of fossil urchins. The echinoids were clearly placed in these graves with care, so perhaps had symbolic meaning or were sacred offerings. In Britain, the practice lingered for thousands of years into Anglo-Saxon times, after Christianity began discouraging the 'pagan' practice of grave goods.

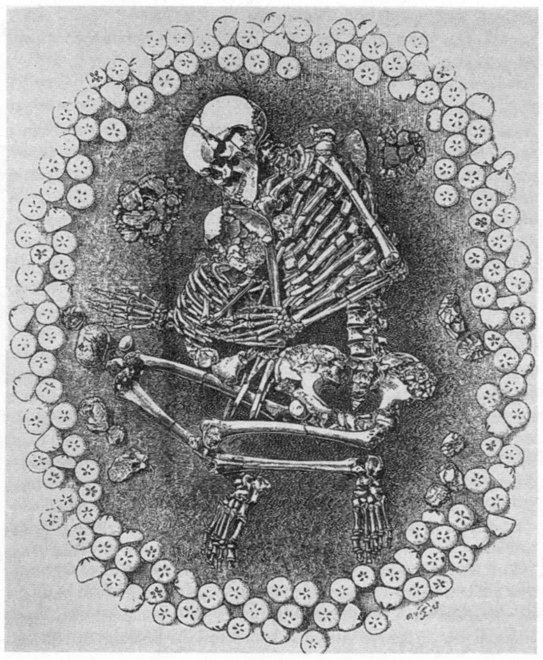

Maud: buried cradling a newborn and surrounded by fossil sea urchins

Long after that, the fossils were used as 'house charms' to keep out the Devil and prevent misfortune. In Britain they were buried beneath the floors of Roman-era homes, kept on twentieth-century windowsills and built into the walls of houses. Echinoids also have a wealth of folk names, among them shepherd's crowns, fairy nightcaps, shepherd's hats and fairy loaves. In *The Star-Crossed Stone* (2011), Kenneth McNamara proposes that some might retain echoes of beliefs with their roots in prehistory. *Shepherd*, he suggests, may actually be a corruption of the Irish *sidhe biorh*, pronounded 'shee-berr' and meaning fairy barrow (with the burial mounds seen as thresholds or portals where the living could enter the otherworld).

Fossil urchins, then, have been collected for millennia. Long before Darwin, those found on the Isle of Wight also helped inspire radical new theories on sea-level change, the Biblical Flood and the origin of fossils. Born a few miles from the Needles in 1635, Robert Hooke was a scientist and polymath, who as a child searched local beaches for what he called 'button-stones' and 'helmet-stones' (no doubt some of these echinoids made their way into cabinets of curiosity). He went on to join the Royal Society, and in a series of lectures in the 1660s addressed the origin of fossils, or 'figured stones' as they were known at the time (when *fossil* meant 'anything dug up'). A subject of debate for centuries, figured stones were considered by many within the Royal Society 'an attempt by the rock to mimic life'. They were thought to grow like crystals in the ground, through some 'kind of Plastick virtue inherent in the earth'.

At the time, the Earth was believed to be no more than 6,000 years old, as in Genesis. Most scientists, then – including leading geologists – believed the Biblical Flood had played a major part in creating geological features. In his lecture series, Hooke sought to explain the more 'problematic' fossils. Among them were stones resembling creatures that did not exist. At the Royal Society, the prevailing view reflected that of the wider population: 'Once God had established His perfect order within the natural world, it was inconceivable that He would allow that natural order to be destroyed by a species becoming extinct'. For some, the figured stones were God's creations that had been unsuccessful, or creatures that hadn't made it onto the Ark. Others considered them tricks of the Devil, planted to lead the faithful astray. Yet although

Hooke believed in the Deluge, as a scientist he didn't believe it explained the presence of fossil seashells found far inland or on hills and mountaintops.

'These shells,' he proposed at one of his lectures, 'could not be from the Flood of Noah, since the duration of that which was but about two hundred natural days'. Instead, they must be 'the Shells of certain Shell-fishes . . . filled with some kind of Mudd or Clay or petrifying Water'.

Almost two centuries before Darwin's *On the Origin of Species*, he came to what was then a remarkable conclusion: 'There have been many other species of creatures in former ages . . . diverse species of things wholly destroyed and annihilated'. Although he wasn't yet thinking in terms of millions of years, he did see fossils as key to understanding the history of the Earth. Proposing dramatic changes in sea level ('many scores of Fathoms'), he argued that before human history, English hilltops – like those on his native Isle of Wight – were once at the bottom of the sea. Hooke's proposal was not well received, either by the public or members of the Royal Society. It was not only radical, but also heretical.

While I knew the Needles must be close, in approaching from Tennyson Down they remain out of sight. Eventually, out on the headland now, the white chalk path turned to tarmac. With no one else around, I wandered past signs for The Old Battery and a Cold War rocket-testing site, before at last finding one to the Viewpoint. Leading out to the edge of the cliff, the path ended at steps to a deserted platform. As I walked out there the Needles came into view. I stopped. At the very tip of Skeleton Ridge, a line of chalk stacks rose to a knife-edge.

Today, they look nothing like needles. Taking their name from pinnacles that eroded away long ago, they looked more like three molars with a noticeable gap. In that space was once the tallest spire: Lot's Wife, which collapsed with spectacular force in 1764.

Way, way below, white surf crashed on a dark flint beach. The scale, like the timescale, was inhuman. With a hand to the rail, I stood in uneasy vertiginous awe, as gulls drifted lazily up the cliff-face on thermals.

Submerged prehistoric field walls
Green Bay, Bryher

3

Lyonesse

Isles of Scilly

In legend, the Isles of Scilly were once the highest hills of Lyonesse. Reaching out into the Atlantic from mainland Cornwall, Lyonesse is said to have been a fertile land of woods and fields, 'fair-sized towns' and 140 parish churches. But in 1099 a violent storm blew up and in a single night the kingdom was lost to the sea. Only one man, Trevilian, survived, on a white horse that outran the waves.

Over the centuries, many have traced the legend back through its earliest written versions. The first mention of 140 churches is in sepia, handwritten Latin, in William of Worcester's notes on his journeys around England in the 1400s. A century later, with the rise of the printing press, other elements appeared and were retained in later versions. The horse turned up in 1580, by which time Lyonesse had become linked with the medieval tales of King Arthur (perhaps due to a misunderstanding of the French *Loenois*, which may instead have referred to Brittany's Leon or even Scotland's Lothian). The first record of a name for this lost land – Lionesse – was in 1584, in the cartographer John Norden's *A Topographical and Historical Description of Cornwall*.

By then, antiquarians had begun making their way down to the tip of Britain's remote south-westerly peninsula, to hear the tale from Cornish-speaking locals. In 1602, Richard Carew, a member of the Elizabethan Society of Antiquaries, wrote of it in his *Survey of Cornwall*: 'The space between the Land's End and the Isles of Scilly, being about thirty miles, to this day retaineth the name, in Cornish Lethowsow . . . Fishermen also casting their hooks thereabouts have drawn up pieces of doors and windows.'

Lethowsow derives from the Cornish name for the Seven Stones Reef – between Cornwall and the Scillies – and is said to mean 'the milky ones', as the waves breaking over it can be seen for miles. One rocky ledge is still known by fishermen today as 'The Town' and according to tradition is the site of the Lethowsow's lost capital, the City of Lions. As well as describing hauled-up masonry, the sixteenth-century fishermen referred to the site as *Tregva* (Cornish for 'dwelling') and told of clear, still days when the ruins could be seen beneath the surface.

Later, as archaeology emerged from its antiquarian origins, others visited the Isles of Scilly in search of submerged ruins. Some also speculated on the truth and evolution of the legend. 'The Seven Stones', wrote the archaeologist O. G. S. Crawford in 1927, 'must once have been a habitable island, now reduced to a bare skeleton'. He concluded that while the submergence of Lyonesse may be true, the legend was not a direct traditional inheritance. Instead, he felt the story was more likely to have grown up in later times, 'through the acute observation of fishermen and other unlettered folk'. 'Provided they are quite unspoilt by book-learning', he wrote, 'their observations are generally trustworthy and their deductions sound, up to a point'.

Further evidence of submergence lies closer to the west Cornwall coast at Penzance. Here the tidal island of St Michael's Mount stands spectacularly in the waters of Mount's Bay. Yet the Mount's Cornish name, *Karrek Loos yn Koos*, means 'Grey Rock in the Wood', and out in the bay the lowest spring tides sometimes reveal the stumps and roots of ancient trees. Along with the

Scillies' drowned field walls, this seabed woodland no doubt helped perpetuate the idea of a drowned Lyonesse, as the legend passed into more recent centuries. In Walter de la Mare's melancholy, romantic poem 'Sunk Lyonesse' (1922), blunt-nosed fish swim over its salt-worn belfries, as Nereids pluck lyres in sea-cold streets. 'Sea cold, sea cold, it certainly is', responded Sylthia Plath in her modernist poem 'Lyonesse' (1962). Here the legendary kingdom – with its 'spidery water-dazzle on field and street' – has been allowed to drown by a weary and negligent God. Today, this Cornish Atlantis remains as popular and evocative as ever, featuring in everything from song lyrics and band names to fantasy novels and role-playing video games.

St Michael's Mount, Cornwall

I left home in Cornwall at dawn and waited at a misty, deserted Bodmin station for the first train to Penzance. From there, I caught the *Scillonian* ferry to the main island of St Mary's, and then another boat out to Bryher, the smallest and most northwesterly of the inhabited islands. At its tiny quay my rucksack and tent were collected by tractor, and I set off along the sandy beach to meet it at the island's campsite. A series of narrow fields divided by old stone hedges, this lay at the foot of Shipman Head Down, between the sheltered Tresco Channel and the exposed granite cliffs of Hell Bay.

After a first night in my one-person tent I headed for Bryher's sheltered side, walking out onto the pale rim of sand at Green Bay. In the early light it was strikingly still, with a faint mist rising from the water and a heron stood motionless in the shallows. I was still distant when it dipped and lifted off, the slow, deliberate wing-beat strangely prehistoric – which felt appropriate as it rose above the lines of boulders I'd come to see. The largest of these were huge, high on shore and half sunk in sand, while others lay where it gave way to mudflats. Out there, the furthest of the rocks were already slipping beneath the rising tide.

Leaving my shoes on shore I headed out barefoot, the water clear as glass and cold as it rose above my ankles. At my feet, sunlight rippled over seabed sand and part-submerged granite boulders, which were remnants of prehistoric field walls. Some date back to the Bronze Age, and they are a feature of the foreshore and shallow waters of several of the islands. From the air, the ruins show up as dark, unnaturally straight lines that trail out from white sand beaches into turquoise water. Tracing the outlines of lost fields, they are a striking reminder of how rising sea levels have been affecting these islands for millennia.

Sea level data suggests that the last time the Scillies could be reached on foot from mainland Cornwall was around 12,000 years ago. Over the next few thousand years – through the period of rapid sea-level rise that drowned both Doggerland and Bouldnor Cliff – the granite landmass was reduced to a single large island.

In 2016, the Lyonesse Project drew together the work of archaeologists, ocean scientists and other diverse specialists to reconstruct its gradual submergence. Along with the dating of intertidal archaeology and remnants of a submarine forest, studies ranged from the analysis of peat-preserved pollen and plankton to 'luminescence dating', in which buried sand grains reveal when they were last exposed to sunlight.

Together, the findings suggest a major inundation of the island, although *after* the steep Mesolithic rise had slowed. By then, over several thousand years, Scilly's prehistoric forest had transformed into open grassland and freshwater marsh. Later, as this flooded with increasing frequency, it formed a broad central area of salt marsh between today's islands. It was then, in the Early Bronze Age, that two-thirds of Scilly's current landmass was lost – over a period of only about 500 years. Some of that salt marsh then appears to have remained useful as summer pasture through the Bronze and Iron Ages – as suggested by the boulders at my feet.

By early medieval times, though, the sea had opened up a channel through the central salt marsh. From then on, high tides could erode the marshes more rapidly, in time dividing the single main island in two. Eventually, this would form the shallow inner lagoon that draws tourists today. Historic place names suggest that in AD 800, Samson, Tresco and Bryher formed the western peninsula of a larger island known as Ryn Tewyn or 'promontory of sand dunes'. By 1200, the three were described as a single St Nicolas's Isle, with Bryher appearing to have cleaved more recently from Tresco. Following a visit in the mid-eighteenth century, the Cornish geologist William Borlase gave a sense of the islands' creeping, ongoing separation: 'The flats between Trescaw, Brêhar, and Sampson are quite dry at a spring-tide and men easily pass dry-shod from one island to another over sand-banks (where, upon the shifting of the sands, walls and ruins are frequently discovered), upon which, at full sea, there are ten and twelve feet of water.'

Today, on very low spring tides, it is still possible to cross between Bryher and Tresco on foot – with care, if no longer with dry shoes. It is even possible to cross by tractor, with locals taking the opportunity to transport heavy loads like machinery (and manure) more cheaply than by boat.

Almost imperceptibly, the tide had submerged the granite boulders at my feet. Closer to shore, many were still smothered by the wrack they anchored: slippery heaps of seaweed that had collapsed as the sea withdrew. Now, though, it was returning to life. Buoyed by air-filled bladders, the drifting fronds fanned out at the surface, drawn lazily to and fro by the swell. In low sunlight, the translucent bladders were incandescent, the same amber as the periwinkles that live camouflaged among them (and whose shells fill many a visitor's pocket). As I stopped to watch, near-invisible sand gobies turned to face my feet, paused for a moment and then swam closer. It was faintly but delightfully unnerving. Although I'd been here less than half an hour, vast swathes of wet mud had transformed into sunlit shallows: inhabited, otherworld gardens magicked to life by the returning tide.

All around me, traces of prehistoric settlement lay obscured by mudflats, beach sand and shingle, by the shine of water. As well as the rubble walls that once marked field boundaries, small plots and a trackway, somewhere between the two islands were Bronze and Iron Age hut circles. Here on Bryher – as with other islands like neighbouring Samson – the submerged farmland is also overlooked by hills dotted with prehistoric cemeteries and entrance graves.

Later that morning, I was ferried out from Green Bay to uninhabited Samson. I caught a lift with Les, a regular visitor from Essex, who was heading out to where he'd scattered his wife's ashes. On the way, we sat across from each other on the sides of the RIB. Barefoot, white-haired and gracious, Les asked after Dan the boatman's family. The eldest, he said, was about to start secondary school, which meant boarding during the week on St

Mary's. For Bryher's nursery and primary-aged children, it was a shorter daily trip across to Tresco (one morning that week, queuing behind them at the tiny quay, I was struck by the mix of Cornish and cut-glass English accents).

Minutes later, the boat grounded on fine white sand at Bar Point, and Les and I waded ashore through water even clearer than Bryher's. Having arranged our separate pickup times, we watched Dan pull away with, I imagined, the usual quips about the boat not coming back.

Unfolding my map, I headed off up the beach in search of a path through the bracken and scrub. To begin with, I had little success. The island's two hills were clearly visible from shore, but the first paths had almost entirely grown over. It was something I'd been warned to expect due to earlier Covid lockdowns. Usually, given Samson's ruins, rich history and stories of abandonment, there were regular summer boat trips from St Mary's. But this year and last, the boats hadn't come, so the paths remained uncut. Today – pleasingly – the only sign of other people was two kayaks dragged high on shore. Eventually, after a series of false starts, I found a likely way in through the bracken. Glancing back, I saw Les making his way with difficulty over boulders at the top of the beach.

Having pushed through bracken that was shoulder and head height, I emerged at the Neck of Samson, a low sandy isthmus also known as the saddle or waist. Less than a mile long, the island is shaped like an hourglass. And between its two hills, sandy paths led off to close but very different beaches. As on Bryher, the western shore faced the open Atlantic, while the curve of East Porth fringed Scilly's inner lagoon. There, the remains of rubble walls trailed out into sheltered turquoise waters, as far as Black Ledge and the foundations of a Bronze Age roundhouse. Other traces of prehistoric farming had also been found at this beach, among them charred Bronze Age barley and the granite 'saddle querns' used to grind it.

As I began the climb up South Hill, the bracken grew taller again, competing with the gorse and bramble that smothered ruined walls. The spurs and ridges of Samson's two hilltops are dotted with prehistoric cairn cemeteries, cists and entrance graves. While Scilly's settlements were often on lower ground near arable land and salt-marsh pasture, the summits of its hills were places for the dead. Strikingly, the islands have one of the densest concentrations of prehistoric burial and ritual monuments in western Europe. For centuries this has led to speculation that they may have been considered sacred 'Isles of the Dead', with bodies or remains perhaps brought over from the mainland (which reminded me of Les, seeking the spot where he'd scattered his wife's ashes).

The granite tombs and monuments echo the natural forms of the island's rocky outcrops, with some incorporating existing 'earth-fast' boulders. Up here by myself, that made it hard to tell the difference between prehistoric monuments and what were just rocks. Or it was until I reached the most striking of the entrance graves, which was unmistakeable. Set high above the lagoon, its great weathered slabs formed the sloping roof of a recessed chamber. In hazy sunshine, its interior was sunk in shadow, as if it opened into the heart of the hill. Above the entrance, eroded by wind and rain for more than four millennia, its granite capstones were a patchwork of green and bone-white lichen.

Like Neolithic long barrows, these entrance graves allowed access to the living, and so presumably some form of ongoing relationship with the dead. More than ninety entrance graves have been recorded on the Scillies. And while many had already been disturbed, others retained at least some of their contents. Among them were disarticulated bones and inverted pots over cremated human remains, glass beads and a bronze dagger, beach pebbles and flints, broken pottery, limpet shells and quern stones.

Another common finding was a 'dark greasy soil'. Following a visit to the islands' 'ancient sepulchres' in 1754, William Borlase described this as 'a strong unctuous earth that smelt cadaverous'. Usually, it is interpreted as either the scraped-up remains of funeral pyres, or 'domestic midden debris', considered by some a symbolic transfer of material from the world of the living to the dead. So while containment of the dead was one of their functions, Scilly's entrance graves also appear to have been the focus of ceremonial or ritual practices.

Entrance grave, South Hill, Samson

Over the centuries, various theories have been proposed for the unusual density of prehistoric monuments on this remote archipelago. Were the Scillies really sacred islands of the dead? Was there some kind of maritime connection? Were they territorial markers, or navigational aids for boats? It's also possible they were a form of communal shrine, with rituals and offerings to protect against a loss of fertility of the land, or the sea.

More recently, archaeologist Katharine Sawyer obtained the first radiocarbon dates from a Scillonian entrance grave for her PhD thesis 'Islands of the Dead?'. This suggested a period of use between 2000 and 1250 BC, so Early Bronze Age. Cremation evidence supports these dates, suggesting a majority of the entrance graves were built following the inundation of large areas of low-lying land in the islands. The loss equates to something like three football pitches a year: an obvious and significant change within a single human lifetime. As archaeologist Jim Leary suggests of Mesolithic Doggerland, it's likely the loss of valuable, fertile land – clearly a shrinking resource – would have provoked tensions among island communities.

This coincidence of timing, writes Sawyer, 'suggests that the construction of entrance graves may have been regarded as a way of "holding the line" against the depredations of the sea'. Perhaps, then, they reflect a community response to environmental stress caused by rising seas. If so, it echoes Jim Leary's suggestion of intensified ritual practices in drowning Doggerland: offerings to placate water spirits transgressing onto the land (which might include the barbed points and aurochs skulls found buried on retreating Mesolithic shores in the Netherlands).

I climbed up onto the tor above the tomb, where the massive, fissured forms of the granite had the look of giant country (it was easy to see why the islands' entrance tombs were once known as 'giants' caves'). Below, Samson was laid out before me, its twin russet hills fringed with the palest sand. Further out in shallow water off the Neck, the dark lines of submerged prehistoric walls were just beginning to break the surface.

Stopping at a natural dip in the granite to sit and look out, I wondered if those who built the tomb might have rested here too. Yet how different the view would have seemed to them, not only with the Scillies still joined, but also alive with very different meanings. As a landscape inhabited by the spirits of ancestors, nature and place, its elements would have featured in stories and origin myths. If so, it seemed likely local deities dwelt in these twin hills, in Samson's spring, in the offshore reefs. Perhaps they were also heard in the distant holler of the Roaring Ledges.

Later that week, I visited the tiny island of Nornour. One of twelve uninhabited Eastern Isles, the four-acre hill is far too small to support a farming community now. It is a place that remained fairly unremarkable until 1962, when the first locals went ashore after a storm so violent that in Penzance it destroyed the promenade and swept away train tracks.

My first glimpse of the Eastern Isles was from the sea. Dark against the sun, they were strung out along the horizon like fins and whalebacks. As we drew closer, the boatman kept an eye on the depth sounder, navigating a route through the channels and necks between islands. Some, like Ragged Island, still had the hilltop remnants of coastal heath and grassland. Many, though, were no more than bare granite rocks and islets, where shags and cormorants dried crucifix wings. Others were reefs that broke the surface only at half-tide. On a few, grey seals were hauled out in the sun: raising wet whiskered heads to watch us pass, then settling back until the rising tide swept them off.

At low tide, a boulder ridge still connected Nornour to neighbouring Great Ganilly. Now, as we stopped offshore to transfer to the tender, only the rounded tops of the stones broke the surface. Beneath the boat, the sounder showed six feet of water. The boatman cut the engine, and we waited in the gently rocking boat, in a new quiet above the drowned land. In clear green water, thongweed rose in columns from the sea floor, to drift eerily at the surface like long red hair.

From the shallows, I walked in barefoot over fine white sand.

This reached almost to the round stone huts first revealed by the storm in 1962. Our visit had been arranged by Katharine Sawyer, who lived on St Mary's, and she led us over to the rubble walls of the largest roundhouse. With cropped grey hair, she was poised and knowledgeable, and we gathered round like children on a school trip. Stood in warm sunshine as she described the aftermath of the storm, it was hard to imagine the force of the waves that tore down Nornour's dunes to reveal its westernmost huts. Later, through the 1960s and '70s, further excavations would reveal a total of eleven rounded rubble buildings, nestled between the hillside and the shore.

This was possibly the earliest permanent settlement on Scilly, with an Early Bronze Age hearth and postholes concealed beneath later Iron Age buildings. Over an extraordinary 2,000 years, through successive phases of alteration and rebuilding, the huts developed as two main groups. New roundhouses and courtyards were added, along with steps, dividing walls and oval rooms. Old doorways were blocked up and new ones added. In telling this, Katharine gestured across knee-high walls to a gap that faced the sea. This was the original doorway, she said, which at some point in the Iron Age was blocked up and replaced with a more impressive entrance. Quite a few of us grinned, at the unexpected connection with those who lived here, at the idea of prehistoric home improvements. On the far side of the hut, the replacement granite of its new Iron Age doorway stood tall above the ruined walls.

Later, after others had left to climb the hill, I crossed its grassy threshold into a circular room. At the centre was a stone-edged hearth, beside what appeared to be a granite sofa bed. Sat on the grass by the hearth, I wondered about those who'd gathered around the fire. I imagined them reaching out for food, passing stone bowls as they listened and talked, told stories, filled dark evenings 3,000 years before Netflix. By firelight the granite walls would have glittered, and the air smelt of smoke and damp thatch: bracken, or perhaps reeds or kelp. Or even the thongweed drifting lazily out there now, above the land where their animals once grazed.

For we do know something of their lives as farmers and fishers, as towards the end of the Iron Age – before the huts and courtyards were abandoned to sand blow – they were filled with rubbish. Among it were ash and flint, a little pottery, limpet shells, stone bowls and saddle querns like those found on Samson. There were the bones of cattle and sheep, of seals and shallow-water fish, and a few from dolphins and stranded whales. Pollen traces suggest Nornour's huts were surrounded by farmland with cereal crops, a little woodland and salt-marsh pasture. This lost landscape also lives on in the old Cornish name for the Eastern Isles: *Enesow Goonhyli*, islands of the salt-water downs.

It made me wonder about the languages spoken around these hearths. How did they evolve over so many generations, over two millennia? Although similar to Welsh, the closest relative of Cornish is the Breton of Brittany, with the two languages once mutually comprehensible. Some research suggests that like Welsh and Gaelic they descend from an early Celtic language dating back to the Iron Age – or even the Bronze Age – which spread by sea along the Atlantic fringes of western Europe. Along with new techniques and technologies, a 'maritime lingua franca' would have brought new ideas and beliefs, new stories and explanations of the world. But how much contact would those living so remotely have had with the outside world? When locals first came ashore after the gales in 1962, one of the Nornour roundhouses contained some extraordinary clues.

I wandered along to the western end of the beach. Today, all that remains of that first group of huts are two crescents of rubble wall set into the hill. When first uncovered, as well as the two adjoining roundhouses, the ruined quarter-circles of two more huts stood closer to the water. In 2004 and 2014, though, this end of the beach took the brunt of further violent storms that tore down walls and buried much under beach stones. Now, I trod over them to the furthest curve of wall. Noon sun shone on stones splashed orange with lichen, but left the crevices deep in shade.

It was inside these that visitors to Scilly placed brooches some 2,000 years ago. By the 1970s, archaeologists had found more than 300 at Nornour, prompting suggestions they might be spoils from a shipwreck, or that the huts were once used as a brooch factory. But a number of things didn't fit. Firstly, the brooches came from many places across Britain and continental Europe, and varied widely in quality and design. Also, while many were plain, others were beautifully enamelled (one of the best was a sea leopard: a hybrid creature that in Greek mythology accompanies the souls of the dead on their journey west to the Isles of the Blessed). Also, the dates of the brooches – like Roman coins found among them – spanned a full four centuries. Taken together, this cast doubt on the theories of a shipwreck or brooch factory.

Another peculiarity was that although the Iron Age building had remained unaltered, the rest of its contents were not the things of daily life. Instead, archaeologists found glass beads and miniature urns, bronze rings and bracelets, a sword with a decorated scabbard, and fragments of white-clay figurines that represented goddesses. All were the types of objects left at Romano-Celtic shrines as votive offerings. Common across the Roman Empire, these places ranged from small roadside shrines to elaborate temples, often sited near water and dedicated to local deities: the *genius loci* or 'spirit of a place'. Seen as successors to Neolithic and Bronze Age ritual landscapes, the shrines typically had an altar where incantations were spoken, and offerings and sacrifices made.

At Nornour, many of the objects were found close to the hut's central hearth. So it is thought to have functioned as an altar or shrine. The two lost huts – revealed as quarter-circles in 1962 – may then have housed the priest or custodian, which was common practice at the shrines. So now, the two western huts are interpreted as an abandoned Iron Age dwelling, later reused as a Romano-Celtic shrine. A stopping-off point for seafarers and traders, it is thought to have been where offerings were made to a local deity, perhaps in exchange for a fair wind and safe passage. As the Roman name for the islands was Sillonia Insula, it's argued this could derive from the name of an Iron Age goddess, perhaps with the root 'Sil' meaning 'she who watches'.

Examination of the Nornour brooches also showed they were missing their pins. And rather than having rusted away, they appeared to have been broken off. Across Britain and Europe, such intentional breakage is often seen where Bronze and Iron Age objects have been cast into water. Described by archaeologists as 'ritual deposition', it is thought to have been some kind of offering. At Flag Fen near Peterborough, for example, many beautifully preserved metal objects were found close to a Bronze Age timber causeway. Among them were intentionally bent or broken swords, daggers and bracelets – as well as brooches with broken-off pins. These metal objects would have been valuable or useful possessions, so their deliberate breakage is often interpreted as a form of sacrifice, a symbolic 'ritual killing' to put an offering beyond human use.

Through most of the four centuries Nornour's shrine was in use, Christianity remained one cult among many in Roman Britain. By AD 323, though, it had become the official religion of Rome. From then on, things began to change, as unlike earlier polytheistic religions, Christianity was intolerant of other gods (the Roman Emperor Constantine hoped it was something that might unite his Empire). Old beliefs would of course linger. But people would also seek new ways to influence the future, and gain protection from forces beyond their control, from famine to storms and rising seas.

Before leaving I wandered back through the huts, ending up at an Iron Age doorway festooned with lichen and heather. Looking out over white sand and turquoise water, it was like the garden gate of one of the Scillies' many boutique holiday cottages. Across the water lay Great Ganilly, with no sign now of the cobble ridge that had linked the islands as we came ashore. Over there were more Iron Age ruins, and a hut circle close to the water. For archaeologists, this suggests other ruins may lie submerged between the islands; that the settlement was more extensive than just eleven huts.

Like the rest of the huts, Nornour's Romano-Celtic shrine was abandoned to sand blow towards the end of the Roman era. With the sea encroaching inexorably on surrounding salt marsh, the dwindling hills of the Eastern Isles would become too small to support its farming communities. After millennia, the challenges of living here would in time have become too much: from repeated flooding and loss of pasture, from windblown sand and freshwater sources turned brackish.

In the centuries that followed, the Scillies' central salt marsh began to flood with increasing regularity. By early medieval times, the sea had made inroads from both east and west, with the channel dividing St Mary's from the northern islands open for most of the tide. Eventually, once the sea broke through for good – perhaps during a violent storm – erosion of the salt marsh would have increased rapidly. Out there now, our boat lay at anchor in more than six feet of water.

Back on Samson I sat on the tor above the entrance grave, drinking tepid coffee and looking out over the inner lagoon. Thin cloud had drifted in from the west, and sky-shine concealed the old land. Within the rim of sheltering islands, the tide was again drawing back to reveal sandbars, rocky reefs and the Half Tide Ledges.

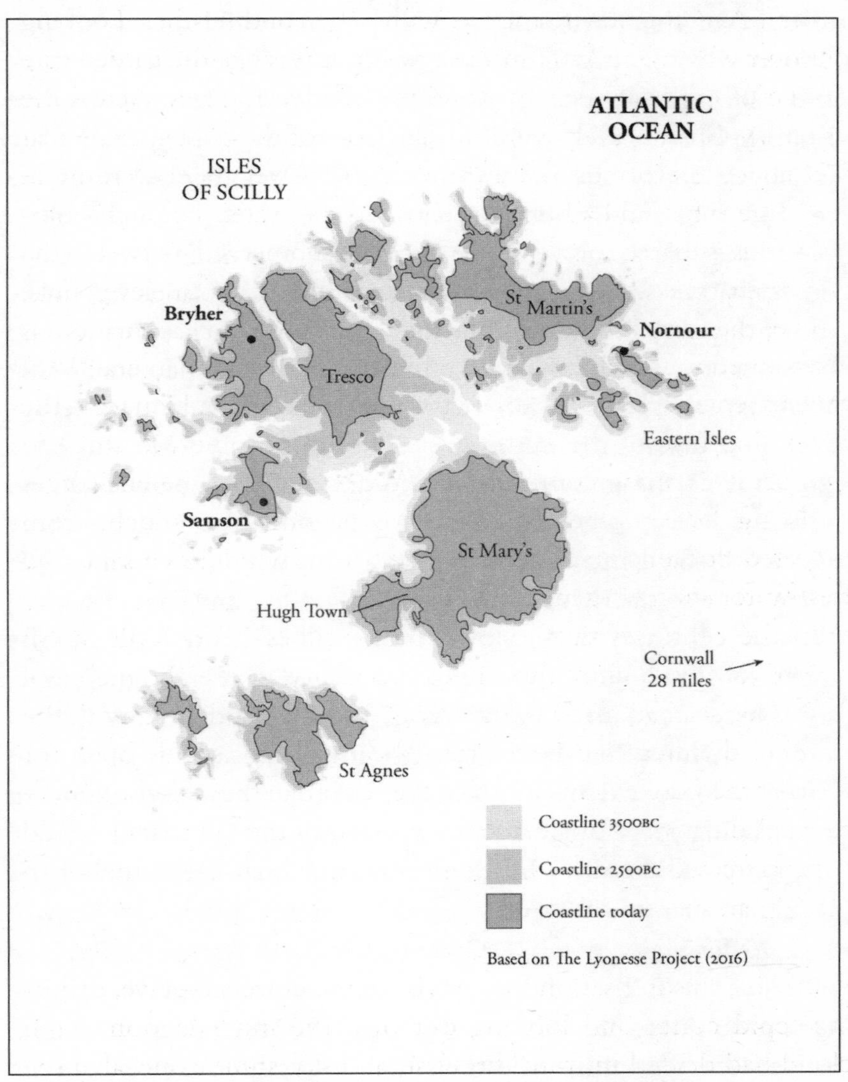

Reconstruction showing Isles of Scilly coastlines in 3500 BC and 2500 BC

Later, poring over maritime charts for a sense of the land that was lost, I traced the intricate whorls of the fathom lines. Swirling between islands like eddies and races, they encircled features of that vanished landscape: submerged hills and tors, drowned pools, valleys and inlets. Now they were Arthur Neck and Chimney Rocks, Crow Sound, Renny Brow and Great English Island Neck (while only five of the Isles of Scilly are inhabited today, the inclusion of skerries and rocks brings the total to over 140 islands).

On the charts, the sea ranged from blue to white – palest, paradoxically, where deepest – while yellow showed land that broke the surface at all states of the tide. Between those yellows and blues, green was for the half-worlds of the reefs and shoals. Out there lay Bars and Banks that appear at half-ebb, treacherous Ledges that vanish at three-quarter flood. Out at what was once the edge of the known world, the draw of their names was no surprise. Many were straightforward: Wee Flat Ledge, Three Rocks, a shoal named Bump and a dozen Round Rocks. Yet there was also the mystery of New Found Out, and rocks I wished I'd seen: Hats and the Rawness, Cowl and Wetnose Rock. Quite a few felt like relics of old tales and tragedies. Cuckold's Ledge, the Three Damned Sinners, Vinegar Ledge, the Tearing Ledges and Tom Butts Bed (later I learned Tom Butts was a boy said to have hidden out there in a sea cave for three days and nights, to avoid being press-ganged on to a man-of-war).

Quite a few of the islands retain anglicised versions of their older, descriptive Cornish names. Some continue to remain fitting: Illiswilgig is still a 'Grassy Island' and Bryher a 'Place of Hills'. Others, though, are reminders of vanished landscapes. One group of exposed barren skerries are known today (fittingly) as Hellweathers, although the name is thought to derive from the Cornish *Hal Weres*, meaning marshy ground. Off Bryher, treeless Gweal is from the Cornish *Gwydhyel*, meaning 'Place of Trees'. And similarly, Crebawethan is from *Krib an Wedhen*, 'Reef of the

Tree'. Yet both Great and Little Crebawethan lie out at the edge of the remote and notoriously hazardous Western Rocks, where white water seethes against granite. Today, they are home to razorbills, puffins and storm petrels. But with little more than the odd patch of scurvy grass, neither has any place a tree will grow again.

From high on the South Hill I could see out over Samson's ruined cottages, which have long drawn visitors to the island. Apart from the odd outlier, the cottages clustered in two main groups: one higher on the hill and the other in a hollow closer to the Neck. Although reluctant to leave my eyrie, I zipped away the flask and headed down towards the ruins.

While the abandonment of the Eastern Isles is lost to prehistory, the last residents of Samson left as recently as 1855. So traces also remain in the records, along with stories – both true and tall – of the families' last decades on the island.

Down on the Neck, the sands around East Porth have also produced pottery dating from the sixth to the thirteenth centuries, along with the remains of an early medieval Christian cell or chapel. From the mid-1200s, though, the island appears to have been abandoned for around four centuries. By then, much of the salt marsh had drowned, and Tresco, Bryher and Samson formed part of a northern St Nicholas's Isle. By 1669, we know Samson had been reoccupied. Sailing past on a tour of Europe, a companion of Cosmo III, Grand Duke of Tuscany, noted a single family living on the island. By then, his overriding impression of the Scillies was its lack of trees, and that the houses had a 'peculiar sort of covering by way of a roof . . . nothing but a simple mat spread over the rafters, drawn tight all round'. By the 1750s, less than a century later, Samson's population had swelled to more than thirty.

Today, with the paths uncut, many ruins near the Neck were overgrown with bracken and brambles. The most complete cottage once belonged to Richard Webber and his wife. Today it stood off on its own, roofless, but with the stone gable ends still tall above shoulder-high bracken. Closer to, the surrounding ferns were trampled enough that a narrow path led round to the leeward doorway. From an old photograph, I knew that somewhere beneath the undergrowth lay the Webbers' vegetable garden and a flagstone path once flanked by stone-edged flower beds.

For those on off-islands like Samson, life was hard. Many relied on subsistence fishing and farming, although for a time there was also a profitable kelp industry (the leathery seaweeds were gathered at low tide or after storms, and burnt to produce soda ash for the soap and glass industries). Given Samson's position out by the hazardous Northern and Western Rocks, there was also money to be made from piloting ships in and out of the islands, and the bonus of salvage from ships that stranded or were wrecked on the rocks. Rarely, as in 1745, there was also a whale stranding (with the valuable, waxy spermaceti sold to make fine wax candles, perfumes and pomades).

Along with its ruined cottages, Samson was also criss-crossed with ruined stone walls, which vanished into thickets of briar and late-summer ferns. Some appeared to have once been continuous with the now-submerged walls out on Samson Flats, linking them with hilltop cairns and entrance graves. On the lower slopes, as Samson's population peaked in the 1800s, the existing prehistoric walls were modified and reused.

Over time, the Samson fields were divided into ever-smaller plots. This was the result of the island's unorthodox system of inheritance, with land on the Scillies leased from an absentee landlord. On Samson, a father's lease passed equally to all his sons, so a family's land could be repeatedly subdivided over several generations. By 1829, this meant the island's eighteen fields – among them several Little Fields, Up-and-Down Field, Old Lay and Back-of-the-Hill – had been split into eighty-four. In time, it left some of those strips or 'stitches' no larger than a 'fair-sized flower bed'.

At the doorway, I passed beneath the granite lintel into a grassy space that was once two rooms. On the southern wall was the stone outline of a large kitchen fireplace, near a single window that faced inland. Ferns now sprouted from crevices, and brambles reached in over walls, hanging tight green blackberries in alcoves that once held crockery and pots.

At the far end was a smaller parlour hearth, set into a granite chimney-breast bearded with sea ivory. Thriving in Samson's clean salt air, more than fifty species of lichen have been found among its ruined cottages. With some dependent on specific microclimates, they'd taken advantage of a sunny chimney-breast, a north-facing joist hole or damp parlour corner. Some thrived untouched by rain beneath a fireplace lintel, others on a gable end wall, exposed to salt spray and the worst of the gales. They clothed the stone with their muted mosaics: grey-green ruffles and off-white splashes, powdery mauve-grey crusts. In the ruined parlour, they were like tester-pot paint patches on holiday cottage walls. Reaching out to the chimney-breast, I touched the oddly stiff hair of the sea ivory. Other species of lichen are named for their resemblance to antlers or jelly, to gold dust and coral, warts or the stalked eyes of crabs. No longer cottages, these stone air gardens were every bit as strange and wondrous as the intertidal half-worlds of the seaweeds.

On the Scillies, those two worlds meet at the islands' granite margins. It is a band that marks the highest tides, where the wrack stops and tar lichens stain the splash zone. Today, that divide creeps higher by almost five millimetres a year – faster than when the entrance tombs were built. In the Scillies, the rate of *relative* sea-level rise is higher than elsewhere in Britain, as glacial rebound is also causing the land to sink. Once again it brought St Mary's to mind, where the Scillies' main Hugh Town is built on a slender sandbar. As sea levels rise, this leaves the town increasingly vulnerable to storms and surges (at high tide, Old Town Quay already slips underwater). So over coming decades, as the islands continue to take the brunt of Atlantic storms, low-lying Hugh Town will be at ever-greater risk.

Ruined cottage, Samson

The story of Samson's abandonment isn't quite what it seems. It often begins in the Napoleonic Wars, with an enemy ship sighted to the west of the islands. Nineteen of Samson's men and boys are said to have boarded the ship. After capturing the French privateer crew, they were then ordered to sail their prisoners to Plymouth. But off Wolf Rock, the ship was struck and went down, taking all hands with it. This left Samson an island of widows, a dwindling community struggling to survive on a diet of limpets and potatoes, until their eviction in 1855.

Yet records show no mass drowning of Samson's men in the eighteenth or nineteenth century. Instead, in 1794, the Reverend John Troutbeck, chaplain for the Isles of Scilly, made note of another local tragedy: nine men drowned in 1788, when a boat went down between St Mary's and Tresco. In other records, the Tresco men left behind seven widows and twenty-eight children. With Tresco close to overpopulation at the time, the loss left Tresco's widows – rather than Samson's – barely able to feed themselves and their children. 'They have nothing but Straw to lie on', wrote Troutbeck after a visit to assess their needs, 'without any Kind of Bed Cloathes, & nothing to subsist on but a Kind of Shell Fish, which they gather on the Rocks'. The shellfish he describes were limpets, and consumption of this 'rubbery and unsatisfying "sea-beef"' would be an ongoing measure of off-islanders' struggles to survive. (In better times limpets were used mainly as bait, not least because a single person would need to eat 400 a day.)

Often, environmental stresses are felt more acutely on islands. And when populations reach the maximum an island can support – as on Samson and Tresco at that time – they become increasingly vulnerable. In 1817, following the notorious 'Year without a Summer' (caused by volcanic eruptions in Indonesia that affected much of Europe), the Scillies' grain and potato harvests failed. This made life hard for the poor throughout the islands, but was felt particularly acutely on the off-islands. By the time Reverend Woodley made a visit to report on Samson, conditions on the island were dire. 'The number of inhabitants here is small and their necessities extremely limited', he wrote. 'They ask only for the means of obtaining just sufficient bread and potatoes to keep them alive. Two or three families are very poor, and have suffered much distress.'

Unwilling to leave their island home, the families hung on and things did improve. Yet there was always the problem of limited resources. Samson, for example, was notoriously short of fresh water, with its families reliant on a single intermittent spring and two shallow wells at the Neck. These sometimes became choked with sand, and during one prolonged drought, from 1825 to 1826, the islanders were forced to row barrels of water from Bryher.

There was also little land for subsistence farming on Samson. So when a crackdown on smuggling coincided with the decline of the kelp industry, it left Samson's men increasingly reliant on salvage and pilotage. This led to fierce competition between islands, with more than fifty men sometimes rowing out to meet a single ship. Inevitably, tensions between the Samson and St Mary's boatmen could run high, sometimes ending in court or erupting in violence and fights.

Despite the hardships, by 1829 there were nine cottages on Samson. By then, seven of the households were Webbers and two were Woodcocks (the story told is of two lawless families descended from shipwrecked privateers, which also appears to be untrue). Then in 1834, a new landlord acquired the lease on the Isles of Scilly. Titling himself Lord Proprietor of Scilly, Augustus Smith came with plans for social reform and soon began making changes. Perhaps inevitably, he proved a divisive figure, admired by some for building schools and a quay, but hated by others. Among the latter were those expelled from the islands as they couldn't find a job, and off-islanders whose leases he set out to 'rationalise'.

For Smith, these smaller islands were 'approaching the final stages of anarchy, dereliction and famine'. Having begun with persuasion, he shifted to compulsion. Within a couple of years of his arrival, Samson's first eviction orders were signed – although Smith did agree to wait for Samson's elderly tenants to die before others in their household were evicted. As it turned out, there were soon several deaths, followed by failed attempts to remove remaining family. On one occasion, constables from St Mary's were brought over to attempt a forced entry. Several Webbers, though, barricaded themselves inside one of the cottages, shouting they'd rather die than leave the island.

Yet by 1841, half the island's cottages were empty. And in 1855, the last three residents were evicted. There is of course a tale of that day, with Smith himself going over to Samson for the final eviction. The very last to leave was Mrs Webber – 'an old woman of strange personal powers' – and before climbing into the boat she cast a spell on the Lord Proprietor. Having lost the use of his legs, he was unable to move, until the boatmen persuaded Mrs Webber to lift her enchantment.

The real ending was that with his tenants gone, Smith went ahead with his intention to turn Samson into a deer park. But despite new boulder walls, some built with stone from the cottages, the project failed. The shallow lagoon proved no barrier to deer, and they escaped to Tresco by wading across the Flats at low tide.

Now, beyond the ruin's parlour window, I could see nothing but bracken. Once, it looked out over a vegetable patch to a cluster of older Webber cottages. Much later, a tamarisk tree would grow inside the oldest of the cottages. In 2006 the gnarled tree was still there, when archaeologists cut a trench into the floor. Beneath the roots and vegetation, they dug down through silt and sand to buried refuse. Among it were door hinges and window glass, prehistoric worked flints, pottery dating from the seventeenth to the nineteenth centuries. Along with several iron candleholders were limpet shells, the bones of rabbits and fish, rats' teeth, a bone-handled knife and a roll of damp preserved leather. This is thought to have been an oar collar, so was perhaps used when various Webbers rowed out to a wrecked or stranded ship.

I stood by the small parlour hearth, where two centuries ago someone knelt to light a fire with driftwood or turf. Above, to one side of the chimney-breast, a striking but precarious-looking lintel capped a window-like opening. Fat pillows of thrift grew from the sill, as the September breeze shuffled papery flower heads on faded stems. From its height, the opening would have led to an attic, and looked out on the Northern Rocks. Up there somewhere, Richard and Mary Webber slept among eaves that were now long gone.

Later, I learned Samson's ruins were also not quite what they seemed. Resonant with loss and impermanence, the hollowed-out homes have attracted visitors for more than a century (one black-and-white photograph shows pre-war picknickers posing before an attractively ruined Webber cottage). Presumably, the ruins also helped draw the tragic story of the widows to abandoned Samson, and away from Tresco with its helipad and luxury timeshares. So today, the intention is 'to preserve the buildings as beautiful ruins'. Wandering through the cottages that day, I had no idea that the walls were threaded and reinforced with steel. High on the South Hill, drawn to the silvered oak of a fireplace lintel salvaged from a ship, I didn't see the stainless-steel rods painted to vanish in shadow. I didn't know that at the peak of gable ends, the granite was fixed in place with unseen resin.

They were careful, sensitive repairs, and I wasn't surprised. Out here, exposed to the full force of Atlantic gales, these ruins can't last. Roots take hold and stones are dislodged, walls bow and collapse into rubble. But it left me with an uneasy sense of illusion, of an invisible framework that held up Samson's past.

It was as if, for a while, time could be stopped on this hourglass island.

Sinkhole, Mutton Island

4

Kilstifeen & the Isle of Fitha

Mutton Island, County Clare, Ireland

From Fishguard in Wales, I crossed the Irish Sea and drove the van across Ireland. By the time I reached County Clare, the roads wound through backlit fields as emerald as the songs, and when at last I emerged from the hills, it was to the panorama of rural West Clare. This was as far as I could go. Beyond lay the silvered Atlantic, split by the molten trail of the setting sun. In Irish mythology this was *Mag Mell*, 'Plain of Honey or Delights'. It was a path to the otherworld, to *Tír na nÓg*, 'Land of the Young', an earthly paradise where Ireland's pre-Christian gods and heroes dwelt. Looking out there now, it led to Mutton Island. Yet despite coming all this way, I still had no idea if I'd be able to get there.

Keen to see the island from shore before losing the light, I pushed on towards the village of Quilty. I was also eager to get to the pub. Before leaving Cornwall I'd spoken to the landlord, who said he'd ask around to see if any of the local fishermen might be willing to take me out there. Notoriously dangerous and exposed, Mal Bay is thought to derive from the Irish *Meall-Bhaigh*, meaning 'treacherous coast'. According to one maritime navigation guide, 'the island and bay are fringed by dangers on all sides . . . a stranger should only approach Mutton Island with sound local knowledge'.

It was a story that had led me to the island. The traditions varied on different parts of this coast, although all involved an enchanted island or city submerged beneath the sea. Among the many spellings of its Irish name were Kilstifeen, Cill Stíopháin, Cill Stuifin, Kilstuitheen and Cillstiffiann (thought to derive from 'the church of St Stephen', or possibly St Scuithin, a medieval Irish saint said to have walked on water across the Irish Sea). North of Mutton Island, Kilstifeen is said to lie at the mouth of Liscannor Bay, the site sometimes marked by a disturbance of the water above Kilstiffin Rocks. Often it is a splendid city built from quartz and precious metals. The streets are paved with marble and the roofs thatched with feathers, with its golden spires and domed palaces sometimes glimpsed beneath the waves. Every seven years the city rises to the surface, but anyone who sees it will die – within the year, or before it rises again. Sometimes Kilstifeen can be disenchanted: by a handful of thrown clay, with a golden key found in a lake or beneath an ancient gravestone, or by a six-fingered girl from Liscannor.

For me, the draw of Mutton Island was also its geology, given certain records in the Irish Annals. Chronicles of medieval Irish history, they refer to a storm or tidal wave devastating this coast between AD 799 and 804. 'On the day before the festival of St. Patrick', states the *Annals of the Four Masters*, 'a great wind arose, accompanied by thunder and lightning, and the sea swelled so high that it burst its boundaries, heaping the coasts of Corcavaskin with rocks and sand, drowning 1,010 persons'.

Other entries describe this 'earth-quake wave' breaking the island of Fitha into three – with Mutton Island thought to be a surviving remnant. But that was all there was: a few lines in the annals, compiled mainly by monks from documents since lost or destroyed. Unsurprisingly, given a culture famed for its storytellers, the tales of Kilstifeen were far more extensive and richly embellished. Occasionally, as in one early 1900s version, Kilstifeen is a humble fifth-century village, with the storm raised by a curse from St Senan when he is refused a bed for the night. But more commonly, legendary Kilstifeen is said to have been lost in the same catastrophe that destroyed Fitha at the turn of the eighth century.

Two days after arriving in Ireland, I drove out to the end of a long sweep of beach, to park up for the night above the pier at Seafield Point. A couple of miles from Quilty, the isolated jetty was sheltered by a rocky outcrop facing Mutton Island, with a handful of small fishing boats moored beside the ruins of an abandoned coastguard station. I was due to meet Anthony next morning on the pier at 5.30 a.m. Earlier, he said they'd be heading out then to check crab and lobster pots, and agreed to make a detour to drop me on the island.

'You'll get wet,' he said, before hanging up.

As the sun set that night in bloodied streaks, Mutton Island was a thin black line on the horizon. All around, the quiet ebb tide revealed reefs that were soon concealed by the gathering dark. Storm-clouds were piled high inland, the stillness a held breath before the first drops of rain. As they came, with an otherworldly rumble of unease, I made a run for the van.

Inside, I sat by lamplight staring out though streaming windows to the floodlit glitter of the pier. Along the distant shore, the lights of Quilty slid into the inky water of the bay. Periodically, though, sheet lightning flashed inside the clouds and laid the land bare. I fell asleep as the rain began to ease, feeling somehow safer in a storm – as who would come out to the pier in this? In the small hours I was woken by lightning and the shudder of the van in the wind. But then it dropped as fast as it came, and I drifted back to sleep to thoughts of Kilstifeen.

Similar tales of enchanted islands are told all along this west coast of Ireland. Out at sea, fishermen are said to have caught the sound of muffled bells far from land, the lowing of cattle or the bleating of lambs, sometimes the scent of wildflowers. Often, a site was marked by a rough patch of sea while all around was calm: the storm conjured to keep mortals away. Other times, far from shore, a magical mist was said to have descended, leaving nothing but a drifting oak leaf or sprig of heather.

Occasionally, the tales describe chance encounters with the undersea inhabitants: an anchor catching on a lintel as a protesting voice calls up from the depths; merrows and shapeshifting seal people; a fisherman who hooks a child with silver scales. Usually, these enchanted islands can rarely be reached by mortals, and many – like Kilstifeen – appear once every seven years.

The roots of these folktales reach back to the otherworld islands of medieval Irish mythology. Sometimes veiled by *féth fíada*, a concealing mist, these fantastical islands were places of everlasting youth, beauty and abundance, with feasting, music and song, and no need to work.

In the eighth-century tale *The Voyage of Bran*, a group of monks embark on a quest to the otherworld. Setting sail in traditional hide-covered currachs, they encounter *Manannán mac Lir*, 'Son of the Sea' and ruler of Land Under the Wave. From a chariot pulled by his horse *Aonbharr* – able to gallop over water – he explains that to him the water is a flowery plain. He then directs them to the Land of Joy, where one of the monks is left behind, 'laughing and gaping'. Later, when the monks hesitate off the Isle of Women, its leader throws a magical ball of yarn and reels them ashore. On the island there is no suffering, sickness or death, and the monks' plates and cups are always full. Every night, beautiful women then lead them away, to 'a large house, in which was a bed for every couple'.

Although first written down by monastic scribes, Ireland's early myths retain echoes of its pre-Christian oral traditions. For Miranda Aldhouse-Green in *The Celtic Myths*, these stories offer 'subtle clues to possible origins in the deep pre-medieval past'. Rich in human-animal shapeshifters and enchanted beasts, the myths are 'shot through with imagery that hints at an underlying tradition of shamanism'.

Yet over time, as Christian themes came to the fore, those elements moved into the background. Like the *Voyage of Bran*, the later *Voyage of St Brendan* relates the travels of another group of monks in search of islands and promised lands to the west of Ireland. While the earliest versions date to around the ninth century, St Brendan was a sixth-century monastic saint who made many pilgrimages by sea. This was part of an early Irish seafaring tradition, in which monks voyaged to islands and remote locations to remain as hermits or establish monasteries to spread the gospel. Others, though, are said to have headed west in search of *Tír na nÓg,* or the classical earthly paradise the 'Isles of the Blessed' (thought to lie in the 'western ocean' beyond the edge of the known world). Later, stories of the monks' sea-voyages would become known as *immrama*: literally, 'rowing about'.

In the *Voyage of St Brendan*, the islands encountered are more clearly 'God's stepping stones', with their wonders and horrors epitomising salvation or damnation. One is a Paradise of Birds

Monks celebrating mass on the back of Jasconius
Voyage of St Brendan, 1621

that sing verses of the psalms; another is the whale-like sea monster Jasconius, which turns up regularly at Easter for the monks to celebrate mass on its back. Approaching one island, the monks are pelted with flaming, foul-smelling slag, while another is inhabited by an Ethiopian devil and a dog.

Towards the end of the journey, the monks meet Judas Iscariot alone on a barren rock lashed by the Atlantic. He is there, he tells them, because it's Sunday: the one day of the week he is granted respite from Hell. The descriptions of its torments vary, not least because a Latin version of the story became something of a medieval bestseller in Europe, and in time was translated into seventeen languages. (The one lingering longest on the Judas scene is a twelfth-century Anglo-Norman version in rhyming couplets. With his flayed body frozen on one side and burned on the other, Judas describes how he is tortured differently each day of the week. On Wednesdays, for example, he is boiled in pitch and forced to drink molten metal, whereas on Fridays he is skinned alive and rolled in soot and salt.) Throughout Brendan's seven-year voyage, the monks – and all the good people they encounter – are sustained and protected by God. Eventually, on reaching the Promised Land of the Saints, Brendan's faith is vindicated, and his monastic crew are richly rewarded for accepting his leadership. By then, any dissenters have died, been left behind, or gone to Hell. For centuries after the story became popular, a St Brendan's Isle – like the similarly legendary Hy Brasil – appeared mid-Atlantic on maps and charts. It also features on the world's oldest surviving terrestrial globe, the Erdapfel or 'Earth Apple'.

Next morning, I woke early to the call of waders in the predawn light. Below, the still-floodlit pier shone in the wet, and five fishing boats kept their mooring lines taut. 'With ludicrous absurdity,' noted the *Parliamentary Gazetteer of Ireland* following an assessment of Seafield in 1845, 'the pier was erected without any care being used to open a channel to it; and it confronts a sea-ground too obstructed with rocks to be possibly navigable.' As a result, only 'wicker-boats covered with tarred canvass' were moored there. Similar in design to those of the voyaging monks, these traditional currachs were used by the local fishermen into the twentieth century. By the 1920s – when families still lived out on Mutton Island – more than fifty three-man currachs still landed their fish at Seafield pier, with each boat named for a different saint (in neighbouring Kerry, currachs are known as *naomhóg* which means 'little holy one').

Down on the jetty in gentle rain, Anthony pulled up beside me in a van. Finbar would be coming out too, he said, before describing the sheep he once ferried out to Mutton Island for the summer grazing. 'I could fit six of them in the boat on the way out,' he said, pulling the braces of orange waterproofs up over his shoulders. 'But not on the way back. By then, they were so fat I could only fit two.'

The island was no more than half a mile offshore, and in the past cattle were also taken out in late spring. At one time, they are said to have waded out knee-deep along the 'old road' on a low spring tide. Yet the reef between Seafield and the island is rocky and hard going, and others found it easier to swim the cattle out. 'Old hands' went first so the rest would follow, and currachs with outboard engines stayed alongside to help keep heads above water.

Busy with the boat, Finbar was quiet as we left the dock. He was perhaps in his thirties, although with skin so browned by wind and sun he might have been almost any age. He'd seemed oblivious to my presence on the boat, then halfway out asked about the book – reminding me of a Seamus Heaney poem:

His fisherman's quick eye
And turned, observant back

With Anthony at the rudder, Finbar spoke with an easy Irish warmth. He'd grown up in Quilty, he said, and his dad was a fisherman too, though rarely went out now. Back in his day, twenty-seven boats had fished out of Seafield, although now it was only four. It was a hard living, Finbar said, and in winter he worked in construction. In the last recession, with so little work, he'd left Quilty and worked abroad – part of a long tradition of Irish emigration that peaked with the Great Famine in the mid-nineteenth century.

From shore, treeless Mutton Island looked low, which proved deceptive as Anthony drew closer, weaving a course through hidden reefs.

'I expect you can climb rocks,' he said, with a glance at my plimsolls.

With the high spring tide pressing up against the island, I grabbed a handhold on steep grey rock and scrambled to the top. By the time I looked back, the small blue boat was already some distance away.

I was alone on the island.

Although its 185 acres stretched away before me, I'd landed close to the abandoned cottages. Finbar had warned that to reach them I'd have to push through nettles, but hadn't mentioned the rabbit holes. It seemed a poor place to break an ankle, so my progress was wary and slow. Ahead, the most complete ruin stood at the cliff-edge facing the mainland, where low cloud still shrouded the Clare hills. Only one roofless building still resembled a cottage. So very carefully, I made my way round to the front, where the doorway was only feet from a sheer drop to the rocks below.

Back in 1887, the Irish antiquarian, archaeologist and folklorist Thomas Westropp visited the small subsistence fishing and farming community that lived out on Mutton Island. Over the course of several surveys, in a field behind one of the cottages, Westropp discovered the 'west wall of a small oratory'. He also described what appeared to be a broken 'rude' stone cross (crudely made, it turned out, not explicit). They are thought to have been relics of a church founded on the island by St Senan in the sixth century, back in the times of the *immrama* (later, he founded a famously austere monastery on Scattery Island further south). Today, any remnants of Westropp's oratory are said to have been lost to the sea, as on this leeward side of Mutton Island, softer clays overlie the rock. At the time of the antiquarian's visit, up to twelve families lived on Mutton Island. Yet it was so exposed to Atlantic storms that in winter there would be weeks – or even months – when it was impossible to fish or reach the mainland. At other times, islanders would stay over on the mainland on Saturday nights, to ensure they were at mass on Sunday. In 1911, twenty islanders still remained in four cottages, but by the 1920s they too had begun to leave. Like so many other abandoned islands on Ireland's west coast – most famously the Blaskets – Mutton Island was deserted by the 1950s.

Stepping across the threshold of this last remaining cottage, I stood on the dirt floor of a single room open to the sky. As ever, it was the stone fireplace that drew the eye. Blackened by the smoke of turf fires, it took up much of one wall. To the east, the only window looked out on the mainland. I wandered the small space beneath fishing rope slung between the gable ends, suggesting someone spent nights out here under a tarp. In a corner by the hearth lay a jawbone: from a sheltering sheep, perhaps, or even a goat (against the odds, a small herd of feral goats had survived Mutton Island's harsh winters until perhaps ten years ago). All in all, it felt very different to the artfully maintained ruins on Samson.

The last person to live here full-time, in this room, was Jer Sexton in the 1940s. The fishermen knew him as Jer de Bull, as he herded cattle, and he too had emigrated before returning to Ireland. Known for his pipe and books, if he needed anything from the mainland, or if something was wrong, he flew a red flag from a pole outside the cottage.

I was turning back to the doorway, wondering if the drizzle still warranted a hood, when the fireplace lit up as if by magic. I stopped and stared. A shaft of low sunlight was slanting in through the solitary window to graze the stone hearth. It was like one of Ireland's passage tombs aligned for the winter solstice. Soon, almost imperceptibly, the faint warmth slipped away. How long, I wondered, since someone was last caught by this tiny cottage's trick of the light.

Jer de Bull's cottage, Mutton Island

Two days earlier, I'd driven up the coast to visit Aindrias de Staic. I'd come across him while searching for recordings of the Kilstifeen story, as he'd told it for a revival of the Clare storytelling project *Dial-a-Seanchaí*. Its original incarnation was in the 1980s, with members of the public invited to 'pick up the receiver' to hear tape-recorded performances by three of Clare's best-known storytellers. Combining Ireland's ancient storytelling art with modern technology, callers were put through to two answering machines in a storeroom in the local library.

'I suppose the old definition of a *seanchaí* was a bearer of old lore,' says the project's 2021 curator (and Irish hip-hop DJ) John Lillis. 'They were historians of the aural tradition. It's easy to call a *seanchaí* a storyteller, but in traditional society, our *seanchaí* were geographers, historians, psychologists. They had deep connections to the landscape.'

As custodians of an indigenous oral tradition, the *seanchaí* are widely seen as having inherited – albeit informally – the function of the *fili*: Ireland's earlier learned class of 'poet philosophers'. A respected and influential profession, the *fili*'s training could last twelve years, and according to one twelfth-century source, involved learning by heart 'seven times fifty' sagas and tales. The stories would then be recited at court before nobility, where the *fili* continued to enjoy high status long after the introduction of Christianity. By Elizabethan times, visiting English nobility were said to have been horrified to see Gaelic chieftains eating at the same table as their poets.

Many of the early Irish myths show traces of their origins in the oral tradition. They include familiar tricks of the storyteller's trade, which helped the memory of both the teller and listeners: short, self-contained episodes, the repetition of certain words and phrases. As usual with oral tales, there was also space for improvisation and embellishment. Yet like indigenous Australian storytelling, the Gaelic tradition also placed great emphasis on the *fili* retaining elements that were considered factual – ensuring information passed down the generations unchanged. As England's first colony, though, Ireland was part of the English and then British Empire for over 700 years, which saw the erosion of these formal *fili* roles.

The *seanchaí* tradition was different, though, with the storytellers as likely to come from lower classes. While some were settled, others travelled from village to village in places like rural Clare, telling stories in exchange for a meal and a bed for the night.

Aindrias lived inland of Liscannor Bay. He'd told me his place was hard to find, so I parked up on the seafront at nearby Lahinch and waited for him to 'drop me a pin on WhatsApp'. As part of Ireland's Wild Atlantic Way tourist trail, the town was busy with summer visitors (unlike Quilty, where wary locals had rejected a public car park proposed for Seafield). Below the promenade, beginner surfers stood within the curve of Liscannor Bay, waiting for non-existent waves. For some, one of the bay's attractions was its proximity to the notoriously dangerous and exposed surf spot known as 'Aileen's'. Around Hag's Head to the north, big-wave surfers from across the world head for a reef at the foot of the spectacular Cliffs of Moher. 'Aileen' is from *Aill Na Searrach*: the 'Leap of Foals'. In myth, it was here that Ireland's pre-Christian deities – the *Tuatha De Danann* – protested the arrival of Christianity. Having transformed themselves into horses, the gods retreated through caves to the otherworld. Centuries later, seven white foals emerged from the dark. But spooked by the light and disoriented, they bolted off the edge of the cliff.

At the other, quiet end of Liscannor Bay, old concrete steps led down to the shore. By halfway down, the treads were increasingly narrow, the edges rounded by powerful Atlantic waves. Towards the bottom it was no more than a scoured concrete slope. Yet today was still, and a big spring low. Rolling my jeans, I walked out into the shallows, with the fine sand warm underfoot and the water like silk. Like so many others between the lifeguards' flags – with their surf gear, bodyboards and hitched skirts – I stood in the sea looking out.

It was from here in Lahinch that people saw Kilstifeen. Yet today there was no horizon; pale sea simply merged with sky. There was no sign of the Kilstiffin Rocks, no visible disturbance of the water, no trace of a splendid city or enchanted island. Instead, the bay's two headlands seemed suspended in the air.

Over the coming days I would pass through Lahinch several times, and it was never the same. The sea was puckered by wind, the horizon a solid grey or deeper blue. But that was all. I saw nothing unfathomable at the mouth of the bay.

When I'd first googled Aindrias, there was plenty to find. He was, I read, from a new generation of Irish storytellers. His performances fused fiddle playing and storytelling with comic lyrics over 'Gaelic beats': jigs, reels and gypsy polka. It was a career that took off in 2007, when he won an award at the Edinburgh Fringe Festival with his one-man show *Around the World on 80 Quid*. This 'highly fictitious' account of his own Irish emigration story told of a fiddle player setting off to busk and play Irish pubs across the world. From the all-night drinking and drugs, Aindrias wound up drifting and couch-surfing in Sydney. Before long, he'd lost his fiddle in a fire ignited by a joint, and ended up homeless and begging on the streets. Eventually, after being saved by a group of Hare Krishnas, Aindrias got sober.

'It's an absolute pleasure,' said the *Irish Times*, 'to witness something so intrinsically Irish, something that is both modern and ancient at the same time.'

'Charming,' others said. 'Seductive.' Watching a recording of Aindrias performing the show in a Galway pub, I could see what they meant.

When the pin arrived, I headed uphill out of town on foot, to a track that led out past wind-bent trees. At its end, a caravan sheltered against a roofless stone cottage, with sweeping views across a wooded valley. It was a striking spot: his family's land, Aindrias said later, inherited when his father died in 2016. Having moved out here temporarily in the first Covid lockdown, Aindrias hadn't left. I knocked on the flimsy caravan door. Soon, Aindrias stood at the stove, boiling water for green tea, yawning and pushing back long dark hair streaked with grey. I found a place to sit among a clutter of books and papers, clothes, a fiddle case and guitars propped in corners. On the wall a poster said *Tír na nÓg*, Land of the Young.

He'd first heard the story of Kilstifeen, Aindrias said, from his father. A storyteller, musician, writer and folklorist, Eddie had grown up in the local pub. The old Clare tunes he knew had been learned from Aindrias's great-grandmother Susan, who also played the fiddle.

'She was shot at by the Black and Tans,' Aindrias said. This was 1920, in the Irish War of Independence, when houses in Lahinch were burned down in retaliation for an IRA ambush on the road I'd driven in on. After that, Susan went on the run and ended up in America. It was there she was recorded playing tunes from back home, which Aindrias would listen to as he learned the fiddle. Later, he'd also heard recordings of Clare folktales from the 1930s. 'There was a musicality to their storytelling,' he said, 'and a rhythm to the way they spoke or used and repeated phrases and words. I loved the dance between the music and the story.'

He showed me a photograph of his great-grandmother back in Ireland, playing fiddle at the age of eighty-two. Aindrias's father remembered musicians and storytellers gathering at her house. This was part of an old Irish tradition, where certain homes became known as 'rambling houses'. People would gather around a fire after dark, to be entertained, educated and informed: with everything from storytelling, local news and gossip to traditional Irish music, song and dance. As well as locals, itinerant musicians and *seanchaí* might also turn up. Earlier, Aindrias had said:

> At that time you'd go to someone's house to hear a story and have to come back the following night. Stories could be fourteen hours long. Or they'd stretch it out for a week – because you might be getting free lodgings. People would be talking about the story next day, wondering what would happen, and then come back to hear the second half.

By the 1950s, though, with the rise of radio and television, the tradition had begun to die out. Today, he said, most people wouldn't listen to a story for more than twenty minutes.

The Kilstifeen tale he'd told for *Dial-a-Seanchaí* was a retelling of the version Aindrias knew as a child. Two fiddler brothers – one happy, one sad – disagree on the ending of a tune. For an answer from an old musician, they row a currach out across Liscannor Bay. Whoever is wrong, they agree, will row back. After listening to both endings, the old man says the happy brother's is right. In celebration, the lad drinks and plays on through the night, then falls asleep as the sad brother rows back. When a storm blows up, and Kilstifeen rises from the waves, only the sad brother is awake to see it. Back home, everyone knows the sad brother will die within the year. So the happy brother becomes sad. At the same time, people want to hear about Kilstifeen, so begin taking the sad brother out drinking. 'What was it like?' they ask. Who had he seen of the people they'd lost? Within the year, it is the once-happy brother who dies, with his empty currach found drifting at sea.

'I should show you an old magazine,' Aindrias said, pacing around the caravan, moving things from one pile to another and reminding me of the piratical energy I'd glimpsed onstage. Eventually the magazine turned up. From 1979, it told a version of the Kilstifeen story involving three brothers and a cattle raid, with one brother drawing the sea over his mansion before he dies. It was a commonly told version today, said to have its origins in a 'wild Irish romance' written in 1760. 'He's done a bit of a Walt Disney on it,' Aindrias said, after reading it aloud. He'd known the cattle-raid version since childhood. 'But I never heard of the six-fingered girl.'

There was something else, Aindrias said and then paused. I leaned in: reeled on the storyteller's line.

> A builder was out here working on my house. Kilstifeen came up, and he said *I saw it*. Well, I didn't act too excited, or sceptical. Oh, really? I said. They were up on a roof in Lahinch, building an extension. You know how it is there. All the tourists, extensions for Airbnbs. Well, when the owner came up with the tea for them, he nearly fainted. It

> was a fine day, like today, and they thought it must be the extension. 'Ah,' they said. 'You think we've done a fine job?' 'No, no,' said the man of the house. 'Look out! Look out!' He was afraid it was only him that would see it. But the builders were from Milton Malbay, so they'd heard of Kilstifeen. They all looked out. And sure enough, way out, they could see this *perfect* village. Like a small town sitting on the sea.

Back on Mutton Island, I left the ruined cottages behind and headed for the wilder west coast. Passing drystone walls, I crossed wildflower meadows with the ground beneath just as riddled with rabbit holes. There was bog and a wide, dark lake: rainwater held by moss and the bowl of the rock. Here and there lay collections of rabbit bones, as if gathered together in some form of ritual. They nestled among stones and succulents, or in dips in the turf: slender and white, with remnants of grey fur parted by the wind.

All the while, I was drawn towards the watchtower. Also vis-ible from the mainland, this stood at the island's western edge: a relic of British rule and the fear of invasion by Napoleon. Today, it also looked like it might offer shelter. I would drink my coffee in there, I thought. Yet an hour or so later, on reaching it I changed my mind. It rose three floors to a crumbling parapet, but inside it was hollow and oppressive, with openings that funnelled the wind. So I headed on out, following a more unsettled sound of the sea.

Ahead, the land fell away to the deep cold of Atlantic blue. From the mainland, Mutton Island was a place of gently rolling green. Yet beneath its thin covering of turf, it was part of the same rock formation exposed at the dramatic Cliffs of Moher. The rock was laid down more than 300 million years ago, when this part of Ireland was a vast, Mississippi-like delta home to forests of one-hundred-foot 'scale-trees'. Later, the unimaginable forces of tectonic collision fractured and deformed the layers of sandstone and softer shales.

With the island's blunt end facing the Atlantic head-on, its cliff-face was spectacular. Below wind-sculpted ledges, the relentless sea had exploited any weakness or fault. There were caverns, gullies and arches, chasms and caves. One was *Iffrin-beg* or 'Little Hell', described by Westropp as 'a great double-arched hall with an up-shaft'. He'd also described the 'Puffing Hole' – a spouting blowhole – although I wondered if anyone had been out here in stormy weather since Jer de Bull's time.

Soon, I was out on a headland that was deeply incised. From a distance, the breaking waves had been no more than a border of lace. Yet from here the water was confined, all its sounds amplified to a roar by sheer walls of rock. With an acute mix of vertigo and awe, I crept towards the edge. Far below, water seethed into darkness at the mouths of caves. I edged closer to see a last vast cavern, its back wall strung – impossibly – with what looked like coloured baubles. It took a while to understand the scale: hurled by waves and wedged on ledges high above the sea, they were lines of plastic fishing buoys.

From there I headed to the island's barren north-westerly tip, passing a pool with the remains of a gull beneath the surface shine, its spread wings hinged only by bone. It was up here that the geologist Dr Andy Pulham thought he may have found traces of the 'great wave' recorded in the annals. In 2013 the Marine Rescue Service dropped him out on the island for a programme by the local radio station *Raidió Corca Baisicinn.* Following in his footsteps now, I walked out on bare pavements of rock that felt wildly exposed. Somewhere out here – some thirty or forty metres above high tide – Pulham saw great angular slabs of sandstone he described as 'imbricated'. In geology this refers to their orientation, and implies transport by fast-flowing water. Where surfaces also show the rocks haven't moved for centuries, as here, it shows they lie out of reach of more usual storm waves. They are, then, often considered evidence of a tsunami. Out here at the edge of Mutton Island, the slabs' alignment suggested to Pulman that a 'great wave' from the south-west could have hurled them up.

For him, despite the hardness of the rock, it *was* possible that a tsunami had 'divided the Isle of Fitha into three'. As I'd seen earlier by the ruined cottages on the island's leeward side, the eroding cliff exposed deep boulder clay above the bedrock. Left by retreating glaciers, this may once have covered a much larger area, infilling and extending the island (perhaps once as far as the mainland). This could explain a loss as sudden as the annals imply, with thick clays swept out by the force of the water – to leave fresh areas exposed to erosion.

Records suggest the AD 800 catastrophe caused massive loss of life along this coast (with the *Annals of the Four Masters*' oddly specific figure of 1,010 often interpreted to mean 'more than a thousand'). Westropp proposed that 'a whole barony' had fallen away at the Cliffs of Moher, with the precipices of Malbay and Mutton Island 'but a remnant of the great loss'. His findings suggest that at the time of the 'great wave', a church of St Senan may have stood on Mutton Island for more than two centuries. I imagined other stone buildings too, wondered about pasture and vegetable gardens tended by the monks. Out on the desolate headland now, it was impossible to imagine anything withstanding the force of waves able to hurl huge slabs this high. It's quite possible that following a tsunami, a reduced Fitha divided more slowly into three – but no one remained as witness.

Today, its remnants are thought to be Mutton Island, tiny Inismattle to the south and rocky northern islets known by the fishermen as Carrick and Little Carrick (Rock and Little Rock).

It was late morning now, with the ebb tide exposing numerous reefs that ringed the island. Some barely broke the surface, while others rose black and ragged from the water, a few where cormorants held their eerie pose (in Irish, the bird is *cailleach dhubh*, the black hag). In many places, reefs extended out from the island's rim: denuded, it seemed, of their boulder clay. When I'd arrived at high tide, they were concealed by the sea, which left me wondering how fast the local knowledge of routes out here would dwindle.

Further north in Liscannor Bay, the same bones of old land rise from the seabed – out where the distant Cliffs of Moher were re-emerging as the rain moved away. Later, poring again over fathom lines on charts, I would trace the ghosts of that retreating headland. Underwater, it reached out into the mouth of Liscannor Bay, to end at Kilstiffin Rocks. Surrounded by much deeper water, the reef is likely to have once been an island. This was perhaps in the very deep past (sometimes, after storms, remnants of ancient submerged forest and bog are exposed at the edge of Liscannor Bay). Proposing local origins of the Kilstifeen tradition, some suggest a small island may still have existed when the 'great wave' struck (perhaps, as with so many remote Irish islands, with a monk or hermit's cell that went unrecorded).

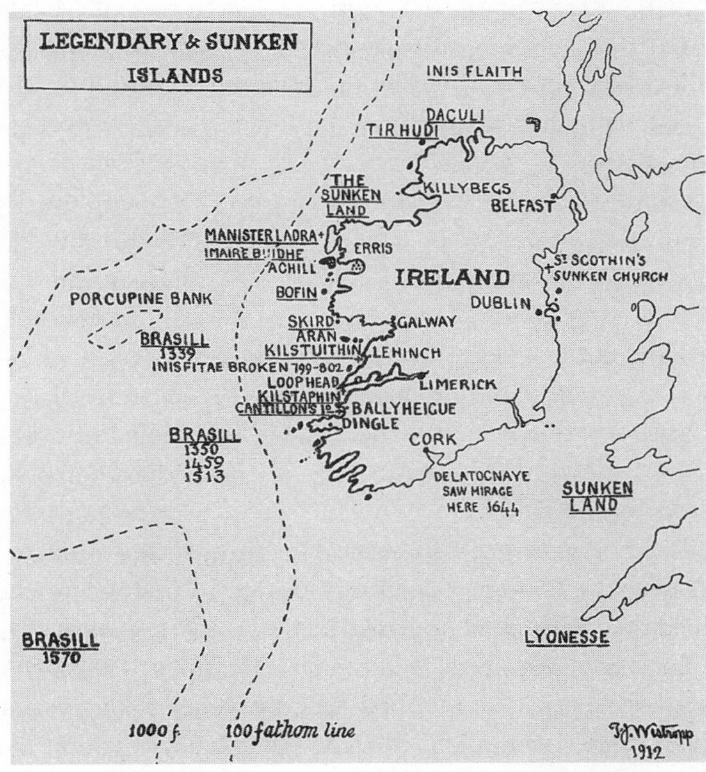

Legendary and Sunken Islands by Thomas Westropp, 1912

Following Thomas Westropp's visit to Mutton Island, he went on to survey other places along Ireland's west coast with a tradition of enchanted islands. While many were glittering cities like Kilstifeen, others mirrored ordinary life (an island with stone cottages and a simple chapel, its inhabitants having 'a taste for cabbage and potatoes, poteen, tea and tobacco'). Almost everywhere, these phantom islands coincided with some geological feature of the coast: a shoal or shallow bank, a rocky reef or barren fragmentary islet. In conclusion, he believed actual islands 'may have existed within traditional memory at all the alleged sites'.

At some places, including Lahinch, it's also possible the tradition has been kept alive by an optical illusion known as a *fata morgana*. This happens when warm air sits above cold water and refracts the light, bending it around the curve of the Earth. Distorted images can then appear at the horizon, sometimes of boats or headlands that remain out of sight. The images may also be layered, stretched or inverted, causing the mirage to appear as towers, columns or domes.

The illusion may be a clue to Westropp's enduring fascination with enchanted islands. In a paper he gave to the Royal Irish Academy, the antiquarian described having seen the illusion himself as child in 1872. Afterwards he'd made a sketch, of an island with wooded hills and towers, and rising curls of smoke. Later in the year, I would also see it for myself at the mouth of the Humber: 'castles in the air' above, of all places, Grimsby. Perhaps it explained the perfect village seen by builders from the Lahinch extension.

There is another intriguing idea around the tradition of Kilstifeen: that it may once have served as a warning. In the stories, anyone seeing Kilstifeen is said to die. Before the devastating impact of a tsunami, the sea recedes unnaturally. Far lower than the lowest spring tides, this would reveal reefs and parts of the seabed that had never been seen before.

Following the 'Boxing Day' tsunami in 2004, the idea of

nat-ural disasters living on in local traditions drew worldwide attention. In the Indian Ocean, the tiny Andaman Islands lay directly in the path of the tsunami. Yet when relief workers finally reached the islands, they found their death tolls were deeply skewed. And it soon became clear that geography was not the only cause. One group, the semi-nomadic Moken – meaning sea-people – had a traditional story of the *Laboon*: the 'wave that eats people'. When the ground began to shake, they were told as children, the *Laboon* had stirred in his lair. Immediately, they must seek deeper water or run to higher ground. As a result, there was no loss of life among the Moken. Similarly, on other islands where such traditions had passed down the generations, many more survived the tsunami. In contrast, by far the highest number of deaths was on an island now home to many outsiders.

The geology shows tsunamis have hit the west coast of Ireland before. Most recently, they followed the Lisbon earthquakes in 1755 and 1761. Some suggest, then, that the story of Kilstifeen may once have been a warning, perhaps with roots in folk memory of the 'great wave' that split Fitha in three.

Following the coast back towards the cottages, I reached a circular stone wall I'd passed on the way out. This surrounded a sinkhole, walled off long ago to stop livestock falling in. As parts of the wall were no more than rubble, I wandered in. I'd been told, unreliably, that this was *Poul Tabbac* – Tobacco Hole – although Finbar wasn't sure (like the route out, it made me wonder about the loss of names on abandoned islands). Somewhere on Mutton Island was also *Poulaneena*, 'Hole of the Wine', with both said to be named for their use by smugglers (in Georgian times, the island's owner – Sir Edward O'Brien, Fourth Baronet and Member of Parliament – was apparently a keen customer). Once again I edged closer to the brink, over thrift to where the land fell away. This time, I dropped to my hands and knees. Below, a vast sea cave had been gouged from the rock. Roofless for perhaps millennia, one thick, dark wall was pierced by light from an archway to the sea. Inside, the troubled waters were a deep blue-green. As at the 'giant's cave' on Samson, it was like looking into the heart of the island.

Heading out around a last deep inlet that almost cut Mutton Island in two, I searched for a sheltered spot out on the headland. I wasn't far from the beach where I'd arranged to be picked up, and had more than an hour to spare. Tired from the hours of walking over rocks and rough ground, I settled down in a dip among pillows of thrift. The rain had stopped a while ago. And already, the turf and most of my clothes had dried in the breeze, although not my shoes and socks. So I pulled them off, and lay down beneath the wind with relief. Not only had I made it out to the island, there was also sun on the soles of my feet.

I closed my eyes. The sound of the sea came from all around: from reefs still emerging with the tide, from the inlet's cobble beach, and rocky shores of the islands to the north. Beneath that, from the headland's fissures and caves, a deeper boom travelled through the ground itself. Given the rabbit holes I'd spent hours avoiding, the entire island – from its thin soil to its ancient sandstone – felt hollowed out. Like a wind instrument, I thought, drifting off.

I woke with a start – afraid I'd missed the boat back – but sat up to find only twenty minutes had passed. Later, due to be picked up from the island's easterly spit, I trod out over sea-rolled cobbles as big as the fishing buoys scattered high on its storm beach. Although I was on time, there was no sign of a small blue boat. Back when they'd dropped me off at the rock and pulled away, I'd imagined catching reassuring glimpses of Anthony and Finbar checking lobster pots between the island and the mainland. But in more than seven hours, I'd not seen a single boat.

As the sound came, the hairs on my arms stood on end. Eerie and mournful, it was from the direction of Carrick and Little Carrick. My first thought was it must be a trick of the wind, whistling through some fissure or chasm in the rock. Belatedly, I realised it was seal song. This was something I'd heard only once before, off the west coast of Scotland. Later, I learned it is specifically the lament of grey seals competing for haul-out sites. In Westropp's time, these barren remnants of Fitha were known as *Roanshee* or *Carrig na Ron*, Seal Rock. It wasn't hard to see why Ireland's enchanted islands were often inhabited by those who wore sealskins. Or the shapeshifting Irish merfolk known as merrows, sometimes translated as 'sea singer'.

When at last I saw a distant boat, it weaved an odd course, presumably to avoid unseen reefs. Trying to guess where the boat might land, I made my way out to the water's edge. With the tide so low, the boulders were dark and slippery with weed. Repeatedly, they shifted without warning and my feet slid into gaps.

'The tide's still running out,' Finbar called from some way offshore. 'I can't come any closer.' I was still slipping on stones as the water rose above my shoes, then the knees of my jeans and my thighs. Finally, waist deep, I got a hand to the solidity of the boat.

I *would* be leaving Mutton Island.

Yet on the otherworld islands of Irish myth, time passes differently. In the *Voyage of Bran*, one monk has a longing to return to Ireland, until Bran finally relents. But once the currach is in sight of land that was once their home, the monks see the forests have gone. The coast they knew so well has changed. When they call out to people on shore, no one knows them. Instead, the *Voyage of Bran* is one of their ancient stories. Eventually, unable to accept they've been gone for centuries, the homesick monk leaps ashore. But as he touches Irish soil he turns to ash.

With some relief, I hauled myself in over the side of the boat.

Failed sea defences, Spurn

5

Ravenser Odd

Holderness Coast, Yorkshire

As Europe's fastest eroding coastline, Holderness has lost at least twenty-nine villages and towns to the sea since the eleventh century. Their names are recorded on Thomas Sheppard's 1912 'Map showing the Lost Towns of East Yorkshire', which marks the Roman coastline an estimated three miles further east. Among them are Owthorne and Out Newton, Monkwike, Hornsea Beck, Orwithfleete, Auburn and Old Withernsea. A few, like Sand-le-mere, live on in the names of caravan parks that 'roll back' as the sea encroaches. Yet many smaller hamlets and farmsteads will have gone unrecorded, leaving no trace that they ever existed. Of those that did make it into the record books, the largest and most wealthy was Ravenser Odd. A thriving medieval port town with a reputation for piracy, it stood out on shifting sands at the tip of the peninsula – and the story of its rise and fall is remarkable.

Although headed there in the van, I first made a detour to Skipsea, where the losses to erosion are far more recent and also imminent. A week before the start of the summer holidays, I came to a halt at the end of Skipsea's sea road, at concrete barriers and a forest of warning signs: 'DANGER, Coastal erosion, DO NOT PROCEED'. Beyond, the tarmac ended at a gaping inlet that cut down through clay to the shore. Nearby, a derelict building stood closest to the edge, with 'AMUSEMENTS' in peeling yellow above roller-shutter doors rusted shut. Across the road, abandoned hardstandings marked the periodic retreat of static caravans.

As at Happisburgh, the train line never reached Skipsea. So it never benefitted from the Victorian rail boom that brought promenades and piers to neighbouring resorts, and its attractions have remained more modest (one reason its cliffs are undefended, in contrast to others' rock armour and concrete sea walls). Instead, seaside Skipsea began in the 1930s, with farmers allowing visitors to camp in cliff-top fields. With caravan parks opening up from the 1950s, bingo and fairground stalls began pitching up nearby. By then, a stretch of the Skipsea cliff-top had become a shanty town of post-war prefabs, makeshift chalets and converted train carriages.

Seaward of the warning signs was once a cafe and wooden store with adverts for Woodbines. There were old-style petrol pumps and ice cream kiosks, and the now-demolished Skipsea Beach Social Club (which lasted eighty years). Opposite, the derelict arcade was remembered by some as Joby's Amusements, and by others as Charlie's Amusements. Long-term returnees recalled other Skipsea attractions with nostalgia; depending on the decades when they were young, these ranged from pinball and swingboats to 1980s Pac-Man. By then, like the cliff they stood on, the early prefabs and shacks were long gone. As far as people remembered, they were dismantled or left to go over the edge, with one rusting railway carriage craned away shortly before the cliff reached the bricks it stood on.

As I looked out to where the shacks once were, an older couple wandered out past the concrete barriers. Much as I had, they edged closer to the drop: unsure what was safe but drawn to look. Where summer grasses pushed up through ruptured tarmac, the woman scanned the cliff for some way down, expressing surprise that Skipsea ended with no access to the beach. Beside her, the man pointed past the abandoned arcade to a row of sheared-off gardens.

'When there's a storm, I feel the house moving,' resident Natalie Day had told a reporter, after losing more of her garden to the sea. 'It feels like I'm on a ferry. In the morning, I look out of the back window to see if the cliffs have moved closer. Sometimes the doors are hard to shut, and you can tell the walls have moved by looking at the decorating.'

She lived on Skipsea's Green Lane – known once as Millionaire's View – and her neighbours described their windows being smashed by wave-flung stones. They told of opening curtains to find a back fence and several feet of garden gone, a shattered greenhouse, a sodden lawn full of stones. When built in the mid-1980s, the row of bungalows looked out to sea over thirty-metre gardens, a road and cliff-top green. Now, the gardens were half their original length, with the sea encroaching by an average of two metres a year. For some time, one couple had been gauging the loss of their garden with one-metre marker posts, and a neighbour with golf tees.

Today, fallen fence posts hung from the ragged ends of their gardens, and a birdbath stood precariously on a slab that jutted out over the cliff. Periodically, people from the council flew drones for aerial photographs, and measured the distance between each house and the edge. When this reached 9.32 metres (allegedly the most land lost here in a single fall) residents were served an eviction notice, and owners a demolition order. Already there were gaps in the row, where in recent years several of the original nineteen bungalows had been pulled down. At the time of my visit, those that remained were thought to have five more years at most.

Once the couple left, I wandered closer to the edge. Offshore of here, Thomas Sheppard's map showed Cleton or Cleeton, Withow and Hyde. Furthest from shore was Hyde or Hythe (a Saxon word for a harbour), which paid its tithes in fish, but by 1396 had been 'totally destroyed'. Below, the shadow of the cliff

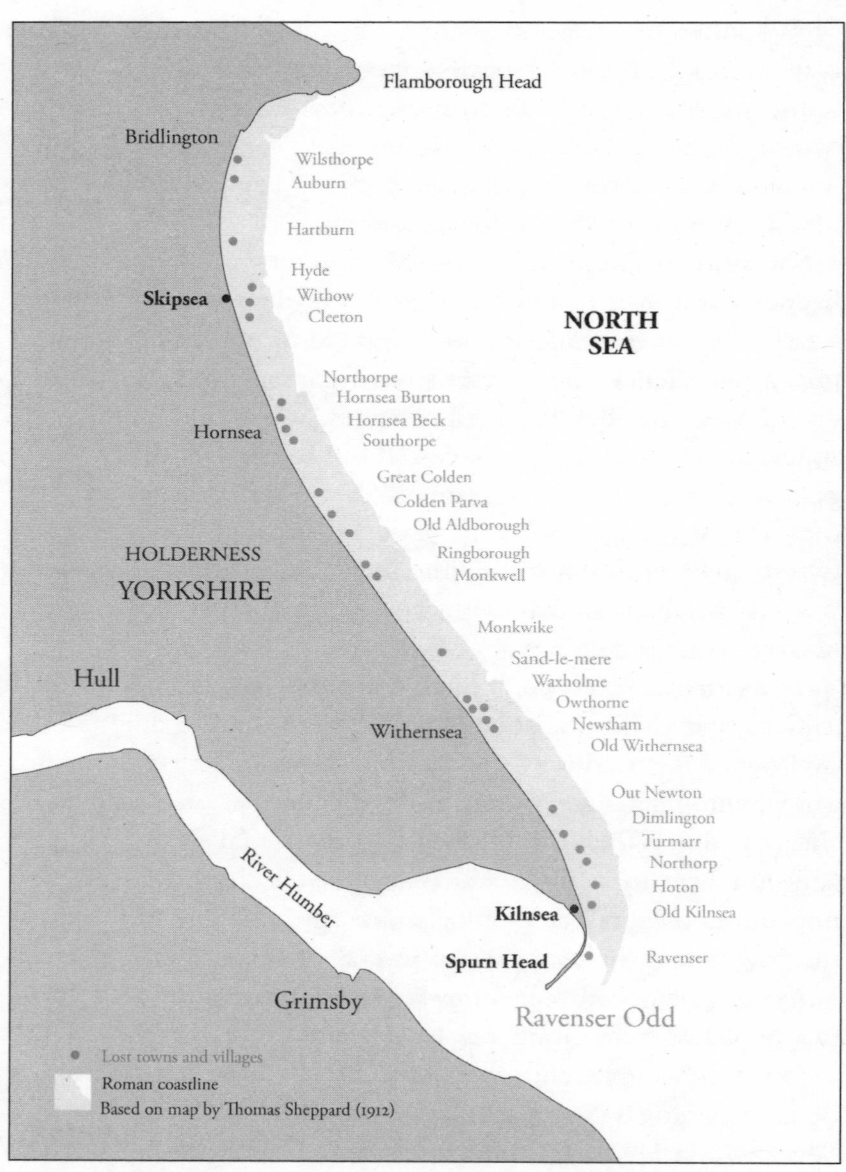

Towns and villages lost to the sea along the Holderness coast

reached out across the shore and lay on the water. In the stillness, the sea was distant and benign, sleep-breathing beneath a violet haze. It reminded me of Happisburgh, as here too a web of ghost roads and trodden paths connected those long-vanished settlements. Out above the shallows was once a 1950s shanty town. From there, the tracks led back in time as the water deepened, branching off to forgotten hamlets and nameless farmsteads, villages and medieval havens. Further offshore, they headed on to a deeper past, out beyond a Roman coastline to the drowned encampments of Mesolithic Doggerland.

The next morning I drove south as far as Kilnsea, where the narrowing peninsula is only a third of a mile wide. So while some Holderness villages can relocate further west as their cliffs erode, Kilnsea is caught between the North Sea and the Humber. I'd booked a campsite online and as I manoeuvred into a space marked with my name, it came as a surprise. Little more than a medium-sized back garden, the site's most striking feature was the unusually spacious garden-shed toilet and shower room, with knotty-pine panelling, quilted toilet paper and a wing-back armchair (this was frequently praised in the online reviews, with one camper finding it 'better than in most posh hotels'). Tacked near the door was a sobering copy of the local Flood Action Plan: 'gather family and leave your caravan immediately; do not attempt to walk or drive through floodwater'.

The site of Old Kilnsea now lies offshore, but in the late eighteenth century its cottages stood on a hill, with a church, an inn and an alehouse, a pond and village green with a high stone cross (said to have been relocated from Ravenser, the first time it was threatened by the sea). Old Kilnsea was originally surrounded by four fields – North, South, East and West – but by the early 1800s, all of the East Field had gone. By then, the village itself was falling into the sea. Many residents, though, surprised outsiders by choosing to remain 'til the ground was almost torn from under their beds'.

In 1824, the chancel of St Helen's Church went over the cliff, although for a while the wardens simply walled off the sea end and continued services. But during a storm the following year, another wall and several arches went over the edge 'with a tremendous crash', leaving the pulpit, reading desks and service books scattered on the shore below. For a few more years, the striking three-storey tower remained at the edge of the cliff, with the church bell hung from a beam in a local farmyard and struck by thrown stones. Then in 1831, the tower finally collapsed onto the shore. By then, erosion was also exposing bodies in the adjoining graveyard.

Old Kilnsea Church, 1829

In 1835, the traveller and writer George Head was returning from Spurn along the beach by horse,

> when among the pebbles at my feet I perceived a bone, which it appeared to me immediately was a human one, and a few seconds afterward I saw another, and another still – a leg and a thigh bone; till, last of all . . . I picked up what was sufficient to dissipate all doubt to what creature the bone belonged – a human scull [sic].

Making his way into the village to find someone to tell, he was met without surprise, and told 'human bones at the village of Kilnsea were as coals to Newcastle'. A local then took him out to where the ruined church lay on the shore below the cliff. 'The latest avalanches of earth,' wrote Head, 'were heaped almost level with the summit, and consisted of rich churchyard mould, in which were profusely scattered bones, sculls, fragments of coffins, remnants of garments, buttons, &c.'

The man with him described how some of the dead were not local, but shipwrecked mariners, with some exposed in the clay still 'interred in their clothes – skeletons with silk handkerchiefs round their necks'. In the decades before the church was lost, almost half of those buried in Kilnsea's graveyard were shipwrecked strangers, the very last 'a negro from a ship called the *Armentus*, wrecked in 1823'. Distressingly, though, many of the exposed bones would have been from relatives and friends of those still living in what remained of Old Kilnsea.

Leaving the van snug in its pitch, I set out for Spurn along the road that once linked old and new Kilnsea, keeping an eye out for the replacement church. This was built in 1865, three decades after the loss of the medieval church, using stone from its eroding foundations. When the new church opened, objects scavenged from the old were returned: lintels and the font from local gardens, the holy water stoop from the Crown and Anchor pub. I found the church set back from the quiet road, and wandered in through an open gateway beneath overgrown bushes. To one side, a disintegrating noticeboard was missing many of its letters: beneath 'St H ENS', it gave details of a last Evensong at 2.30 p.m. Inside, the red-brick church was closed up, its leaded-light windows blind with sky-shine, and weeds grown tall around the gravestones. Later, I learned it closed in the 1990s, after the Kilnsea congregation had dwindled to single figures.

At the crossroads, rather than turning right for Spurn, I crossed over to a last stub of road that led to the sea. On the corner stood what was once the Blue Bell pub. Built in 1847, this was Kilnsea's initial replacement inn, thought to have originally been angled to face the old village and the sea. By the end of the century, though, so little remained of Old Kilnsea that the building was altered, so the front faced west towards the new village. For 110 years it remained as a pub, and through the wars was often raucous with soldiers based at both Kilnsea and Spurn. By 1957, though, with most of the military gone, the pub closed its doors for good – although in later years, some who stayed there claimed to have heard the playing of a ghostly piano. On the wall now there remained two plaques:

BUILT in the Year 1847, 534 YARDS FROM THE SEA	RESTORED 1994 190 yards from the sea

Beyond the old pub, as at Skipsea it was mainly static caravans – this time the Sandy Beaches Holiday Park. Towards the back, its caravans were a tin-boxy, corrugated green, while those closest to the cliff shone white. With apex roofs and patio doors, their wide plastic-railed balconies overlooked the sea. In front there weren't any fences, just an oddly distinct line where laid turf ended at rough ground along the edge of the cliff.

Today Kilnsea's cliffs are low, as the hill Old Kilnsea was built on has eroded away. As elsewhere along this coast, the seafront caravans were periodically moved inland, leaving old hardstandings jutting out over the edge. On the shore below, wave-worn concrete lay broken on the sand, with more scattered further down the foreshore. As well as the debris from retreating caravans, a failed sea wall lay out in the shallows, along with the massive concrete ruins of military installations from the Kilnsea Battery (three decades earlier, when the gun emplacement fell from the cliff, those in caravans said they felt it like an earthquake).

As it was summer and the cliff fairly stable, fallen slabs had been fashioned roughly into steps. So I made my way down to the shore, and headed for the end of the Old Kilnsea road, which now lay on the sand. Above, the apex roofs of caravans peeked warily over the edge. Protruding from the cliff-face, rather than the bones that dismayed George Head, were terracotta drainpipes and blue plastic water pipes spooling down to the shore.

From the air, the slender curve of Spurn Head looks strikingly and beautifully fragile. Three and a half miles long, this sandy extension of the Holderness coast reaches out across the mouth of the Humber. I first came here in 1989, struck by its shape on a map, when you could still drive out along a windswept road to the Point. Yet Spurn is continually shifting and changing, and in 2013 a series of storms washed away the road at the spit's Narrow Neck. By then, wave damage and blown sand had caused problems for years, so the rupture wasn't unexpected. Only the previous year, Spurn's last, isolated community had left for good, when the RNLI decided that after two centuries stationed on the Point, the families of the lifeboat crew could no longer live out there. Until then, people had been making their homes on this wind- and wave-swept spit for over 1,300 years.

I walked out onto the peninsula at half-tide, Spurn curving away like a sheltering arm around the mud of the Humber. In the distance, a pale industrial rim hung between water and sky. It wasn't long, though, before I could no longer make out the horizon. Drained of colour, the spit and decommissioned lighthouse were little more than tracing-paper outlines. Everything beyond was gone. It was a receding of the outside world I found pleasantly unsettling: a glimpse perhaps of the remoteness felt by those who once lived out here, as the weather closed in before a storm.

The earliest record of someone living on Spurn is from the seventh century, when the Christian hermit Wilgils built a cell there. Later, the spit was mentioned in the Icelandic Sagas – a series of medieval tales based on historical events – once after a Viking poet-warrior was shipwrecked here in AD 950. Appearing several times in the Sagas, the Old Norse name for Spurn was *Hrafnseyrr*, meaning 'raven's promontory', which went on to become Ravenser and later Ravenserspurne.

Lying at the mouth of the Humber, Spurn was strategically important for the Vikings. As many went on to settle in the area, it had a considerable influence on the culture and dialect of Yorkshire (among its words with roots in Old Norse are bairn, arse, dollop, flit, muck and gaum – as in gormless). Crucially, the spit allowed control of access to a network of rivers leading into the heart of Northumbria, which at the time was part of the Norse-controlled Danelaw region. As skilled sailors and revolutionary shipbuilders, the Vikings and their longships could navigate the muddy Humber and its tributaries to their inland capital of *Jorvic*, or York. Calmer waters in the lee of the spit also offered safe anchorage from a turbulent North Sea. So Spurn became a key staging point for the Norse fleet before and after Viking raids. Its final appearance in the Sagas follows what is considered the symbolic end of the Viking Age. This was the 1066 Battle of Stamford Bridge, in which some 300 Norwegian longships advanced on York. But following the English defeat of this 'Great Heathen Army', less than thirty ships made it back to Spurn. With the King of Norway also killed in battle, his son Olaf the Peaceful led the surviving Vikings from England, setting sail 'from the port, called Hrafseyrr (the raven tongue of land)'.

The name reflects the symbolic importance of ravens to the Vikings. Seen as iconic, magical creatures, their image was carved into the hulls of longships and featured on banners and shields, invoking the Norse war god Odin. Referred to in the medieval *Prose Edda* as 'raven-god', he is often depicted with two ravens on his shoulders: Huginn (thought) and Muninn (memory), which flew around the world and returned with information.

Spurn's shipwrecked poet appears in the thirteenth-century Egil's Saga, which offers a glimpse of the Danes who settled this coast. The saga follows the family of the Viking warrior Egil Skallagrímsson over several generations, beginning with his grandfather, *Kveldulf* or Night Wolf: a berserker who could take the form of a wolf. Associated with Odin, berserkers were infamous Norse warriors who fought in a trance-like fury, the origins of which can be found in ancient shamanic traditions. Like his father Ugly Skull, Egil had inherited his grandfather's berserker traits, yet was also a *skald*: a poet to the Scandinavian court.

The saga tells of Egil's tenth-century feud with Erik Blood-Axe. This began when Egil and his companions were slighted by the King's bard, when he pretended to have run out of ale. Instead, he served them *skyr* (curds), so Egil retaliated by composing a poem that mocked the bard. The bard's response was to try to poison Egil. Yet Egil was skilled in magic; warned by protective runes he'd carved into his drinking horn, Egil stabbed the bard. The result was a string of killings that included the son of Erik Blood-Axe, who went on to become King of Norway as well as Northumbria. As part of the ongoing feud, Egil was outlawed and headed to Iceland, and later England on Viking raids. There, following the Spurn shipwreck, he was taken to York and brought before Erik Blood-Axe. Sentenced to death the next day, Egil stayed up all night composing a poem. This was *Höfuðlausn,* or Head-ransom: a 'mighty poem' he recited next morning, that so impressed the King he freed Egil and forgave him the murder of his son.

★

Today, Spurn's road came to an end at the Wash-over, where ragged tarmac jutted over windblown sand. Spurn's fragile neck is where the road washed away during the 2013 storm, and the place that struck me most when I first visited twenty-five years ago. As a first-year student missing the sea, I'd bought a map and driven out to this odd hook of land in a Ford Escort inherited from my mum. After months in an unfamiliar city, that first sight of the Narrow Neck was exhilarating: the exposure; the thin strip of road between two sandy shores; two vast bodies of water pressing up against the land.

Back then, I'd driven on to the Point. Now, though, wave-strewn slabs of the old tarmac lay half-buried in sand. Unable to resist – this was after all the road I'd driven out on – I chose a sea-worn chunk the size of a breakfast bowl and stowed it in my pack.

In 2013, no one witnessed the loss of the road. By then, repeated storm damage meant a temporary road already ran alongside the old, edged with marker stakes for when it was buried in drifting sand. Driven south by hurricane-force winds, the 2013 tidal surge reached Spurn after dark on Thursday, 5 December. Although the wind had begun to drop, the height of the swell increased as it swept down the coast, funnelled by the narrowing North Sea. Along the Holderness coast, this coincided with a high spring tide – already forecast to be one of the highest of the year – which it raised a further six feet. No one is sure whether the road washed away that night or on the morning's high tide. But by daylight, there was a scene of devastation. The two shores at the Narrows were now one, with almost a third of a mile of Spurn's road washed away. Fallen telegraph poles lay on wet sand, with the power lines looping over pools of seawater. Exposed water pipes snaked across the beach, severing services to the Point. It was soon clear that in a single night, not only had parts of Spurn shifted eighty yards west but the Narrow Neck had become the Wash-over. Spurn was now Britain's newest tidal island.

Trailing out across deep, dry sand, I passed several warnings: of extreme danger at certain high tides; to leave enough time to make the journey back; to never walk through waves or standing water. Today, this stretch of Spurn can be covered by up to four feet of water, with deceptively strong cross-currents as the North Sea floods into the Humber. Where the road resumed at the far end of the Wash-over, I passed a 'High Tide Shelter' in the lee of the dunes, for anyone mistiming their return. Beyond there, the road cut like a holloway through Spurn's dune-spine, known locally as the Bents after the marram grass that created 'bent hills'.

At one point, embedded in a stretch of concrete road, the bright metal of railway tracks caught the light. This was a legacy of the First World War, with storm damage including a surge in 1942 that left a thirty-metre section of track suspended in the air across a dune gap. Yet the wartime line was repaired, and until the 1950s was used by the lifeboatmen and lighthouse keepers, who ran Spurn's famous wind-driven 'sail bogeys': wheeled trolleys with a mast and sail. Ahead of me now, just a short section of track remained, crossing the road at what seemed an inexplicable angle: leading off into the dunes and out to sea. Later, I learned the track points to what was once the terminus at Kilnsea (where an extra platform was put in behind the Blue Bell pub for soldiers based at Spurn). In 1981, a series of scouring storms offered a last, brief glimpse of those Kilnsea sidings out on the foreshore.

To date, no trace of Ravenser Odd has ever – reliably – been found. Yet church and court records offer a glimpse of the rise and fall of this extraordinary town, known also as Ravenserodd, Odd and Lodd. The story of the town's birth 'by the casting up of the sea' was first recorded at a 1290 inquiry into accusations of piracy against 'the men of Ravenserodd'. Initially, the site appears to have been little more than a sandbank where fishermen stopped to dry their nets, and where ships came to grief.

> Forty years ago a certain ship was cast away at Ravenserodd, where no house was then built, which ship a certain man appropriated to himself, and from it made for himself a hut or cabin, which he inhabited for so long a time that he received ships and merchants there, and sold them food and drink, and afterwards others began to dwell there.

By then, there was already a small, unremarkable settlement on Spurn, which became known as Auld Ravenser, once overshadowed by its upstart neighbour. It's possible that Odd developed on a tidal island like Spurn today, with records describing the two Ravensers connected by a sandy road, 'covered with round and yellow stones, thrown up in a little time by the height of the floods, having a breadth which an archer can scarcely shoot across'.

Taking advantage of its position at the mouth of the Humber, and supported by the Third Earl of Albemarle – 'a feudal adventurer of the worst type' – the rise of Ravenser Odd was rapid. By 1251, it was already attracting merchants from neighbouring ports, and had permission for an annual fair and twice-weekly market. As the town continued to grow in wealth and importance, there was increased rivalry with nearby Grimsby ('Grim's village' was also Norse-settled, with Grim a name used by Odin when 'masked' among mortals).

It was the mayor of Grimsby who in 1290 accused the new town of piracy, in particular the practice of 'forestalling'. This involved the men of Odd rowing out to intercept merchant ships that were headed for Grimsby or Hull, and 'persuading' or forcing them to dock at Ravenser. The men were also accused of spreading lies about poor prices in rival ports. As a result, jurors heard, merchants were abandoning Grimsby; its port was in decline and residents were unable to pay their rents.

Yet less than a decade later Ravenser Odd was granted borough status, no doubt further provocation for Grimsby. This allowed the new town to levy taxes and harbour dues in return for supplying the King with ships and armed men for ongoing wars with Scotland and France. By the early 1300s, Odd had become a desirable place to live, and was represented by two MPs (one of them Peter Atte See or 'Peter At Sea'). While no record of the streets survives, such medieval new towns were often laid out on a grid system, with mainly wattle-and-daub buildings and a few built of brick. At Ravenser, some are also likely to have incorporated beach cobbles.

As well as wharves and a quay, Odd had boatyards, tanneries and a marketplace, taverns, a chapel and fairground, a gallows, a prison and a court. There was a thriving fish-curing trade, along with warehousing for the import of goods such as wool, French wine, skins, tallow and whale oil, along with swords, armour and falcons.

Like the word 'Ravenser', 'Odd' too is derived from the Old Norse: *oddi* meaning point of land. Yet the town's apparent rise from the sea – 'like Aphrodite' in the words of one thirteenth-century chronicler from Grimsby – was almost three centuries after the end of the Viking Age. The name, then, is a reminder of the continuing Norse influence in this North Sea port town, which at the time would have been a melting pot of Anglo-Saxon, Norse and Norman cultures. Ravenser's MP Peter Atte See, for example, was recorded at the piracy inquisition as Peter de Mari (in Latin that had spread with the Roman conquest) and in court as Peter de la Mer (in French from the Norman conquest). Linguists trace the loanwords of these languages like fossils, and find those associated with conquest often enter a language 'top down' – introduced by a conquering elite. Yet the relics of Old Norse are often everyday words, suggesting settlement following Viking raids and integration through trade and marriage.

In Odd, as in other North Sea port towns, this history of raids, conquests and migration produced a rich meld of cultures, languages and beliefs. The Viking settlers' adoption of Christianity, for example, was often a pragmatic decision based on social or political benefit (not least as English nobles and bishops were often critical of trade or treaties with 'the heathens'). One result was temporary Viking baptisms; another that early converts, already having many Norse gods, simply accepted a Christian god alongside their own.

'When I am on land, I pray to Christ,' says Helgi the Lean in the Sagas, 'but when I am at sea, I pray to Thor'.

Unlike the Christian Church, the Vikings had no concept of sin and salvation (their Hel was not a place of punishment), so they made no real attempt to proselytise or spread their faith – a notable difference between such polytheistic traditions and the Abrahamic religions of Judaidsm, Christianity and Islam. Archaeology suggests that for the Viking settlers, the religious crossover period could be lengthy, with Old Norse beliefs lingering despite conversion to Christianity. So as Odd began to slip beneath the sea – little more than a century after its remarkable rise – those who stayed on are likely to have invoked the power of more than one god.

By the early 1330s, flooding had become more frequent and the damage more severe. Merchants were already moving away, with Odd repeatedly requesting money to repair its damaged quay. Given the exodus to Grimsby and Hull, by 1332 around a third of the population had left. Through the following decade, as the island continued to erode, Odd's decline was rapid. With more than 200 buildings already lost to the sea, an inquiry in 1346 heard that 'two parts of the tenements and soil' had already gone, with the town 'daily diminished and carried away'. In a reflection of shifting fortunes, Grimsby and Hull now supplied many more ships to the King.

The final years of Ravenser Odd are described in the 'Chronicles of Meaux Abbey', written by its retired abbot in the fourteenth century. He describes 'floods and inundations of the sea . . . welling up every fifteen days, as is their custom . . . sometimes exceeding beyond measure the height of the town, and surrounding it like a wall on every side'. By then, those who could afford to leave already had, 'with their goods and chattels, as the dangers there continue to increase from day to day'. Of those who remained, the Church recorded many who were unable to pay their tithes.

Within a few more years, high tides had reached Ravenser's Chapel and graveyard, leaving the building in ruins and – as at Kilnsea five centuries later – exposing 'the corpses and bones of the dead'. After decrying the looting of chapel ornaments, the Abbot of Meaux went on to describe the residents' last desperate attempts to save what remained of their town.

> And so terrible vision of waters seen on every side, the enclosed persons, with the reliques, crosses, and other ecclesiastical ornaments, which remained secretly in their possession, and accompanied by the viaticum of the body of Christ in the hands of the priest, flocking together, mournfully imploring grace, warded off that time their destruction.

This was almost the end of Odd. 'Afterwards,' wrote the Abbot, 'daily removing thence with their possessions, they left that town totally without defence, to be shortly swallowed up'.

By 1358, the once-thriving port was all but abandoned. High tides now washed over much of the island, reducing the last of its buildings to ruins, and sweeping sand and gravel out to sea. For the Abbot of Meaux, there was no doubt as to the reason for Odd's destruction: 'By its wicked works and piracies,' he wrote, 'it provoked the wrath of God against itself beyond measure'.

Four years later, on 16 January 1362 – the Feast of Marcellus – fierce south-westerly gales blew in from the Atlantic. This followed a series of intense, damaging storms that swept across northern Europe as the Medieval Warm Period came to an end. In the North Sea, the storm's hurricane-force winds coincided with spring tides, leading to a devastating storm surge that would become known as *Grote Mandrenke*: the 'Great Drowning of Men'.

As the sea swept inland, destroying ports and overwhelming coastal and lowland communities, at least 25,000 people lost their lives. In a single night, the coastlines of Denmark, Germany and the Netherlands were dramatically reshaped, with towns and entire districts submerged. As well as carving new islands from mainland Germany, in the Netherlands the surge formed a vast inland sea: the Zuider Zee, which would lead to the rise of the village of Amsterdam. At Spurn, the last remains of Odd were 'altogether consumed', with much of the island itself washed away.

Given the constantly shifting nature of Spurn, there has long been controversy over the site of Ravenser Odd. From the 1960s, the accepted geographical theory – put forward by George de Boer – was of cyclical phases of the spit's destruction and regrowth. According to this, Spurn reformed in a new location around every 250 years. The fourteenth-century loss of Ravenser Odd, it proposed, had coincided with the end of a cycle of development.

Later work, though, led by the coastal geomorphologist John Pethick, disputed de Boer's theory. Rather than repeated patterns of erosion and renewal, it suggests the position of the Head remains relatively constant, held in place by an under-sea moraine ridge known as the Stony Binks. Replenished by material eroding from the Holderness cliffs further north, Spurn acts as a hinge between this stationary ridge and a shifting 'root' at Kilnsea. Due to erosion, this moves progressively west. In recent centuries, perhaps due to land reclamation in the Humber, the spit has also lengthened by more than a mile.

Since the seventeenth century, when 'panier men' began removing shingle with donkeys, Spurn was also altered significantly by the gravel trade. By the 1800s, vast quantities of sand

and shingle were being transported from the spit by barge, for use in building and as ballast on sailing ships (without a sufficiently weighty cargo, the masts and sails left the ships top-heavy and in danger of capsize). At the time, whalers were also leaving Hull for Greenland, which meant much of Spurn's gravel was dumped overboard in Arctic waters – to be replaced by the weight of slaughtered whales.

By the 1840s, Spurn's gravel trade had reached an unsustainable peak, with up to 45,000 tons removed every year. Crucially, much of this was from the weakened Neck. Already, that stretch had suffered a series of minor breaches. Then in December 1849, north-westerly gales combined with high spring tides to cause a more serious breach. As winds remained strong over several days, the gap between Spurn and the mainland continued to widen and deepen. Eventually, on some high tides, almost three-quarters of a mile of the Neck lay underwater, with one stretch deep enough that fishing vessels began using it as a shortcut out to sea. By then, dangerous currents and shifting sands had given it the name Chance Bay.

With the sheltering spit crucial to shipping and trade, the breach was a wake-up call for the authorities. In 1850, Spurn's gravel trade was banned, with gangs of labourers instead set to work repairing the breaches and constructing sea defences. Even so, it wasn't until 1857 – eight years after the initial breach – that Spurn Island was finally reconnected to the mainland. For the next century and a half, the Neck was then held in place by artificial defences that ranged from massive chalk embankments, groynes and sea walls to dunes. In 1959, Spurn was bought by the Yorkshire Wildlife Trust. Since then, due in part to prohibitive costs, the Trust has left its defences to deteriorate, allowing the spit 'to resume a more natural response to storms'.

While sea defences kept Spurn in place, the Kilnsea cliffs had continued to erode by an average of two metres a year – similar to Skipsea further north. So today, still acting as a hinge, Spurn is in the process of 'catching up'. Usually, these are jerky realignments through the 'wash-over effect', with storms and surges pushing shingle up over the Neck as in 2013. While recent studies suggest a future Spurn will be thinner and lower, it is expected to continue to exist and evolve for at least another century – or perhaps many more.

More than six centuries after its loss, the site of Ravenser Odd remains unknown. Many believe it lies off the Humber side of Spurn, close to a shoal long known as Old Den. This has appeared on nautical charts since the sixteenth century, and was often shown as an island. Other times it was marked as a shoal exposed at low tide, along with other Humber shipping hazards like the Stony Binks, Sunk Sand and the Dreadful.

On older maps, shapeshifting Spurn appears in silty colourwashes, with hand-drawn galleons and the radiating lines of wind roses. In the earliest, its slender neck curves to a bulbous head. Later maps show it spoon-shaped or tapering to a point, others with a straight neck or forming a tight hook. One shows it 'clumsy and shapeless', and by 1728 the peninsula is a dangling sepia epiglottis. Yet it's not clear how much of this variety reflects the evolving nature of Spurn or the challenges of early mapmaking. Usually, though, the Den or Old Den was shown in the lee of the spit or close to what was once the point.

Keen to look out and wonder myself, I left the road after Chalk Bank (named for its eroding sea defences) and headed out to Spurn's Humber shore. There, the sand soon gave way to estuarine silts, the tide still ebbing beyond a vast, ribbed mud sea. Although separated from the North Sea by little more than a strip of dunes, this inner shore was very different to the clean sand beaches facing east. Just offshore, in the shelter of the spit, the Humber mudflats were dark with eel grass. Out beyond there lay the Old Den: a muddy and unremarkable shoal, barely rising above pools of sky-shine and a channel known as Greedy Gut.

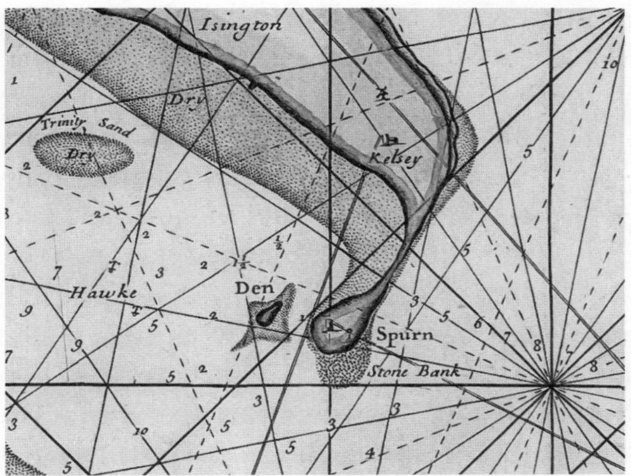

Chart showing Spurn and the Den, 1693

Tantalisingly, in the nineteenth century, a man out digging on the Den claimed to have found dressed 'Ashlar Stone, chiselled and laid in lime; seemingly the foundation of some building of note'.

Today, fishermen out regularly in lobster boats describe subtle 'disturbances' at the water's surface as the tide ebbs and floods. Such changes in texture – like those seen on rivers – are often caused by uneven features on the seabed. A few hundred metres offshore of Spurn, they occur close to a supposed site of Odd. In recent years, geoscientists from the University of Hull have surveyed the area using high-resolution echo sounders (more commonly used by the department to track the movement of sediments).

'Yorkshire's Atlantis nearly found' ran one premature headline before the 2022 survey, testament to our enduring fascination with places submerged beneath the sea. But despite hopes that the technology would locate foundations and sea or harbour walls, the team found no trace of Ravenser Odd.

Tradition has long claimed that on that same night the last of Odd washed away, the Frisian town of Rungholt was also lost.

East of Spurn across the North Sea, it is said to have stood on the island of Strand, much of which now lies beneath the Wadden Sea off the coast of Northern Germany. Yet in medieval times this was part of the *Uthlande* or 'outer lands' of Frisia: a patchwork of low-lying salt marsh divided by meandering watercourses. In the stories, the inhabitants of Rungholt were wealthy and arrogant. And in building dykes, they challenged the sea.

'Defy us, Blanke Hans,' they shouted during gales, 'if you have the courage!' *Blanke Hans*, meaning 'White Hans', is a Frisian name given to the raging North Sea in a storm. Then one night in the town, a group of drunken men played a trick on a priest. In many versions, the men get a hog drunk and dress it in human clothes (sometimes it is simply a man 'drunk as a pig'). Pretending the pig is dying, the men put it to bed and call the priest to read it the last rites. The 'godless revellers' then force the priest to drink beer, either at an inn or from the sacramental chalice. He refuses, and afterwards calls on God to punish them. When a storm blows up, the arrogant townsfolk remain unafraid and again taunt the sea. As the waves surge inland, drowning wealthy Rungholt, the priest is the only survivor, along with 'two or maybe four virgins'.

For many historians, the lack of medieval records made it unlikely Rungholt had ever existed, at least as a major settlement. Yet in 1921, a local farmer out crossing the mudflats made a striking discovery. Previously, fishermen and locals were used to glimpsing pottery and bricks out on mudflats near what was once the island of Strand. Andreas Busch, though, was crossing near the tiny island of Südfall when he came across timbers lying in the mud. They turned out to be part of two huge tidal gates. Subsequently radiocarbon-dated to 1331, they were the kind used to secure a harbour – with gates of a similar age and size known only from the medieval harbour of Rotterdam.

Convinced they were from legendary Rungholt, Busch went on to spend much of the next fifty years searching the mudflats.

Marking his finds on hand-drawn maps, he recorded dykes, fields that had retained the plough marks, graves, the posts of a lock, and the distinctive circles of ninety wells. To archaeologists, this number suggests a population of maybe 1,500–2,000, so a major settlement for the sparsely populated Uthlande. This was settled in the same waves of migration and invasion of Britain by the Angles, Saxons and Danes, and the Frisian spoken today remains the most closely related language to English (highlighted in a 2003 episode of *Mongrel Nation*, when in stilted Old English the comedian Eddie Izzard tries to buy a brown cow from a Frisian farmer). Cultural life in medieval Rungholt, then, is likely to have had many parallels in Ravenser Odd.

Marked on Andreas Busch's maps of the Frisian mudflats were also remnants of twenty-eight *terps*: raised 'dwelling mounds' still found today along much of the Wadden Sea coast. Long familiar with flooding and storm surges, the Frisians have been building their homes and farm buildings on *terps* since the Iron Age. 'There this miserable race inhabits raised pieces of ground or platforms,' wrote Pliny the Elder in AD 77. 'Living in huts built on the chosen spots, they seem like sailors in ships if water covers the surrounding country, but like shipwrecked people when the tide has withdrawn.' In truth, many lived comparatively well, given rich resources out on the Frisian marshes. During periods of flooding – known as *Landunter* or 'land under' – the *terps* provided refuge for both people and livestock (while the flooding usually lasts no more than twelve hours, it can be days). Excavations of some of the earlier mounds have found 'ritual deposits' buried beneath walls and roof poles, among them the skulls of dogs and horses, bowls – perhaps once containing offerings – and locks of hair. Similar deposits are also found buried in drainage ditches encircling the homesteads – so perhaps as protection against Blanke Hans.

Another Frisian local, Hellmut Bahnsen, has been searching the mudflats since the 1970s, and on the nearby island of Pellworm houses the Rungholt Museum in his outsize garden shed. Along with the medieval jugs and bowls that crowd its shelves, his finds have included green-glazed stove tiles and pieces of window-lead, fire-blackened cooking pots and coffins holding mud-stained skulls. More recently, in 2023, geophysicists wheeling a trolleyed contraption out across the mud discovered a medieval *terp* containing the foundations of a major church.

Back at Spurn, such archaeological relics of Ravenser Odd remain no more than a dream. When I contacted the team from Hull several months after the sonar surveys, the disappointment was clear.

By the time I got back to the Wash-over, the tide had turned. I took the path behind the High Tide Shelter up to where the sea now cut into the dune. Below, the smashed sea defences were on a massive scale. Great chalk boulders lay wedged between concrete and wooden groynes, beneath fallen walls built from bags of hardened cement. Further down the shore, slabs of a failed sea wall balanced drunkenly over cavernous dens. Later, I would return at high tide, to waves rushing these confined spaces with an eerie and ominous boom. It left me wondering, if remnants of Ravenser Odd lay off this side of Spurn, what little would remain today?

Now, I made my way out to the foreshore, where scattered chalk boulders were the dirty white of snowmen after a thaw. Down here the wooden groynes were more than three times my height: a glimpse of the magnitude of the defences needed to hold Spurn in place. Now, only the posts remained. Darkly sculptural out on the mud, they decreased in height, like a museum display of human evolution in reverse. On some the wrack hung like beards; on others it was plastered to wet heads. Where currents had torn cross-planks away, the indents suggested necks and waists and jutting chins. Black against mud-shine, one stood taller than the rest, leaning gently back as if countering the swell of her belly. Although the tide was coming in, their human strangeness drew me out. Further from the beach, powerful North Sea currents had lent an arbitrary grace, a nonchalance, or something hunched and withdrawn. Far from shore now, the sodden wood was pocked with barnacles or smoothly malformed.

While the waves still felt distant, it wasn't long before two pools merged and the water pushed on. Quietly, it surrounded the sand where I stood. I scanned the foreshore for a safe route back, with a jolt of old fear. It came from growing up on Sheppey, and looking up from childhood absorption to find your sandbank encircled (sometimes followed by a panicky wade back thorough cold water that tugged at your knees, your thighs and then your waist). Today, I was keenly aware this was a shore I didn't know. So I hurried back, leaping shallow but broad gullies as I neared the beach, hoping that where I landed would be firm.

By the time I set off back along the beach towards Kilnsea, the Holderness cliffs were dissolved in mist. Seaward, the old groyne posts lined up at the edge of my vision: a disquieting, watchful presence like the ghosts of Spurn.

Submerged forest, Borth

6

Cantre'r Gwaelod

Borth, West Wales

After a freezing night in the van outside a friend's place in west Wales, we set off for Borth. They'd suggested a particular route for its first view of the village, and we headed north into steepening hills that showed no sign yet of winter giving way to spring. There had been snow little more than a week ago, and meanders in the road gave distant glimpses of the mauve-white peaks of Snowdonia. After a last cautious climb, with road signs warning of previous fatalities, we crested a hill. At the sight of Borth I let out a long breath, and glanced over to see if my fourteen-year-old daughter was looking at a screen.

Like an amphitheatre, the hills around Borth faced the Irish Sea. Below, sheep pasture and drystone walls fell away to the plain of the Dyfi valley and the glint of caravans. Out at the edge of the land, Borth was little more than a single street wide: a strip of houses stretching away along the shore. It was the thinness of that rim between marsh and sea that gave the village its air of vulnerability. From up in the hills, it seemed a tentative hold on the land.

Inland of the village, the morning sun lent a gold flush to the expanse of Cors Fochno, or Borth Bog. While I was drawn to Borth by its extraordinary submerged forest – along with some wild legends – ultimately I was here because of the bog. Thousands of years ago, when sea levels were lower, this stretched out beyond the modern coastline into Cardigan Bay. And recently, after winter storms had dragged sand and shingle offshore, low tides had again exposed the striking sight of ancient tree stumps preserved by the bog.

Borth Bog began to form more than 7,000 years ago. It is a raised bog, now a rare habitat of northern Europe famed for its remarkable powers of preservation (in the last century Britain has lost a shocking ninety-four per cent of its raised bogs, which are natural carbon sinks). Originating in wet hollows and shallow lowland lakes, these bogs grow so slowly they take millennia to form their characteristic dome shape. The bogs' preservative properties are due to sphagnum moss, and its sponge-like ability to retain water. This allows surface mosses to grow on their own slowly decomposing remains, and the bog to grow upwards. Eventually, over thousands of years, the moss becomes isolated from groundwater supplies, leaving it fed only by rainwater. In places a lens of water also lies beneath the surface, so it quakes underfoot. Raised bogs, then, can be illusory places to walk: lightless, watery worlds hidden beneath russet-gold carpets.

As well as retaining water, the bog's blanket of moss prevents oxygen reaching microbes in the under-layers, so these engines of decay can't survive. Additionally, sphagnum moss soaks up calcium, turning bog-water acidic and further retarding decay. For most species this makes the bog inhospitable. Yet the dearth of nutrients means strange, carnivorous plants can do well. Deep in Borth Bog, rare great sundews – their sugary 'dew' glistening at the end of red tendrils – can trap insects as large as dragonflies (days or weeks later, their leaves unfurl to release the exoskeleton). Yet it's the sphagnum moss that dominates here, even in the bog's acidic pools. There, if lifted from the water, one Borth species has the look of wet fur and is known as 'drowned kittens'.

It is a dark, fairy-tale world. So it's perhaps unsurprising that for centuries – or millennia – stories have leached out of the bog into the Welsh imagination. *Yr hen wrach ddu y figin* was the old black witch of Borth Bog: a seven-foot marsh hag that entered houses to breathe in people's faces, so they woke 'with the shakes' (this was actually malaria, which in medieval times was endemic on British marshes). Another well-known legend of the bog is the 'Old Toad' of Cors Fochno, one of the four oldest creatures in the world, 'Who feels the cold skin sagging round his bones'. Although the wisest creature in Wales, anyone seeking his wisdom will be sucked down into Borth Bog before they reach him. Presumably, it is a legend that grew from the way the bog stills the decay of what slips beneath its surface.

For it's not just trees these raised bogs preserve. Most unsettling are the infamous 'bog bodies', which have been found across northern Europe since the seventeenth century. While some are so well preserved they were first mistaken for recent murder victims, the majority are more than 2,000 years old and date to the Iron Age. One peculiar quality of the sphagnum moss is that while calcium is leached from the bones – leaving them soft and pliable, or occasionally dissolving them completely – many bodies retain their skin. Some still wear the clothes they were buried in, while others retain internal organs and even traces of last meals: apple pips, oats and dried sloes, and plants that today we call weeds. But it's the preservation of ancient skin that draws us in. Often bronzed and leathery, it is 'tanned' by the peat, which preserves extraordinary details: toenails and body hair, skin pores and forehead creases. It leaves the bodies eerily lifelike, and museum visitors with the unsettling sense that the dead are only sleeping.

More than a hundred bog bodies have been recorded, and most suffered violent deaths. They have been variously stabbed, disembowelled, decapitated, cut and strangled. Some, such as Lindow Man, also show signs of what is known as 'overkill' (found face down in a Cheshire bog, he appears to have not only stab wounds but also a slit throat, fractured skull, broken ribs and a broken neck). To archaeologists, this suggests execution and ritual sacrifice, with the bodies appearing to have been deliberately placed in the bogs. This is sometimes linked to the Iron Age practice of deposition in watery places, and the idea of a 'ritual killing' of objects as sacrificial offerings. It's also quite possible that those interring the bodies were well aware of the bogs' uncanny powers of preservation.

Not long after arriving in Borth, I met Anthony on the beach. Drill in hand, he was kneeling beside the solid sleeper wall that divided his backyard from the top of the shore. After a brief chat, he waved me in over the wall to a sheltered spot by his beach-cobble shed. Beyond a protective ridge of imported stone, the cold-blue sea showed no sign yet of the forest it concealed.

Anthony was in his seventies, the fifth generation of his family to live in the village. With his childhood home 150 yards along the shore from where we sat, he'd had a lifelong interest in Borth's succession of sea defences (along with a ringside view). Settling down on his bench in the sun, he spoke with an easy, unhurried warmth about the village's evolving relationship with the sea. Built on what coastal engineers describe as a 'mobile shingle bank', this seafront road was once the entire village. From 1863, though, everything began to change with the coming of the railway. Before then, most of Borth's men made their living from the sea, and English was spoken only as a second language.

The new railway, though, brought visitors and a need for boarding houses. This was something I'd noticed as we drove into Borth: the striking up-and-down heights of the houses either side of the road. Taller houses like Anthony's, built in 1865, dwarfed Borth's older beach-cobble cottages. This influx of both Welsh and English tourists also brought new opportunities for the locals. Soon, they were moving into attics at the height of summer, to let the rest of the house to holidaymakers. Anthony's own grandparents would move the family down into the cellar, for what became known as 'Birmingham fortnight'.

Later, he showed me postcards of Borth beach in his parents' childhood. In one, above wooden rowboats drawn up on shore, his grandparents' house stood near the edge of the frame. At the window was the ghostly blur of a child: his dad, Anthony presumed, or perhaps his aunt. 'That sinister-looking black shed,' he said, pointing to where it sat at the top of the beach, 'was the outside toilet. It was reduced to matchwood by a storm when Dad was a young lad.' On the beach below, the tops of groynes protruded from the shingle. Other postcards showed them more clearly: palisades of wooden stakes driven into the shore, forming terraces at the top of the beach. At the time, people were responsible for their own defences, so some houses were more solidly defended than others. Today, storms occasionally shift the stones enough to reveal even earlier defences: the stubs of groynes said to have been put in by a local carpenter in 1880.

Postcard showing Borth's old palisade sea defences

As children, Anthony said, with gales and a massive sea, at high tide they'd gather at alleyways between the seafront houses 'that took the biggest hits'. Looking out to a quiet sea now, he shook his head, his childhood awe at its power still vivid. 'You'd feel the houses rattle and shake.'

Most destructive were south-westerly gales, which drive Atlantic waves straight through the channel between Ireland and Wales to the shore at Borth. One of the worst to ever hit the village peaked on a Wednesday morning in October 1896, as hurricane-force winds coincided with high spring tides. In Borth, a local reporter described waves that 'rose mountains high and crashed in through the windows and doors. Not a house in the village escaped from the effects of the waves.' He wrote of torrents rushing through the seafront houses, and bursting from front doors to sweep furniture and clothes into the street. Three days later the journalist returned. 'The whole of the surrounding country was, even on Saturday, under water. There was just the narrow strip of land on which Borth stands between miles of water at the back of the place and the open sea.' The village itself 'was in a pitiable condition': smashed windows and doors, downstairs rooms filled with tons of stone and shingle, collapsed walls and upper storeys held up by props. The wind, he wrote, was 'causing the water to run in waves from field to field and from garden to garden, which left the houses between two waters, and in a highly dangerous position.'

In the 1970s, Borth's old palisade sea defences were ripped out and replaced with wooden groynes and tons of imported shingle. Approaching the turn of the century, though, they clearly needed replacement. With decisions made by weighing costs against the value of property, the policy agreed for Borth was 'Hold the Line' for fifty years. This was followed by more than a decade of discussions, surveys and 'endless public meetings' where local disagreements and tensions were aired. Today, a minority of Borth's residents are Welsh, and in summer its population more than quadruples. In general, Anthony said, second homers didn't want a sea wall. They wanted nothing that would 'spoil their gin and summer views,' he said. 'But it can be scary for those living on the shoreline in winter.'

Eventually, sixteen years after the consultations began, a defence scheme was agreed and completed in 2011. So today, rather than the 'four miles of sand' the old adverts describe, Borth's seafront houses look out on a bank of imported grey pebbles. Beyond that, great boulders shipped from Norway form a series of massive breakwaters and offshore reefs, which cause waves to break before reaching shore. So it's not the view it once was. Some also complain that the pebble banks are hard to walk on. But for Anthony, it's meant each generation of his family has seen less destruction. He was, though, well aware of future uncertainty, given Met Office warnings of perhaps a metre of sea-level rise by the end of the century. Long before then, Borth's policy of 'Hold the Line' would change to 'Managed Retreat'.

A decade earlier, the council had announced that the seaside village of Fairbourne – twelve miles up the coast – would be 'decomissioned' by 2054. From then on, officials said, its sea defences would no longer be maintained. With a population of around 700, low-lying Fairbourne sits at the edge of the Snowdonia National Park, so can't retreat inland. Based on current rates of sea-level rise, council representative Lisa Goodier said the council planned to begin in 2045. 'It means we would eventually return this land to the sea,' she said. 'We would have to move everybody out, and then every ounce of infrastructure to return it to a salt marsh over time.'

Since the announcement, Fairbourne residents have been described in the press as 'Britain's first climate refugees'. As house prices subsequently nosedived and banks stopped offering mortgages, villagers described their fury, distress and disbelief. Afraid for the future, and angry at a lack of compensation or support, many said they would refuse to leave. 'Until the water actually comes in here,' said the owner of the Fairbourne Chippy, 'until we physically can't work, we'll carry on.'

I'd known for a week that the forest was exposed, but ever since had worried that by the time I got to Borth it would be gone. Earlier, Anthony had described how the new sea defences meant the trees now appeared and disappeared more rapidly. With increased shelter from waves at the village end, marine life flourished on the artificial boulder reefs. Yet to the north, the shore had become more dynamic. Not only did the forest now appear more often, but heavy seas also scoured away more sand to expose the ancient roots. In the past, Anthony sometimes went years without seeing them. But not anymore. Once the weather settled, he said, calmer seas also returned the sand more rapidly, accelerating the cycles of revelation and concealment.

Today, though, I was in luck. As the sea slipped from shore, dark, irregular shapes began to break its mirror shine. Very gradually, more and more tree stumps were revealed out on the glistening mud. Although the trunks were rarely more than a foot or so high, waves had scoured away the bog's ancient peat to expose some spectacular roots. Radiocarbon dating suggests most of the trees died between 4,000 and 6,000 years ago, although oaks at the Borth end were still alive around 3,000 years ago. Lying just offshore of the village, the remains of ancient, mature oaks were the most impressive. Gnarled and twisted, some retained the slow-grown magnificence of the trees they once were. Now, though, their great, buttress-like roots shouldered up out of pools like giants, the ancient wood sculpted into crooked spines and wet backs. Further out, immense thighs and forearms seemed to flounder as if rising from the mud.

Having strayed into Irish mythology during my visit to Clare, the oak roots brought to mind Fomorians. Malevolent and grotesque, they were the mythical enemy of the Irish: goat-headed or one-armed, one-legged giants, with a single destructive eye. Seen later as raiders from the sea, they are thought to represent the destructive forces of nature. So it seemed fitting that they might rise from the Irish Sea onto Borth's storm-battered shore.

Prehistoric roots exposed on the foreshore at Borth

From Borth, the beach stretches north for several miles to the dunes at Ynyslas. Yet it wasn't until roughly the halfway point that I came to realise the extent of the forest. And it was extraordinary. Remnants of similar – if less impressive – submerged forests are periodically exposed around much of the British Isles, and were first recorded by Gerald of Wales in 1188. Following a visit to a Pembrokeshire beach, he wrote:

> A very remarkable circumstance occurred . . . The sandy shores of south Wales, being laid bare by the extraordinary violence of a storm, which had been covered for many ages, reappeared and discovered the trunks of trees standing in the very sea itself . . . like a grove cut down, perhaps at the time of the deluge, or not long after.

In 1665, Samuel Pepys mentioned similarly preserved trees in his *Diary*, after a conversation with a Blackwall shipbuilder:

> In digging his late Docke he did 12 foot under ground find perfect trees over-covered with earth. Nut trees, with branches and the very nuts upon them . . . Their shells black with age, and their kernel, upon opening, decayed, but their shells perfectly hard as ever.

At the time, the presence of the trees was hard to explain. In Borth and other places around the British coast where they stood in the sea, they were often known as 'Noah's trees' or 'Noah's woods', and widely believed to be a glimpse of lands lost in the Flood. The first study to set the trees in a wider geological context was Clement Reid's *Submerged Forests* in 1913 (for which he'd boiled the Doggerland moorlog to reveal plant species that once grew on what was now the North Sea bed). His wide-ranging survey covered sites all around the British coast, including dock excavations like that described by Pepys. Yet most of the sites had been only briefly exposed and were poorly recorded – a neglect Reid attributed to widespread acceptance of the theory they were relics of the Deluge. Towards the end of *Submerged Forests*, following his painstaking survey of the many varied sites around Britain, he asks: 'To what conclusions do the foregoing somewhat monotonous pages lead?' The only explanation, he concluded, had nothing to do with Noah. Instead, it could only be relative sea-level rise. Either the land had sunk, or the sea had risen. While less shocking than Robert Hooke's similar proposals in the 1660s, it was still controversial.

★

Underfoot, Borth's wave-worn peat was bituminous: somewhere between the give of preschool playgrounds and the thud of forest floors. In places it was drying between tides to the taupe of animal hide, but in shadow it was dark as tar. Surrounded by wet sand and the shine of mudflats, roots and fallen branches were still embedded in these islands of peat. For now, without the protection of sand and silt, at each high tide the currents exposed a little more. Seen closely, the raised surface of the peat was flecked with traces of that ancient forest floor. Even the finest of twigs were exquisitely preserved, the winter sun casting their angles in sharp relief. Sometimes, where fragments had washed away with recent tides, just the imprints and shadows remained.

Like the strokes of an ancient language, the marks reminded me of cuneiform cut in clay tablets – not least as I'd just read Irving Finkel's *The Ark Before Noah* (2014). With Cardigan Bay's rich inundation legends stretching back to the thirteenth century, I'd been considering much earlier flood tales. These remain among our oldest written stories, with their origins attracting endless speculation and controversy. Finkel describes his work as Assistant Keeper of Ancient Mesopotamian Script at the British Museum deciphering the language, and his 2008 discovery of what became known as The Ark Tablet. It was, he writes 'the biggest shock in 44 years of grappling with difficult lines in cuneiform tablets'. With the tablet's clay surface abraded, he describes angling it under a light for the slightest shadow to make out the marks, and then searching for matches in the Assyrian dictionary. 'I found the following entry,' he writes, 'and nearly fell off my chair as a result of the words . . . *Two each, two by two*.'

A thousand years before the Bible, this ancient language described animals entering a boat two by two to survive a flood. The same clay tablet also contained detailed instructions on how to build a circular, coracle-like boat. While the ark-like information was new, this wasn't the first cuneiform tablet to show that earlier versions of the Genesis Flood story predated the Bible; George Smith, a predecessor of Finkel's at the British Museum, made the initial discovery in 1872. Through the previous decade, this working-class ex-engraver and self-taught historian had been sorting, cleaning and translating the museum's chaotic collection of cuneiform tablets retrieved from a Mesopotamian site in modern-day Iraq.

This particular tablet contained a fragment of what would become known as the Epic of Gilgamesh. Dating to the second millennium BC, it is recognised as one of humanity's oldest written stories. This fragment tells of a catastrophic flood conjured by the gods to rid the world of humans. Too populous and noisy – rather than sinful – they have begun to keep the gods awake. Yet one good man, Utanapishtim, is chosen to survive with his wife. So the god of wisdom instructs him to build a boat and fill it with animals and seeds. Later, as the flood begins to recede, Utanapishtim releases a raven, a sparrow and a dove to find dry land. Much of which feels very familiar.

On first making the connection at the British Museum, Smith is said to have 'rushed about the room in a great state of excitement, and, to the astonishment of those present, began to undress himself!' For the implications of the discovery were huge. Most significantly, it contradicted the belief that the Old Testament was the word of God. Instead, it implied earlier versions of the Genesis Flood story had long circulated in oral traditions. As with early Irish myths, many Mesopotamian stories recorded in the clay also include tricks of the storyteller's trade such as repeated phrases. Finkel suggests some version of the Mesopotamian flood story may have passed down generations for millennia, perhaps with origins in remote memory of catastrophic local flooding (meaning 'the land between two rivers', Mesopotamia was bounded by the great Tigris and Euphrates).

More famous is the 'Black Sea deluge hypothesis'. First argued by the oceanographer William Ryan in 1997, this instead proposes that the origins of these ancient flood stories lie in a breach of the previously landlocked Black Sea by the Mediterranean, as Mesolithic sea levels rose. While there is disagreement as to whether this breach would have been gradual or catastrophic, the geology shows it occurred around the same time Doggerland slipped beneath the North Sea. For Ryan, survivors of a Black Sea flood are likely to have fled into Mesopotamia, with their ancestors preserving the tale that evolved into elements of both the Epic of Gilgamesh and Genesis. In the light of other findings, given well-developed storytelling traditions, such longevity does seem possible.

By the time I was halfway to Ynyslas, I was surrounded by hundreds of trunks. And these were quite different to the roots at Borth. I couldn't tell from the stumps, but learned later they were from birch, hazel and pine trees that died some 5,000 years ago. Unlike the earlier oaks, many of these stumps had worn to fin-like points that stretched off into the distance with an eerie, devastated beauty.

Preserved by the time-defying magic of the bog, the trees were spaced much as they would have been in life, when sunlight filtered down through their leaves to the forest floor. Pressing my fingers to nearby peat, I touched the edge of an ancient leaf. Darkly pliable and patterned with veins, it still lay more or less where it fell.

Weaving a path through the knee-high forest, I made detours for more spectacular roots. Typical of trees that have grown in fen woods, many splayed out along the surface (the high water table restricting deeper growth). Their sinuous limbs now snaked across the foreshore, darkly waterlogged or scoured bone-white by the waves and sand. A few reached out towards neighbours, their roots entwined in oddly familiar poses: an enfolding arm or the grasp of a wrist.

By late afternoon the winter sun cast sculptural shadows. No giants here, but the twists and curves suggested equally mythical forms, some reflected in the stillness of pools: talons and serpentine tails, stranded selkies or shapeshifting fin-folk. Good grief. It was the strangest and most awe-inspiring place I'd ever been. And for more than a thousand years, it had been appearing as if by magic after storms, as the seething tide withdrew to reveal a forest standing in the sea.

There are many versions of the story of how this land drowned. The earliest is a poem from *The Black Book of Carmarthen*: the oldest surviving manuscript written solely in Welsh. A collection of mainly ninth- to twelfth-century poetry, the irregularity of its text suggests it was written by an amateur, sometime before 1250. Perhaps part of a lost prose saga, the poem '*Boddi Maes Gwyddno*', 'The Drowning of the Plain of Gwyddno', is again likely to be a remnant of an earlier oral tradition. It also echoes other Celtic legends, where inundation is due to an overflowing well. In this short poem, the flood is caused by Mererid. She is described as both a maiden and a 'fountain-cup bearer', which is thought to imply she was the guardian of a sacred well. The duty of these 'well-maidens' – often seen as goddesses or virgin priestesses – was to protect a freshwater well or spring (with the openings sometimes interpreted as gateways to the otherworld). If left unprotected, those waters might overflow to form rivers or lakes, or rush to the sea and reshape a coastline. The cause of the floods is often the well-maiden's neglect of her duty, or the loss of her virginity. While translations and interpretations of the poem vary, most blame Mererid for the flood: for neglecting her duty through either pride, arrogance or presumption.

Later versions retain the same seventh-century characters, but the sins are new. In the sixteenth century, Mererid is distracted from her duty by lust, when seduced by a man named Seithennin (sometimes 'Seithennin of the feeble mind'). In succumbing to the pleasures of the flesh, Mererid neglects to close the gates and the low-lying kingdom is drowned.

By the eighteenth century, the well-maiden has gone, and the version told is well known today. The lost land is now Cantre'r Gwaelod, 'The Lowland Hundred' or 'Hundred of the Bottom', said to have extended some twenty miles out into Cardigan Bay. A rich and fertile plain, its sixteen wealthy towns and villages depended on dykes and sluice gates as protection from the sea. But one night, around AD 600, a storm blew up from the south-west. Now the King's friend or a prince of Cantre'r Gwaelod, Seithennin was appointed watchman responsible for the floodgates. Yet he was also a notorious drunk (in another medieval Welsh text he is listed as one of the Three Immortal Drunkards of the Isle of Britain). Later that night, partying at the King's palace, Seithennin fell into a drunken stupor and failed to close the gates. This allowed the sea to surge across Cantre'r Gwaelod, which was lost forever. Only the King and a few revellers escaped, by running to higher ground along the Sarn Cynfelyn ridge.

Sarn Cynfelyn is a boulder and shingle formation to the south of Borth. One of three similar ridges, it extends out into Cardigan Bay, roughly at right angles to the shore. Partly visible at low tide, the sarn ends seven miles out to sea at a rocky reef known as Gwyddno's Palace or Fort (where in the legend Seithennin falls down drunk). Sarn means 'causeway' in Welsh, and these oddly linear geological features can appear man-made. Today, we know they are glacial moraine ridges: debris left behind by melting ice sheets after the last Ice Age. Yet they could look like sea defences that failed long ago.

Perhaps tellingly, a similar legend is also told of a rocky reef two miles off the North Wales coast. This is known as Llys Helig – meaning 'Helig's Palace or Court' – with the earliest known use of the name thought to date to the early 1600s. Visible at low tide, this too appears to be debris left by retreating glaciers.

According to tradition, though, it is the ruined palace of the sixth-century Prince Helig, and all that remains of the sunken kingdom of Tyno Helig.

Here, the story of its loss is revenge for ancestral crimes. In the version most often told today, the blame falls on Helig's beautiful but cruel daughter Gwendud and her lover Tathal. When he proposes, she refuses to marry him – as he does not wear the golden torque of a nobleman. Vowing to obtain one, he tricks and murders a Scottish chieftain held prisoner at the palace. Later, when her lover returns wearing the stolen torque, Gwendud agrees to the marriage. But at the wedding feast, the ghost of the murdered chieftain appears, threatening vengeance over four generations. With the couple living well into old age, the curse is forgotten – until the birth of their first great-grandchild. Celebrations are held at the palace and by nightfall the revellers call for more wine. So the maid heads down to the cellar, to find fish swimming in rising seawater.

Later, I came across an earlier version of the story by chance, in an old copy of William Ashton's *The Battle of Land and Sea* (1909). The thick yellowed pages were deckle-edged, and after Ashton introduced the legend of Llys Helig, it was followed – thrillingly – by an uncut page. Slicing it carefully open with a knife, I found a version of the legend recorded in the 1850s. In this, while the ancestral crimes are left to the imagination, vengeance was also prophesied over several generations. Following the crime, every night in Tyno Helig a wailing cry was heard through its hills and valleys.

'*Dial a ddaw*' – 'Revenge will come'.

One evening, during a feast at the house of Helig, the jovial, carousing guests called for more wine. As the servant went down to the cellar, the old minstrel found himself unable to play. Tears fell on his harp strings, as he foresaw the fate of Tyno Helig. As the servant rushed crying from the drowning cellar, the harper ran with her as far as the mountains, with the sea at their heels.

Looking back in daylight, they saw the kingdom's fields and villages were submerged, and that no one else had survived. With drunkenness a recurring theme in the later Welsh legends, the pair are often the only ones sober. Given the longevity of these Welsh stories, they offer – as ever – a fascinating glimpse into the shifting weight of society's sins.

Along with other similarities between these two Welsh inundation legends, a seventeenth-century reference also describes Helig as 'Lord of Cantre'r Gwaelod'. It suggests to many that both traditions may have their origins in the same earlier story. Like many of the early Irish legends, the two Welsh stories feature legendary or local semi-historical figures from around the sixth century, the period following the break-up of Roman Britain. For Celtic scholar Rachel Bromwich, it was to 'the beginning of their national traditions, that medieval *cyfarwyddiaid* [Welsh storytellers] attached the legends of the great inundations'.

Perhaps, then, the legend of Cantre'r Gwaelod is really a story from elsewhere, which became localised around curious geological features that appeared man-made. There are further striking parallels with Brittany's legend of the drowned city of Kêr Ys (returning me to the Celtic seaways I'd glimpsed on the Isles of Scilly). Meaning 'Low City', Kêr Ys is often said to lie off Finisterre beneath the waters of the Bay of Douarnenez. Yet as one of the best-known stories in Breton folklore, there are many regional variations. Interestingly, a number centre on submerged sites at a similar depth to Cardigan Bay, which were likely lost around the same time.

Early versions describe Ys built on land reclaimed from the sea, and that like Cantre'r Gwaelod it was protected by dykes and a floodgate. The city was ruled by the good and pious King Gradlon – fifth-century hero of many an early Breton folktale – who wore the key to the floodgate around his neck. His daughter Dahut, though, was wayward and easily tempted. One night, during a storm, her lover persuades her to steal the King's key to let him in. Succumbing to flattery – and sometimes too much wine – Dahut opens the gate and Ys drowns.

Like the Welsh legends, the story is set in the early centuries of Christianity. And in later versions, Ys becomes increasingly wealthy and degenerate. While the King converts to Christianity, his daughter refuses, and – like the rest of the city's inhabitants – continues to follow the old pagan ways of the Celts. Like Sodom and Gomorrah, Ys becomes known throughout the land for its feasting, wickedness and debauchery. One night, while Dahut is drinking and dancing, she falls for the Red Knight, who persuades her to steal the key. Another version describes Dahut as an unrepentant sinner, responsible for turning the city into a place of drunken, fornicating debauchery. Every night, she lures a different man to her bedchamber, and afterwards dashes their corpses on the rocks beneath her window (alternatively, they are sacrificed in the *Baie des Trépassés*, the 'Bay of the Dead'). One night, though, the man she takes to her chamber is a knight dressed in red, who turns out to be the Devil.

Many stories of Ys end in a similar way, with King Gradlon the only survivor – after he attempts, but fails, to save his daughter. Taking her with him, the King escapes on his magical horse *Morvarc'h*, which like Lyonesse's white horse can gallop on water. But the weight of Dahut's sins drag the horse down. Otherwise doomed, Gradlon is finally persuaded – often by a saint – to throw his daughter into the sea. The good King is then free to escape. Dahut, though, is transformed into a morgen: a Breton water spirit similar to a siren. To this day, her singing continues to lure sailors to their death in the Bay of Douarnenez (nineteenth-century versions also describe how at low tide people hear the chimes of a *carillon*: an organ-like instrument connected to many brass bells in a tower).

The story of Ys was often told by traditional Breton storytellers known as *conteurs*. Like the Irish *seanchaí*, similar traditions of travelling storytellers thrived at the Celtic fringes of Britain, among them the Welsh *cyfarwydd* and the Cornish 'droll-tellers'. As with all oral traditions, the stories told were inherently organic. Embellished with each retelling, they evolved over generations: repeatedly modified to fit the times, an audience or locality. Features of a local landscape were no doubt woven in. And those stories would then be passed on within a community. At family firesides and local inns, the stories would have changed again and again – through being misheard or misinterpreted, half-forgotten, embellished or simply improved.

The earliest handwritten versions of the Welsh inundation legends are vague on where they take place. It is only later that the stories attach to specific locations: to curious reefs and moraine ridges that spark the imagination or beg explanation. Along with its striking similarities to other Celtic legends, this leads many to suspect the story of Cantre'r Gwaelod originated elsewhere. With the Welsh, Cornish and Breton cultures so closely linked by sea since prehistoric times, stories inevitably travelled by boat. Others have also linked the story to the Old North, suggesting origins in Scotland or perhaps Northumbria, before it migrated to Wales.

At the water's edge, I followed a wave-cut channel out through a peat outcrop that was several feet high. It was through here that currents surged on the incoming tide, with eddies and rips undercutting and sculpting peat walls. As well as exposing roots, this also revealed layers of sediment in cross section beneath the peat, among them fine grey clays laid down on ancient estuary mudflats. These too contained the telltale remains of molluscs and insects, ancient plants and seeds, pollen and single-celled diatoms.

For those who could read it, they told a story that reached back thousands of years – and it wasn't of steady encroachment. Instead, the ground at my feet was previously salt marsh and mudflats, before the sea retreated and the forest thrived, along with bog and reed-swamp that would later preserve it. Closer to Borth, an even more complex layering of sediments suggests conditions fluctuated there, with repeated periods of flooding and withdrawal – which allowed the more recent oaks to grow. The final inundation then appears to have been gradual, with no evidence of catastrophic flooding as the stories describe (here, researchers find no 'chaotic' layer of sand and broken shells like those left by the Doggerland tsunami).

Instead, there are suggestions that the stories may have been influenced by the Great Flood of 1607, which devastated vast swathes of low-lying land in South Wales, Somerset and the Bristol Channel. In *Sunken Cities* (1957), F. J. North proposes that later versions of both the Cantre'r Gwaelod and Llys Helig legends were influenced by reports of that disaster. This Great Flood hit south-west Britain in January 1607. Driven by gale-force westerlies, Atlantic storm waves were funnelled by the narrowing Bristol Channel, increasing both their height and speed. Unfortunately, the peak of the surge also coincided with an exceptional high tide, and in places the floodwaters rushed more than four miles inland. According to one vicar, 'In Brysto by credyble report that mornyng tyde was hygher than that Evenyng tyde by nyne foote of water.'

In the weeks following the disaster, news pamphlets across Britain described houses in the south-west 'carved quite away', 'huge and mighty hills of water . . . faster than a man could run', and how people spent days clinging to the tops of trees. One woodcut showed drowning livestock, a child adrift in a crib and a church submerged to the roof. Echoing the feelings of many, one report described the 'lamentable' catastrophe as 'God's warning to his people of England by the great overflowing of the Waters of Floudes'.

Another pamphlet described the drowned lands as 'reputed the richest and fruitfullest place in all that country'. It was only after

1607.

A true report of certaine wonderfull ouerflowings of Waters, now lately in Summerset-shire, Norfolke, and other places of England: destroying many thousands of men, women, and children, ouerthrowing and bearing downe whole townes and villages, and drowning infinite numbers of sheepe and other Cattle.

Printed at London by W. I. for Edward White and are to be solde at the signe of the Gunne at the North doore of Paules.

News pamphlet on the Great Flood of 1607

the 1607 floods, F. J. North suggests, that the extent, richness and fertility of Cantre'r Gwaelod became central to the story (as with Cornwall's Lyonesse). Inevitably, there is also the tolling of drowned church bells: immortalised in the popular song 'The Bells of Aberdovey' (while often cited as an old Welsh poem, its origins appear to lie in an eighteenth-century English comic opera). Other details were also added by seventeenth- and eighteenth-century Romantics, as they reshaped older legends for print. Many later versions retained their embellishments. Which was all part of the revolution that came with the rise of the printing press, changing both how stories spread and their influence on each other.

The legend of Cantre'r Gwaelod has no doubt been influenced by events and stories from elsewhere. Yet the search for historical local roots continues. After all, the Roman 'father of cartography' Ptolemy suggests that 2,000 years ago this coastline lay some eight miles further west. In the summer of 2022, after my visit to Borth, *Atlantic Geoscience* published a study by geographer Professor Simon Haslett and historical linguist Professor David Willis, who specialises in Celtic at Oxford University.

'"Welsh Atlantis" mystery SOLVED', ran a headline in the *Daily Express*, 'after Mediaeval map reveals location of TWO "lost" islands'.

The study included a 'reassessment' of the Gough Map: the earliest surviving map of Great Britain. Held at Oxford's Bodleian Library, it takes its name from the antiquarian Robert Gough, who in 1774 bought the worn map at a sale for half a crown. Drawn on two skins of vellum, it is coloured with ink washes made from woad, buckthorn yellow and gall. And while the map dates to around 1360, it may include copying from a prototype created as early as 1280. No one knows how or why the map was compiled, but for its time it is considered surprisingly accurate.

And off the coast at Cardigan Bay, it clearly shows two islands – each about a quarter the size of Anglesey.

Both lie close to a sarn, one of which is Sarn Cynfelyn (along which the King and several revellers are said to have escaped the inundation). Roughly where the islands are shown, Haslett's bathymetric analysis of the seabed revealed two raised areas of coarse broken rock: the same glacial moraine that forms the sarns. For the researchers, then, it was entirely plausible that the islands were remnants of a low-lying landscape lost to erosion. As the surrounding land was dissected by the outflow of rivers, they suggest, and truncated by the advancing Irish Sea, the sarns could have acted as 'anchors' for the islands. With later maps showing no sign of any islands in Cardigan Bay, they appear to have been lost by the sixteenth century.

Professor Haslett also suggests the islands' eventual erosion would have released boulders that contributed to the sarns – which appear to have played a major role in perpetuating the legends. If the Gough Map does have origins around 1280, the prototype would have been almost contemporary with *The Black Book of Carmarthen* – in which the well-maiden Mererid allows the sea to overflow Cantre'r Gwaelod.

If those islands existed as shown, people may have lived out there. It brought to mind the council's plans to decommission Fairbourne. Given the extent of the land that's been lost in Cardigan Bay, inundation stories may well have been told here for much longer than the records suggest. So might their origins reach back as far as when the forest began to drown? This *was* possible, as Borth's intertidal peats also preserved traces of humans here at the time. Among them were a cluster of footprints, made by an adult and a barefoot four-year-old. Left around 4,000 years ago, the prints were sealed beneath a fine layer of silt laid down as the forest was submerged. So might they have stood beneath its dead and dying trees?

'As woodlands died and land submerged,' writes Jim Leary in *The Remembered Land* (2015), 'the whole environment irreversibly altered.' The drowned forests would 'have been eerily quiet, devoid of leaves, growth and much of the life that once dwelt amidst them.'

'It is possible,' he says, 'that mythologies grew up to explain this phenomenon – perhaps dead woodlands became taboo areas or lands of the spirits'. Today, across the Atlantic on America's east coast, climate change and rising sea levels are creating similarly haunting landscapes, which are known in the scientific community as 'ghost forests'.

By the time I headed back to the fantastical oak roots at Borth, it seemed this prehistoric Welsh forest must once have had its stories. Which made me smile when I finally caught sight of my daughter, exactly where I'd left her. Still in the lee of the breakwater, she was staring at the screen of her Kindle – doing much the same thing we always had.

Sunken Lane
Once a main route into medieval Dunwich

7

Old Dunwich

Dunwich, Suffolk

I pulled up in a car park at the end of another Beach Road, this time in Suffolk. Beyond the closed cafe, a shingle bank obscured the sea, and I sat for a while as their colours ran together in the rain. Perhaps it was better to wait until it eased. For a while, lulled by the steady thrum on the roof, I dozed in the back of the van, thinking of the ruins of old Dunwich on the seabed. Before leaving, I'd taken to watching grainy divers' footage on a loop: cold stone encrusted with sponges and soft corals; the red eyes of velvet swimming crabs retreating into darkness beneath the remnants of medieval churches. In the snug of the van, the images merged with the sound of the rain. Tomorrow, hopefully, I would be visiting Stuart Bacon, the first diver to find the ruins more than fifty years ago.

Once the rain let up I headed out to the shingle ridge, where a misty drizzle still veiled the marshes and sharpened the calls of waders. Cresting the top of the bank, I stopped. After all I'd read, there was nothing but the curve of shingle. To the south it dissolved into distance, where later the Sizewell B nuclear reactor would emerge like a white orb rising on another world. Now, out at the horizon, there wasn't even a ship. It was hard to believe that out there once was medieval Dunwich, which at its height was one of the largest port towns in Britain.

By the sixteenth century, old Dunwich was already slipping into legend. In the 1570s, it led a London publisher to commission someone – widely believed to be the historian and antiquarian John Stowe – to investigate the true extent of what had been lost. Three centuries after its heyday, Stowe found Dunwich 'now decayed, and is supposed more than half swallowed up in the sea'.

'The oldest inhabitants of the neighborhood', he wrote, 'report that Dunwich, in ancient time, was a City surrounded with a Stone-Wall, and brazen Gates.' There were 'fifty-two churches, chapels, religious houses and hospitals, a King's Palace, a Bishop's Seat, a Mayor's Mansion, and a Mint, as many Top-Ships as Churches . . . and not fewer wind-mills'. Others spoke of 'more than seventy parish churches'. Today, in gentle drizzle, I could easily have got the wrong place.

By the time of my visit, the retreating cliff had reached the inland limit of the gated town boundary, the Palesdyke. Almost everything within it was now lost to erosion, leaving little more than a sliver of cliff-top land that was once the cemetery of All Saints Church. The last of at least seven (rather than seventy) Dunwich churches lost to the sea, the final service was held there in 1754. By then the town was all but abandoned, and throughout the Romantic era All Saints gradually fell into ruin as the cliff drew nearer. As at Blackgang Chine, crumbling Dunwich drew a fashionable crowd: artists, writers and aesthetes in search of inspiration, reverie and a sense of the sublime. In 1824, Turner would paint All Saints spectral against the dark of storm-cloud. By the 1860s, as well as a landmark for seamen, the cliff-top ruin remained a magnet for Victorian sightseers, its tower girded by a blacksmith's band to keep it from collapse.

'I defy any one,' wrote Henry James in *English Hours* in 1905, 'at desolate, exquisite Dunwich, to be disappointed in anything . . . a month of the place is a real education to the patient, the inner vision'. A year earlier, the eastern end of All

Saints – including a chancel that once echoed with choral song – had crashed to the shore. The bell tower stood furthest from the sea, and a series of black-and-white photographs taken over the next fifteen years show the arched bays of the nave lost one by one. Stark against the white of the sky, some collapsed to leave pillars at the edge of the cliff. At Dunwich this was a period of particularly rapid erosion, and the postcards are like a sequence from school geography: a rocky headland reduced from sea caves to arches, to stack, to stump. By 1912, all the arches were gone. For the last seven years, the tower stood at the edge of the cliff, battlements crumbling above an empty belfry before it fell to the shore.

Long gone from the beach today, the last of the fallen tower remained visible until the 1970s, if only at low tide. Searching for images of ruined All Saints on the beach, I came across the strangest of promotional films in the depths of the East Anglian Film Archive. Released in 1959, it was styled as a travelogue, with the twitching subtitles of projected film.

An exploration of the coast
of East Anglia
introducing Ransomes Lawn Mowers
encountered on the way

On reaching Dunwich a disembodied voice describes the loss of the town, in the Queen's English of early radio. 'One after another the churches went down the cliff,' intones the male narrator. 'And when south-east gales lash the sea, folk tell you they still hear the death toll of the bells.'

In age-faded colour, waves wash in over the last of ruined All Saints to the strains of violins. There is a cut to the top of the cliff, and the eerie whine of soundtrack wind. Slowly, the camera pans down the crumbling cliff-face. A pause, a dramatic orchestral sting, and earth-stained bones protrude from the

Old Church Ruins Dunw

Postcards showing the loss of All Saints, *c.*1905–19

mud: human thigh bones and arm bones eroding from the All Saints graveyard. The camera lingers, before a last climactic cut to the foot of the cliff, where the eye sockets of a half-exposed skull face the sea.

Moments later the tone turns cheerier. 'After the gales,' says the narrator, 'all kinds of flotsam and jetsam litter the beach.' We see a log adrift in the shallows. 'Driftwood. Maybe merchandise from ill-fated vessels. Contraband, perhaps. Whisky galore.' On the shore, a wooden cask and a box of Johnnie Walker lie half-buried in the Dunwich shingle. 'And . . . what's this?' the narrator asks. 'A mower!' A hand enters from the edge of the frame, to push away pebbles from the gleaming green paintwork of a Ransomes lawnmower. 'This is it, with its super high-class finish, perfect order, untouched by the ravages of time . . . all rescued from a watery grave.'

Today Dunwich is a rural hamlet, little more than a pub, a tea room and a single street of houses. For the past fifty years one of them, Reading Room Cottage, has been a small museum. So the next morning, I stood in its doorway before a marble tombstone, brought up from the seabed near the ruins of All Saints. Found by a dive team led by Stuart Bacon, it dated to around 1320 and is thought to have memorialised a knight.

Inside, Jane – who'd run the museum for years – was speaking to a family of three over a scale model of medieval Dunwich. Pointing out yellow tape that marked the modern cliff line, she told the story of the lost town with relish and efficiency, undaunted as the child sidled off to roll a shipwrecked cannonball out across the floor. With one ear on the conversation, I wandered around, touching stones retrieved from the seabed ruins of several Dunwich churches. There were carved blocks from columns and arches; fragments of limestone tracery; the sill of a mullioned window cut with slots for stained glass. It was strange to run fingertips over stone worn smooth by centuries of wind and rain, and later the sea. Scoured by sand, shingle and waves, the stone from St Peter's had spent three centuries on the shore and out on the seabed. Here, in the heated museum, it still felt cold.

Nearby, a yellowed copy of *An Historical Account of Dunwich* lay open behind glass. Written in 1754 by Thomas Gardner, the local Salt Officer, it proved invaluable for the divers searching for ruins on the seabed. Of most use was the map hand-copied for Gardner before the original was lost. It showed the course of the old Dunwich River, and the town's main streets and buildings in 1587 – when around half of the town had already been lost. The original was on parchment made from calfskin, drawn by the skilled sixteenth-century cartographer Ralph Agas.

Steering the child away from the shipwrecked cannon – also found by Stuart – the family left, and Jane came over to where I stood peering into a cabinet. Inside were medieval spouts and the handles of jugs, pots and an earthenware pipkin: a saucepan-like cooking pot placed in an open fire. Other cabinets contained spurs and spoons, metal fish hooks, brooches, bronze needles and buckles. Among some wonderfully idiosyncratic keys, one was double ended.

Much of what was in the museum, Jane said, had been found on the beach at the foot of the cliffs. 'All from that narrow strip of land lost in the last century.' How much more was out there, we wondered, buried in sediment, that would never be found. Out in the murky blackness of the North Sea floor, it was hard enough for divers to find ruined churches. She told me then about things members of the public had brought into the museum. Often they were bones eroded from the All Saints graveyard; while some had been reburied at nearby St James Church, others lay in boxes in the museum's storeroom. Once, when Stuart was exhibiting his finds, a woman from London had come over and said 'I thought you'd like this'. She handed him a carrier bag and inside was a human skull.

Jane glanced into the cabinets alongside me: grey hair pulled back in a ponytail, horn-rimmed glasses on a cord around her neck. Over the years, she said, quite a few people had come in and described relics they'd found from old Dunwich.

'Things that sound wonderful,' she said.

Excited, she'd ask where they were. Perhaps they could bring it in to the museum for her to see?

No idea, they'd often say with a shrug. By now it was probably lost.

'I'm friendly to them,' Jane said. 'But really I'm thinking, well that's a bit shit.'

The earliest record of local land lost to erosion is in the Domesday Book, so almost a thousand years ago. In the twenty years since the Norman Conquest in 1066, the entry for Dunwich shows the town's cultivable farmland had halved, with 200 acres reduced to one hundred. By then the town was already a thriving fishing and trading port. Through previous centuries, like other towns on this coast, Dunwich had been raided and settled by Angles and Saxons, and also by Vikings. The waves of invasion and migration were reflected in the names of the wealthier Dunwich townsfolk: Ulf the Rich, Brithmar son of Gotha, Walter Leadenpenny, Snotyng the Rich. Following the Norman Conquest, French surnames also appear, with the prefix Fitz – from *fils* meaning 'son (of)' – becoming common among the Dunwich merchant class.

The town's early growth relied on a natural harbour at the mouth of the Dunwich River, as well as plentiful herring. The Agas map shows a high point in the town known as Cock Hill, which an early panorama shows topped with a lookout tower. These wooden structures were known as *conders*, where a 'huer' watched for shoals of herring to alert the fishermen (who dried their nets on neighbouring Hen Hill). Although the season lasted only six weeks, cured – or 'red' – herring remained a staple in Britain all year. Salted at the Dunwich harbourside, the fish were dried or smoked, then taken to the market in barrels by 'pykers'.

Traces of this eleventh-century seaport are also buried out on the marshes. Beneath layers of 'high energy' silts – left by the storms and floods that would later devastate Dunwich – core samples show soils dominated by the pollen and seeds of cannabis. With the amount indicating 'industrial scale production', this inevitably caught my attention. Yet it turned out to be hemp used to make rope and sails. At the time, this was commonly grown close to harbours, with the stalks 'retted' (rotted) in nearby ditches and wetlands to separate the fibres.

By Domesday, Dunwich already had three parish churches. Yet little is known of them, perhaps as they were among the first to be lost to the sea – which would suggest they lay either to the east or on low-lying ground near the harbour. There may also be clues in their dedication to particular saints. With St Michael the patron saint of fishermen and mariners, his church may have been near the quayside. St Bartholomew, on the other hand, was the patron saint of butchers, tanners and leatherworkers: foul-smelling industries often sited to the east of medieval settlements, due to prevailing westerly winds.

By the thirteenth century, Dunwich was a Royal Borough with a population thought to have been around 5,000. Bounded by the defensive wooden Palesdyke, the town covered roughly a square mile, similar to London at the time. A centre for shipbuilding, trade and religion, medieval Dunwich also had chapels, monasteries and a convent, hospitals, a Guildhall and Great Market Place, annual fairs, a prison and a mint. As a result, merchants flocked to this 'Town of good note abounding with much riches and sundry kind of merchandise'.

The town's prosperity depended on the safety of its natural harbour, where maybe a hundred vessels could moor: everything from fishing smacks and Icelandic barques to naval galleys and clinker-built cogs. By then, low-lying land around the quay would have been crowded with stores and warehousing, smokeries and fish-curing sheds, quayside taverns, sail yards and rope-walks. With herring on the wane, Dunwich fishermen now sailed as far as Icelandic waters to fish for cod and sturgeon, and traded corn for Icelandic furs, whale oil and walrus ivory. These sold well at the Great Market Place, along perhaps with the spiral tusks of narwhal (passed off as unicorn horn at the time, their legendary healing properties made them worth more than their weight in gold). Most of the town's wealth, though, came from more everyday trade like the export of wool, grain and hides. Among the imports were cloth from Flanders, pottery from Germany, steel from Spain, flax from Prussia and furs from Scandinavia. Most celebrated of all were the wines from Gascony, with the ships carrying them armed against the threat of piracy.

This was of course not the only threat faced by the Dunwich traders, with every voyage a risk for sailors and a gamble for merchants. In the days of sail everything depended on the weather: the strength and direction of winds, and the dangers of storms and shipwreck. So as seafarers have done for millennia, those setting sail from Dunwich would invoke what protections they could. Among common medieval practices were prayers to Christ, Woden and Thor; carrying pagan or Christian charms and amulets; and paying 'wind-sellers' for more favourable winds. First described by a Benedictine monk in 1342, these wind-sellers were often local cunningfolk, among them women believed to be witches. The usual practice was to tie three knots in a rope or string – sometimes a rag or lock of hair – to 'bind up the wind'. Loosening the first knot was said to summon a gentle breeze, the second a brisk wind and the third a gale. So the magic could be put to various uses: to raise a wind if a ship was becalmed, say, or 'lay a storm' when conditions kept sailors in port.

In the museum, a number of local finds evoked trade in the town's Great Market Place. Among them were small medieval weighing scales – used to weigh something of great value like silver or gold – and tiny thirteenth-century French and Spanish coins. Groats and silver pennies were cut into halves and quarters (the original halfpennies and farthings or 'fourth-things'), with a twelfth-century Cut Halfpenny of Dunwich evidence of a mint. Other favourites were metal purse frames and lead tokens imprinted with the names of hosiers, grocers, apothecaries. 'It would be difficult to think of an every-day commodity in existence in the late 13th century,' wrote Rowland Parker in *Men of Dunwich* (1980), 'which was not obtainable in Dunwich market-place, either immediately or when the next ship comes in from Copenhagen, Hamburg, Barcelona or wherever.'

Woodcut of 1555 showing a wind-seller
holding a rope tied with three wind-knots

Whereas most English town markets were held weekly or closed on Sundays, a king's charter allowed Dunwich's Great Market Place to open seven days a week. It stood between the town hall and the wealthy, cruciform St John's Church, where bells were rung to open and close the market. A 'market cross' covered rented stalls, and the surrounding streets would have been crowded with wattle-and-daub shops under weathered thatch. As well as the fishmongers, wool sellers and wine merchants, there would have been all the usual trades and artisans, from brewers, butchers and shoemakers to blacksmiths, hatters and saddlers.

By this time, Dunwich also traded in more exotic luxuries. Much of this was due to new trade routes opened up by the religious wars of the Crusades (among the town's grandest buildings was the circular church of the wealthy Knights Templar, a chivalric order founded to defend Christendom). So beneath the pall of fish smokeries and damp North Sea fogs, Dunwich marketplace offered lemons, nutmeg and figs, frankincense, perfumes and silks.

Elsewhere, locals haggled for staples like bread and ale, with peasants bringing produce to market in handcarts and baskets: eggs, butter and cheese, crates of chickens or geese, faggots and reeds. Herbs were also widely sold, for cooking and brewing, and as a vital part of medieval healing and medicine.

Two early texts – both rich in herbal remedies – provide a rare glimpse into popular beliefs in a place like medieval Dunwich, where Christianity had integrated with folklore and Anglo-Saxon beliefs. Both *Bald's Leechbook* and the *Lacnunga* ('Remedies') are a complex mix of herb lore and charms, classical theories, prayers, incantations and faith healing. Alongside cures for 'mad-heart' and oozing galls, a 'light drink against the devil and insanity' involved twelve masses sung over an infusion of ale, wormwood and nightshade. 'Elf-disease' features frequently, a concept with its origins in Germanic animistic beliefs, whereby pain was inflicted by elves and invisible flying beings. One remedy 'against elf-kind and night goers' was first left beneath an altar, and another required lichen grown on a crucifix. Anyone 'fiend-sick' was encouraged to drink a lupin infusion from a church bell, and the 'Nine Herbs Charm' famously invoked both Woden and Christ.

By the thirteenth century, Dunwich was at its height, and the Great Market Place thronged with people from all walks of life and many seafaring nations. Sailors, merchants and nobles passed among fishwives and friars, beggars, pilgrims and minstrels, street hawkers and even the odd knight. As the town was a Crusader port, leprosy had also arrived by ship. Where today's main village street ends at the cliff, it once entered the Palesdyke at Bridge Gate, which was also known as Leper's Gate. This led out to a leper colony and chapel on the outskirts of town, where its ruins still stand today. At the time, sufferers entering towns to beg for alms were often required to wear a 'leper's costume' – perhaps rags or a robe with a mark – and carry a warning clapper or bell. While disease would increasingly be blamed on sin and moral corruption, at the time it was also seen as a Christ-like suffering before death.

In this melting pot of North Sea trade, those going about their business in the Dunwich marketplace would have spoken a variety of languages, dialects and traders' pidgins. By the thirteenth century, the nobility in Britain no longer spoke a version of Old French – as they had after the Norman Conquest – but a hybrid Anglo-Norman. Yet among the wider population a language had evolved that could now be recognised as English: a blend of mainly Germanic Anglo-Saxon dialects influenced by Old Norse. (The word English derives from *Englisc*, which by the ninth century referred not just to Angles but all invading Germanic tribes, and may originally have meant 'the fishermen's language'.) Later, as the language spread north and west, it went on to displace the native Celtic dialects spoken across Britain.

With the town's prosperity reliant on its harbour, it in turn depended on the protection of a natural shingle spit known as Kingsholme. However, as the Medieval Warm Period's changing climate was strengthening North Sea storms, this increasingly affected the spit. At the time, the town was bounded to the north by the Dunwich River, with the harbour entrance close to its mouth. North of there, the sheltered haven stretched some two miles to the mouth of the River Blyth at Walberswick. Like neighbouring Blythburgh upriver, Walberswick had access to the harbour, but not to the sea. So their ships and traders were forced to pay tolls to 'the men of Dunwich' who controlled the harbour entrance.

Predictably, this led to long-standing tensions between Dunwich and its rivals to the north. Among them was animosity over the right to claim 'wreck' on the spit (shipwrecks and goods cast ashore, known in Old English as *sae-upwarp*: 'what the sea throws up'). Far worse, though, were disputes over tolls and harbour boundaries, not least when storms altered the harbour by shifting the spit.

Records show tensions coming to a head as early as 1216, when a band of merchants and other Dunwich men raided Walberswick. After setting fire to a dozen homes and the manor house chapel, they 'dragged a certain image of St John by its neck as far as Dunwich'. By this time, parts of lower Dunwich were already prone to flooding; in the ensuing court case, the widowed Lady of the Manor agreed that neither she nor her heirs would 'entice any of the townsmen of Dunwich to go and live in her towns of Walberswick and Blythburgh'. Yet inevitably the rivalry continued. Later, in a subsequent court case, the burgesses and men of Dunwich would be forced to agree that merchant ships headed for the rival towns would not be 'maliciously hindered'.

In 1249, following a series of North Sea storm surges, gales coincided with unusually high tides. Overnight, the force of the waves dramatically remade the shared harbour. Crucially, the shingle spit, which had long been creeping south towards Dunwich, now blocked the harbour entrance. With rising water trapped in the harbour, the swollen River Blyth finally broke through Kingsholme, forcing a new route out to sea. And this time it favoured Blythburgh and Walberswick. With their ships no longer having to pass Dunwich, there was no need to pay tolls to their rivals. In fact, ships bound for Dunwich would now pay tolls and taxes to Walberswick. Temporarily, this crippled trade at Dunwich, and relations between the towns became increasingly bitter. Yet Dunwich still had the support of the King, and help came in the form of pardoned rent. Over the next two years, a new channel was cut through Kingsholme: a huge undertaking that involved the shifting of vast quantities of sand and shingle. With their own entrance reopened, the Dunwich men then 'stopped up' the outlet at Walberswick.

Yet they were only really buying time. With the new harbour entrance no longer a natural outlet to the sea, it was repeatedly silting up. This would become an ongoing battle with the sea: repeatedly strengthening and repairing sea walls, dredging sand and shingle to clear the harbour. As the stormy period continued, high spring tides made increasingly frequent incursions into lower Dunwich.

Four decades later, on New Year's Eve in 1287, another severe storm approached Dunwich and coincided with spring tides. By now, residents of the lower town were well used to flooding, and I imagine them preparing with apprehension as high tide approached. As winds strengthened to gale force, furniture, bedding and possessions were moved upstairs and into lofts. Locals and traders drew fishing boats up into yards and alleyways, secured moorings, and lashed ships together in the harbour. While some people moved to higher ground, others no doubt stayed on, seeking protection through ritual and prayer, amulets, charms and the wind-sellers. From storm-watching in Cornwall, I know the roar of a rising gale over the surge of waves, the whine of the wind through rigging. From the harbour at medieval Dunwich, there would also have been the creak of ships' timbers straining against ropes. With the sickening crack of collision, splintered masts were cast adrift in the swollen harbour, along with the wreckage of devastated lives and livelihoods.

Amid the cacophony at the peak of the storm, there would also have been the tolling of church bells. For in medieval times, bells were not only rung to call people to prayer, mark time and lament the dead, but also to sound the alarm and invoke protection. Consecrated in a ritual known as the 'baptism of the bell', they were believed to have supernatural powers over invading enemies, demons and evil spirits. While the Church believed the Devil feared the sound of church bells, the wider population also broadened this to include pre-Christian spirits, elves and invisible beings. Baptised in saltwater and anointed with oils, the bells would be named and often inscribed. 'Do thou Peter, when struck, calm the angry waves' reads one medieval church bell in County Durham. Unlike the tonal peal of church bells today, this was more a loud and violent clanging, intended to drive away demons thought to raise storms. At the time, church bells were also rung to ward off lightning strikes on bell towers: a practice that led to the deaths of hundreds of bell ringers across medieval Europe.

On the night of the storm in 1287, in Dunwich as elsewhere, the tolling of church bells did not ward off devastation. As the storm abated, the flooded streets were left deep in silt and the timber and thatch of wrecked homes. And by morning it wasn't only the lower town buildings destroyed and washed away. In the east, a cliff-top strip of Dunwich 'a good hundred yards wide in places – maybe a tenth of the whole – had crashed to the shore'. In *The Lost City of Dunwich* (1994) Nicholas Comfort suggests that in a single night, the town lost 'over two hundred houses'.

Once again, the spit had blocked the harbour entrance. And as before, the River Blyth had broken through two miles north, sweeping away the old Dunwich barriers to cut a direct route out to sea. As a result, the Dunwich River was now reduced to a tributary of the Blyth. Although in Dunwich the wealthy lived more safely on higher ground, the loss of the harbour was catastrophic for livelihoods and the economy. Once again, the town began the huge task of clearing the harbour entrance, and closing the channel that favoured their rivals. The process of rebuilding also began, although this time with fewer houses. Enticed or not, people were moving away from Dunwich.

In time, the harbour entrance was reopened. But with their neighbours again forced to pay Dunwich tolls, the feuds grew increasingly bitter. On occasion, old hatreds and resentments spilled over into local courts. One of the worst was in 1324, after Dunwich built a toll house on Kingsholme so a bailiff could row out to collect tolls from incoming ships. With the toll house considered a provocation by Walberswick, a gang set out to burn it down. In the ensuing raid, they killed the Dunwich bailiff and broke the arm of his assistant.

By then, Dunwich was clearly in decline. The fight was not only with northerly rivals but also the relentless sea, as residents waged an ongoing battle to keep the harbour from silting up. In January 1328, a third catastrophic storm eroded cliffs and shifted vast amounts of sand and shingle, again blocking the harbour entrance and also burying the stone quay. 'The Old-Port', wrote Thomas Gardner, 'was rendered utterly useless'. Although a new wooden quay was built in Dunwich, this time efforts to reopen the choked harbour entrance were in vain. All the while, the feud between the towns continued to escalate. Two years later it appears to have peaked, with Dunwich men accused of sinking a Walberswick ship and killing sixteen men on board. By then, relations were so bad the King ordered Dunwich to stop, complaining of almost daily 'assemblies of men at arms, burnings, homicides, robberies, etc.'

Even before that storm, an inquiry into reduced Dunwich rents had found people abandoning their homes due to 'obstruction and deterioration' of the port. Without a decent dock for overseas trade, the Great Market Place fell into decline, and through the 1330s and 1340s the exodus gained pace. Then in March of 1349, the plague also reached East Anglia, bringing further devastation to weakened Dunwich. With medieval church bells also believed to drive out evil spirits that brought the Black Death, those of the remaining Dunwich churches would have rung out in desperation that spring.

With the passing of the stormy Medieval Warm Period, Dunwich did enjoy a century of relative stability, and a temporary halt in the town's decline. Yet the climate in northern Europe was changing again, and the Little Ice Age saw resumption of the intensity of North Sea storms. By the sixteenth century – when the Agas map was drawn – the sea was encroaching on the heart of old Dunwich. Visiting in 1570, John Stowe found 'the remains of the rampart . . . foundations of down-fallen edifices – remains of dead exposed – naked wells divested of the ground about them by the waves of the sea . . . and part of the old key [quay]'. By then, only two Dunwich churches remained: All Saints and St Peter's.

At the museum, Jane had mentioned the key to St Peter's. Originally in Thomas Gardner's private collection, it later passed down to his family. Ten years ago, when Jane was in the museum, a woman had brought it in – although only to show them. Almost a foot long, the weighty, near-black iron key beautifully evoked a medieval church door. Possibly one of the three Dunwich churches recorded in Domesday, St Peter's was described as 'a spacious fine old church . . . curiously glased with painted glass . . . and many gravestones with inscriptions upon brass'. A decade before its closure, the church's listed ornaments included '63 Cherabims, 60 at least of JESUS, written in Capital Letters, on the Roof; and 40 superstitious Pictures'. The last service was held there in 1654, with the abandoned church remaining on the cliff-top for decades as a landmark for

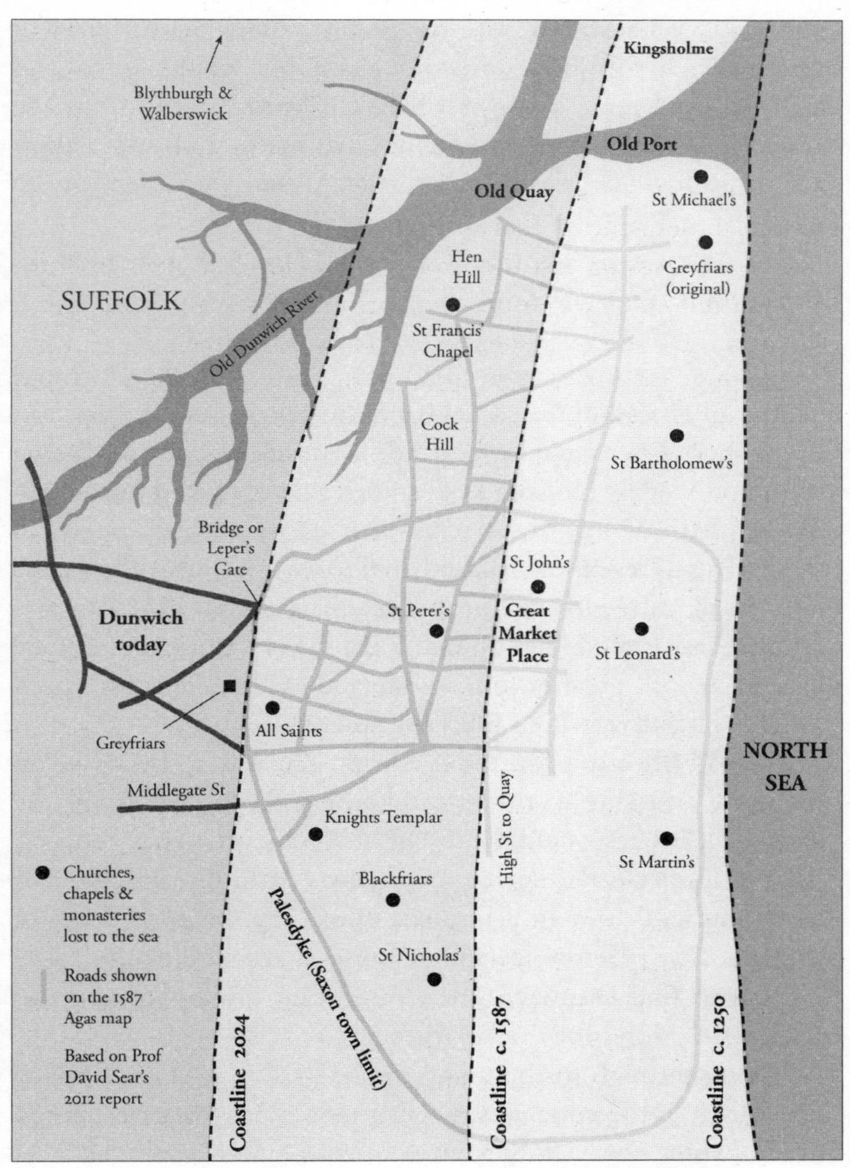

Reconstruction of old Dunwich based on historical documents, maps and coastal change analysis

mariners. Then in December 1688, after thirty-four years of abandonment, the east gable crashed to the shore. Nine years later it was joined by the bell tower. Just before the tower went over, its peal of four bells – that once rang out against storms and plague – were removed to All Saints. Bones eroding from the cemetery were also collected for reburial there, with some likely to have already been moved when more westerly graveyards were lost to the sea.

In 1702, noted Thomas Gardner, 'The Sea extended its Dominion to St Peter's Church'.

Almost three centuries later, finding the ruins of St Peter's would become an obsession for Stuart Bacon. Later that day, I drove out to meet him. On a rural lane outside a Suffolk village, his cottage was surrounded by blossom trees and an acre of garden once carefully tended. Woody roses scrambled up white-painted walls, now flaking to reveal the bricked-in doorways of what were once three small sixteenth-century cottages. At the front door I knocked and waited. Beside me, a big carved stone was shaped like the base of a pillar or font, and furred green with moss. Later, I would learn it was lifted from the seabed.

I'd already heard a lot about Stuart. He was well known in Dunwich, and Jane – along with others I'd spoken to in the village – clearly respected the things he'd achieved. They spoke of his drive, his persistence given tough dive conditions and frequent disappointment, how he'd inspired others 'by the sheer force of his personality'. Before learning to dive at the end of the 1960s (in order to find Dunwich), he'd raced cars, climbed mountains and flown Spitfires for the Air Force.

Walking through to the living room, I had a sense of stopped time. Much in the cottage was centuries old: the dark beams and uneven plaster, the thickly painted tongue-and-groove walls. Yet the kitchen and faint smell of cigar smoke reminded me of the houses of uncles who lived alone in the 1970s. I found Stuart in his armchair, with a blanket drawn across his lap. He would have lit a fire, he said, but birds were nesting in the chimney. Although now in his nineties and finding walking difficult, as we settled in to talk, he retained an air of the self-assured rigour others had implied.

Stuart had begun his search for drowned Dunwich as a newly qualified diver in 1970. By then, the All Saints ruins – that he'd climbed as a child in the 1940s – were no longer on the beach. Given the cliff's retreat, by then the last of the rubble was only visible on the foreshore at low tide, out at the water's edge. All Saints, then, wasn't hard to find. The divers could also line up with its last remaining gravestone on the cliff (while still there today, it has been moved inland). Their main problem was poor visibility.

'The North Sea is a very hostile sea,' Stuart said. 'You can't see. The water is black because of sediment in suspension. Sometimes a diver's lamp will penetrate a little over a metre, and at other times the water is so black the lamp won't illuminate a compass or depth gauge.' For much of the year, it is also both rough and cold. Given the dangers of being trapped by fishing nets snagged on the seabed, the divers took to strapping multiple knives and cutters to their legs, as things were easy to drop with numb hands.

'The young divers wore gloves,' Stuart said. But his own hands stayed bare, as down on the seabed, in near total darkness, they had to feel their way along the bottom for stone. Staying down as long as the air allowed, he sometimes surfaced shaking. Later, diving the site with experienced American divers, they would tell him: 'If you can dive at Dunwich, you can dive anywhere.'

As a result, the early dives were plagued with disappointment. Even when they did find something, the Dunwich seabed was constantly changing. So despite the use of marker buoys, ruins found one day might be gone the next, buried beneath shifting sands. But Stuart persisted and in September 1971, he found his first piece of carved stonework, out where the All Saints' chancel had fallen at the turn of the century.

'Part of the tower lay over the site,' he said. 'When I first saw it, it was covered in pink sponges, and thousands and thousands of crabs and lobsters. It was quite a sight.' Finding All Saints was easy, he said. But St Peter's would be a much harder task. From the beginning, his wife Jean had helped with research to locate potential dive sites. In winter, with conditions too poor to dive, the couple worked together on a series of local guidebooks, and later *The Search for Dunwich City Under the Sea* (1979).

I asked Stuart if Jean had dived too.

'No,' he said, shaking his head, cheekbones still high and strong. 'I didn't let her.'

'She was very important,' he said after a pause. 'Much better educated than me. We worked well together.'

He closed his eyes and was quiet for a while.

'She died of cancer an incredible thirty-three years ago,' he said. 'And I've rattled around here with my various cats since.'

He described Jean's dream of living in the countryside, and them finding this cottage. As I looked around the room, the sense of stopped time fell into place. 'Do you mind if I smoke?' he asked, and took a thin cigar from a tin.

As St Peter's had fallen from the cliff two centuries before All Saints, the divers knew any ruins would lie further out. Crucially, St Peter's was also marked on the Tudor Agas map. So if that was accurate, its ruins should lie almost a quarter of a mile from shore. Over the next four decades Stuart would dive Dunwich more than 600 times, but clearly remembered the day he found St Peter's. It was May 1973, and attempts earlier in the year had been thwarted by the usual challenges. This time, Stuart was trialling a new technique to measure distance: a weighted line attached to his dive belt, running out from a spool on shore. From Stuart's own calculations based on the Agas map, St Peter's lay roughly 400 yards east of the old Leper's Gate.

Early that Sunday morning, he arrived in Dunwich with a rope of that length. And for once, the North Sea was flat and blue, perfect conditions for a dive. He waited, but the other diver didn't show.

'I was ready to go,' Stuart said. 'So I broke the rules and went alone. I anchored the drum to the cliffs and attached one end of the rope to my weight belt.'

Entering the water, he began to fin east. 'The visibility was unbelievable,' he said. 'I could see for at least twelve feet.' Used to near total darkness, he swam out over a gully and up the first Dunwich sandbank, to where sunlight filtered through shallow water.

'As I swam down the bank, the water darkened and the rope began to pull.' Visibility, though, remained good. At the foot of the sandbank the seabed began to change. Soon, there was no longer any rippled sand. 'The rope dragged and I had to fin very hard. Minutes later, when the rope had almost halted my progress, the ruins came into view. They were about ten feet below. I was almost too excited to breathe. I shouted, with great bursts of bubbles.'

Later, when he surfaced and swam back to shore, a couple were walking on the beach. He couldn't help himself.

I've found St Peter's Church, he called out. 'And they looked at me as though I was mad.'

With the Dunwich sandbanks constantly shifting and changing, more recent surveys show the ruins of St Peter's are now buried in sand. For decades, though, they remained accessible to divers, and were occasionally captured on film. In darkness on the sea floor, grains of sand streak past the camera like rain under street lights. Caught by the divers' headlamps, the ruined stone is strangely ethereal. At times, parts of the fallen walls and tower stood a metre or more above the seabed, with one diver surfacing to describe entering a 'room-like arrangement' of flint and mortar walls.

A rare solidity in the shifting sands, the exposed stone was soon colonised by larvae drifting in the plankton. Out on the floor of the North Sea, a quarter-mile from shore, the remains of medieval St Peter's blossomed into the strangest of gardens. Too lightless for seaweed, the scattered church ruins were encrusted with colonies of gently pulsing creatures. Sponges competed with soft corals, and feathery hydroids swayed with the currents. Luminous in the diver's torchlight, dahlia anemones flowered in the dark. Eeriest of all were the colonies of dead man's fingers: reaching up from the gloom, the pallid coral frays into filaments like flesh too long in water – which at Dunwich can feel a bit much.

'That's from St Peter's,' Stuart said from his armchair, gesturing to a block of limestone built into a ledge beside the fireplace. Above it, the television stood on a granite gravestone from All Saints. 'You passed a bit by the garage too,' he said. 'A coffin from St Peter's.'

He then handed me a pre-war black-and-white photograph, taken before the All Saints tower went over the edge, and said:

> There are cart tracks in the sand so people were taking away debris then. The stone must be all over East Anglia now. I know there's a garden wall in Ipswich where they've incorporated part of a church window that was found on the beach. There's a wooden fireplace from a Dunwich church in Swilland. If you go round the village, you'll find bits of medieval Dunwich built into garden walls and rockeries.

I handed back the photograph. Stuart said that back then – in the years of rapid erosion – the beach below All Saints was sand.

But by the 1970s, a shingle ridge had formed, which made shifting the dived stone hard (later each piece would be precisely weighed and recorded, so in future someone could check where a stone was found). 'We had a sledge you could tow along the shingle,' he said. 'It was part of a bed head that was curved at one end. So it was ideal.' He closed his eyes and smiled at the memory, at the aptness of a solution to a problem. By now it was late afternoon, and the panes of old rippled glass cast pools of watery, magical light on the cottage floor.

'There's something about Dunwich that gives you this awesome feeling,' he'd said before. 'Once you're down there in the dark, and certainly when you're on a ruin, your mind goes a bit wild.'

Early the next morning, I walked the Dunwich cliff-top. Just inland of the lost Palesdyke, the path led through scrub stunted by onshore winds, while earlier disused sections ran closer to the edge. Beyond there, the path turned inland, and emerged from trees into an open field. At the centre stood the imposing ruins of Greyfriars monastery. Built just outside the Palesdyke around 1290, it replaced an earlier Greyfriars – that was abandoned to the sea only sixty years after it was built. (Out at the end of Dam Street, which led to the Old Quay, the original monastery was damaged in the devastating storm of 1287 and left close to the edge of the cliff.) Now, I crossed a field to stand alone within its imposing flint and cobble walls. Beyond the sagging tape of an electric fence, a horse lifted its head from a plastic bucket to stare.

Back on the path to Greyfriars Wood, I reached a lichened gravestone fenced off in undergrowth close to the edge of the cliff. Known as 'The Last Grave' from All Saints' churchyard, it was the headstone used by divers in the 1970s to locate the ruined church.

In Memory of
JACOB FORSTER who departed
this Life March 12th 1796 Aged 38
Years

Writing in 1754, a year before the last service at All Saints, Thomas Gardner described what remained of Dunwich. 'This once famous *Town* or *City*', he wrote, 'is reduced to a narrow Compass, the Buildings few, and most of them mean . . . and about one hundred Souls subsisting.'

By then, Dunwich was one of Britain's most notorious 'rotten boroughs': as a legacy of its historical importance, the town was still represented by two MPs, making results easy to manipulate.

Beyond the Last Grave, the cliff path entered Greyfriars Wood. At this northerly edge, light filtered through the green of new spring growth, and I stopped to check the map. I was heading for Sunken Lane, which is thought to have once been Middlegate Street: one of the main routes into gated medieval Dunwich. Now, as I wandered further into the wood, conifers began to dominate. Sunken Lane, when I reached it, lay deep in evergreen gloom: a holloway between earth banks in the grip of mossy roots. With my footsteps muffled by the carpet of pine needles, I followed its long-trodden dip towards the sound of the sea. Nearing the end, I passed under the last of what were once three arched bridges. Said to have been built to allow the landowning family to picnic by horse-and-trap at ruined All Saints, the two seaward bridges were long gone. The first, Stuart said, went over the cliff around the time he started diving in the early 1970s, while those that remained had been clear markers of erosion since.

Back in Dunwich's heyday, Middlegate Street would have thronged with those on foot and horseback, with drovers, handcarts and oxcarts, wagons laden with goods on their way to the

Great Market Place. Now there was only birdsong, an insect hum, the soft thud of my plimsolls. It made me wonder what lay beneath. No one was sure, Jane had said, as local concerns around hastening cliff erosion meant archaeologists had never gained permission to dig. Instead, any traces – of dark earth, debris and rubble, perhaps a coin or a lost pilgrim's badge – would eventually wash from the toe of the cliff. Perhaps a few might even end up at the village museum.

With so much now lost to the sea, Dunwich inevitably has its share of ghost stories. Among them are monks and lepers, an Elizabethan sailor who haunts the shore, and Old Maid Eva, who cut out her broken heart and threw it into the sea (when this Dark Heart of Dunwich washes ashore, it resembles driftwood and brings misfortune to the finder). There are of course also stories of church bells that toll beneath the sea. Yet as elsewhere along this east coast of England – where so much has been lost to erosion over thousands of years – there is a curious lack of inundation legends. This is particularly true when compared to the more westerly Celtic fringes of Britain: Cornwall's Lyonesse, for example, or the Welsh Cantre'r Gwaelod. Or, of course, coastal Australia. In *The Edge of Memory*, Patrick Nunn suggests this may be because:

> East Anglia has been substantially repopulated – quite frequently, perhaps, during the past few millennia – as successive waves of migrants and invaders, from Vikings to Normans, overran the country . . . Traditions would have been lost, and connections between people and place forgotten.

Perhaps, then, the lack of local flood myths should come as no surprise. Facing continental Europe, the melting pot of old Dunwich was the very opposite of the cultural isolation that gave rise to some of our oldest stories.

★

Later, I walked back along the shore. Above me, although now largely obscured by cliff-top scrub, crescents of darker earth marked other truncated medieval main roads: St James Street, Scott's Lane, Duck Street. For a while I sat on the shingle below the site of the old Leper's Gate, close to where Stuart had emerged jubilant from his lone St Peter's dive. While he hadn't dived Dunwich now for more than a decade, many of his later dives were with teams led by the geographer Professor David Sear. Sear's fascination with Dunwich began, like Stuart's, in childhood, while playing around the last of the All Saints ruins in the 1970s. By then, Stuart was already diving the site, aided by the pre-measured ropes and bedstead sleigh.

By the time the two worked together, the equipment and technology had moved on. Along with GPS replacing Stuart's ropes, sonar could also now penetrate the murky conditions, 'illuminating' the Dunwich seabed with sound. In time, echo sounders would be attached not just to boats, but also the divers' masks and remote under-sea rovers. From there, pulses of sound were bounced off the sea floor, fanning out like sweeping torchlight to create digital images and 3D video. Once a ruin was located, narrow high-frequency beams could then be focused like a camera lens – even in zero visibility. In the spectral blue of foetal ultrasound, the 'sound shadows' cast by ruins give the illusion of shape and height. Like a familiar landscape in the otherworldly light of a full moon, there is enough detail to make out rubble and rippled sediments, even the angular edges of worked stone. From the site of St Peter's Church in 2010, the sonar images showed scattered debris from the nave and aisles, shadowy scour pits, and great blocks from the bell tower softened by sea life.

Such surveys are expensive, but interest in Dunwich meant money was forthcoming. Over the last thousand years, long after Doggerland drowned, more than 300 settlements have been lost to receding coastlines around the southern North Sea. And while so many were too small to have left much trace, others – like Rungholt – appear to have been centres of regional prosperity and international trade. Among them, Dunwich remains the largest and most important, with its loss comparatively well documented.

By combining their results with other historical sources, the team led by Sear produced a series of striking digital maps. In addition to the 1587 Agas map, they collected old tithe maps, Ordnance Survey maps, maritime charts and seventeenth- and eighteenth-century 'sea atlases' (sailing charts combined with directions that referred to landmarks in 'sailor's eye' sketches of the coast). Once the old maps were scanned, common points could then be located, and the old maps stretched and overlaid in a process known as 'rubber sheeting'. To chart the retreating coastline, the team included data from geophysical and archaeological surveys, historic records of the timing of losses and storm damage, and everything from old paintings, etchings and postcards to aerial photographs and the digital visualisations of seabed ruins.

The resultant map is both clear and evocative, telling the story of the loss of Dunwich over more than 800 years. Close to the modern shoreline, the roads are marked with certainty: Duck St, Middlegate Street, Scott's Lane, Maison Dieu Lane. Just as solid are the buildings shown on the Agas map, with some sites also confirmed by divers and sonar. Mainly, these are churches, and possibly the town hall that once stood beside the Great Market Place. Yet seaward of Agas's 1587 shoreline, the grids of streets are faint and increasingly speculative. Out near the 1250 coastline, early churches and the original Greyfriars are pencilled into swathes of blank space, where no records show parishes existing after 1331.

At the museum, a version of the map models the retreating coastline as the town was lost. The earliest, before Domesday, is a mile offshore today. Later date lines slice through the heart of the medieval town – 1250, 1350, 1450 – marking off centuries until the relative certainty of the Agas map.

A further layer of the Sear map also models future coastlines – 2050, 2080, 2100 – by which time everything within the Palesdyke has gone. The rate of recession, though, depends on the same processes that have accelerated or slowed erosion here in the past. As well as shifting sandbanks affecting the force of waves reaching shore, the height of the beach either protects or exposes the foot of the cliff. In Stuart's photograph of cart tracks on the shore below ruined All Saints, the low sand shore offers no protection at all. Through the years that the church was lost – so clearly documented in pre-war postcards – the sea was advancing by an extraordinary 8.8 metres a year.

More recently, offshore sandbanks have reduced the force of the waves, allowing the shingle beach to build. For now at least, cliff recession at Dunwich has fallen to under one metre a year. Yet as with so many sites across the world, rising seas and more intense storm surges mean future coastlines may advance faster than the models predict.

Ruins of Forvie Kirk

8

Forvie & the Barony of Culbin

Aberdeenshire & Moray, Scotland

I travelled from Cornwall to Aberdeen by train, which at thirteen hours turned out to be Britain's longest single train journey. 'Like the Orient Express,' I'd told my daughter before we left, 'but without the lampshades and dining car.' Instead, we travelled up on the August Bank Holiday in overly upright seats, with staff shortages meaning the only food on sale was crisps and biscuits. Yet my daughter has grown up some distance from the nearest village in Cornwall, so crossing the entire country by train felt like a belated introduction to the English given three days off. Passing through Devon, we were surrounded by four children all under ten, shepherded by a tiny white-haired woman with a walking stick. Heading for Butlin's, with the children close to bursting from the potent mix of boredom and excitement, she leaned in periodically to mouth inaudible but effective threats. An hour later, their seats were taken by three girls on their way to a Bristol Bank Holiday weekender, who spent much of their journey discussing the best time to start drinking. By lunchtime, in the Midlands, it was standing room only, with the seats taken by a group of men drinking cans of lager, and my daughter trying to disguise her laughter at 'how loud their burps are'. By early evening, approaching Newcastle, the air was saturated with perfume and the carriage a sea of bra tops, cleavage and bare thighs.

Then we crossed into Scotland and it was all over. North of the border, it wasn't a Bank Holiday Monday; the summer holidays were over and the children already back at school. Losing the sun and most of the passengers at Edinburgh, we slipped into autumn. Later, our night in Aberdeen was mainly wind tunnels between granite buildings, a vast ship at the end of the street and waiting beside rucksacks at the central bus station. And after that we were out of the city, on a bus heading north up the Aberdeenshire coast into veiled Scottish light.

The closest accommodation to the Sands of Forvie was across the Ythan River in Newburgh, which was once a salmon fishing port. Now, though, the bus drove away and left us in the middle of a deserted village. Shouldering rucksacks, we passed tidy retirement lawns lining the main street, with the gaps between houses giving glimpses of wide-open dunes and distant golfers. At the inn, opening the door to a dimly lit bar with tartan carpets and antler lampshades, we appeared to be the only ones staying.

The next morning, I crossed the Ythan River and walked out to the Sands of Forvie. In 1832, one visitor described them as, 'Huge piles of driven sand, stretching for miles in every direction . . . a loneliness and desolation of the vast Zahara'. From here, though, the approach was through dunes long stabilised by marram grass and dune heath: an odd, other-worldly landscape of tufted off-kilter peaks. Beneath muted skies, Forvie's sand hills were the colours of faded rugs: blue-green bent woven with the mauve of heather and grasses gone to seed. 'Like wet cat fur,' my daughter said on seeing them the next day, and that's exactly how they looked.

I was here to visit the ruins of a medieval village abandoned to sand blow, that in legend was lost when three women lay a curse on Forvie. First, though, I was meeting David Brown, who for the past two decades had been the ranger for this stretch of the Aberdeenshire coast. A tall, dark figure in the pale landscape, he had a brimmed hat pulled low over his eyes, a stick and a black greyhound that was beautifully trained. When I'd first got in touch, it was because he was a storyteller, and I only learned later that he was also the local ranger.

Lying close to the mouth of the Ythan, Forvie had a long history of settlement, and first we headed for the Iron Age hut circles. All greyhound curves, Millie slunk alongside as we left the sandy paths. After a pause while David counted hills – having memorised the route as he did the sagas and epic poems – we headed out into what for me was an unfamiliar and disorienting landscape. Surrounded by bent hills, we entered even stranger 'dune slacks', dropping down out of the breeze into wind-sculpted depressions closer to the water table. I'd worn thin plimsolls to feel the sand underfoot (something I'd later regret), and here the springiness of the dune heath was unlike anywhere I'd walked before. 'Reindeer moss,' David said when I asked. Antlered and almost white, the airy lichen turned out to be a native of the Arctic tundra – here, where so much looked like desert.

By the time we reached the hut circles, I'd lost all sense of direction. In total, thirty-one prehistoric huts had been recorded here, although now only two were visible. Nestled in a carpet of heath, the two circles of kerbstones once held Iron Age roof timbers. Like the other buried huts, their doorways faced east, and they once had floors of red clay; outside, archaeologists also found scatterings of fire-cracked stones. Closer to shore, larger fire-pits appeared to have been used to steam mussels, with the sites of buried shell middens sometimes disclosed by the diminutive, calcium-loving moonwort (a plant long considered to have magical properties, which could 'open locks and unshoe such horses as tread upon it'). Beneath the sandy turf, the prehistoric land surface also showed Iron Age plough marks, later buried by drifting sand and abandoned until early medieval times.

From several routes David suggested to the ruined church, I chose the one that took us south through the 'mobile' dunes.

Like the Holderness clay, Forvie's sand was left by retreating glaciers after the last Ice Age, settling first on the seabed beyond the mouth of the Ythan. Ever since, currents, waves and onshore winds had been pushing the sand ashore.

Today, the Sands of Forvie is the least disturbed dune system in Britain. And as we headed south, the older stabilised dunes gave way to a dramatically different landscape, where the marram grass ended at slopes of wind-rippled sand. Closer to the river, their sculpted peaks reached some thirty metres high, and the sand fell away from a knife-edge. These were Forvie's youngest, most dynamic dunes, and even today's gentle breeze was lifting sand grains to send them creeping and skittering north – an ongoing process over the last 4,000 years. While I could only imagine this place during storms, on Cornish dune beaches I'd sometimes squinted my way through scouring gales that drove the sand head high.

'Dune blowout,' David said, as he'd mentioned them earlier. He pointed to where marram grass had stabilised a dune for some time, until gales had tunnelled sand from beneath its binding roots. Now, after what I imagined was a dramatic but unseen collapse, the sand walls dropped steeply to a hollow. Plimsolling my way through deeper sand, I was reminded that this disorienting landscape could change overnight – and that there was a Sands of Forvie on Mars.

This was something I'd glimpsed online, and after my visit David wrote a letter to NASA asking why. Six weeks later, he received a reply, from a research scientist working on their Mars Project. The Curiosity rover, she said, was currently in an area being named after places in Scotland, and it was 'a delight to hear from someone connected to the real Forvie National Nature Reserve!' She included a map of the rover's recent route around the Martian Sands of Forvie, along with some striking photographs. In the planet's cold, parched atmosphere, its black sands lay under red Martian dust, sculpted in waves like a frozen sea.

The dust storms that shape this can be several kilometres high, and roughly every three Martian years grow to encircle the planet. Incredibly, the storms' colour shifts are visible from Earth, sometimes with the naked eye. While poorly understood, like Earthly tides these vast dust storms are thought to relate to the gravitational pull of the planet's two moons.

Here in Scotland we began to climb, and in this undulating place the line of pewter sea caught me by surprise. I was surprised again as we dropped between dunes to find a beach of wave-worn pebbles nowhere near the shore. I learned later that it lies five metres above sea level: a relic of a time when this land was lower. Having lost the weight of its Ice Age glaciers, Scotland has continued to rise, in the process sinking southern England with a see-saw tilt. For thousands of years this glacial rebound was enough to outstrip global sea-level rise, leaving Scottish beaches in strange places like this. Now, though, Scotland is no longer rising faster than the sea.

As we reached a gap in the dunes above the shore, at some signal I didn't see or hear, there was an explosion of greyhound speed and Millie was off. From here, we would follow the beach to the site of the medieval village.

Forvie is one of a number of settlements around the British coast that were abandoned to sand blow as the Medieval Warm Period gave way to the Little Ice Age. As with Dunwich and Ravenser Odd, the increased storminess of a changing climate accelerated coastal change. Also, settlements in or close to dunes were often made more vulnerable through medieval land-use practices: deforestation for agriculture, overgrazing of dune pastures, rabbiting and the removal of marram grass for thatching. Lost – and sometimes found – on the coasts of Scotland, England and Wales, they range from hamlets and villages to a fair-sized town. And like Forvie, their concealment and revelation by the sand has left them rich in story.

Perhaps best known is Kenfig on the South Wales coast. This was once a prosperous medieval port town, although today just the keep of its ruined castle protrudes from grassy, long-stabilised dunes. A Norman-English stronghold repeatedly sacked by the Welsh, both Kenfig and its castle were largely abandoned to sand blow by the late 1400s (in the 1530s, John Leland would describe the castle as 'in ruine and almost shokid and devoured with the sands'). Yet as sand began to engulf the church, it is said to have been dismantled and moved inland, stone by stone. So, unusually, its replacement has the smallest stones at the bottom and is known as the Upside-down Church.

Legends of the loss of Kenfig echo those of Llys Helig on the North Wales coast (where the harper and maid survive the flood to tell a tale of vengeance over four generations). In Kenfig, the daughter of a local nobleman fell in love with a man her father considered too poor. As in Llys Helig, after committing murder and theft, the suitor grew rich enough that the father consented to the marriage. During the wedding party, though, a storm blew up. Overnight, a voice was heard on the wind, crying three times, 'Vengeance will come'. Asked when, the voice replied, 'In the ninth generation'. Yet the couple remained unconcerned, as by then they would long be dead. In time, as their children had children, all the lands of Kenfig belonged to the couples' descendants. And miraculously, both were still alive to see the firstborn of the ninth generation. Celebrations were lavish, but at their height another violent storm broke over Kenfig. By morning the town was gone, submerged beneath Kenfig Pool. Out in the middle of the lake, all that remained of the town were three chimneys that broke the surface and continued to smoke. Today, the customary church bells are said to toll beneath Kenfig Pool, with the reappearance of the chimneys a portent of storms and death at sea.

Closer to my own home, the ruins of two abandoned medieval chapels lie hidden in the dunes at Penhale Sands on the north coast of Cornwall. The legend of this stretch of coast is of Langarroc: a town of seven fine churches said to lie beneath the dunes. Long ago its inhabitants grew rich from mining, but over time became greedy, lazy and immoral. In some versions of the story, this was the fault of criminal outsiders brought in to work in the mines. Intermarrying with the local population, the incomers introduced bad blood, causing this once-pious town to sink 'to the lowest depths of vice'. In time, God's retribution came in the form of a great sandstorm. For three days and three nights the storm raged, burying Langarroc and its people in sand. Ever since, on stormy nights, their cries can be heard beneath the wind and waves, along with the bells of the seven lost churches.

At Penhale, the historical bones of the legend lie close to the surface. Tiny St Piran's Oratory – the Lost Church – lies closest the sea, and appears to have been abandoned to drifting sand by the tenth century. (St Piran was a fifth-century Irish monk said to have washed up on this beach, after pagans threw him into the sea from a cliff in Ireland with a millstone tied around his neck.) Several hundred yards inland, the oratory's twelfth-century replacement – the Old Church – was built on the far side of a stream. For 600 years this protected the chapel from sand blow. But in the 1700s, the stream was diverted for tin mining, and drifting sand began to swallow the replacement church too. In time, parishioners would have to dig their way through to the door. So in 1804, the Old Church was also abandoned to the sands, with much of its stone reused to build a third St Piran's Church two miles inland.

According to local tradition, the village of Forvie was lost during a nine-day storm in 1413. In support, meteorological records suggest that in Aberdeenshire, severe gales and extreme tides did coincide in the August of that year. Yet little is known of the village, not least as it remained buried until the late nineteenth century, when a local doctor dug the floor of Forvie Kirk from the sand. Inside, later digs uncovered the *piscina* (a basin placed near the altar), and beneath a stone slab a human skull in a clay-built grave. Burial grounds were also found south and west of the church, with the last bodies interred in the century of the legendary storm.

Close to the church, men digging drainage ditches in the 1950s also uncovered square medieval huts built of stone and red clay. Beyond the buried settlement, aerial photographs also show traces of medieval 'rig and furrow' marks. Made by the use of heavy wooden ploughs drawn by oxen, the ridges were preserved by burial in blown sand.

Excavations suggest drier summers in the Medieval Warm Period led to more productive farming on this exposed Scottish coast. Among the crops grown at Forvie were oats, kale and an old form of barley known as bere. Seaweed was also gathered and spread on the fields as fertiliser, and hemp grown for fishing line and net. At the time, in this part of Scotland a watery soup known as 'brose' was cooked daily in cauldrons over open peat fires, and eaten with oatcakes. Further traces of village life were also glimpsed in a midden found south of the church. As well as beef and mutton, the Forvie villagers appear to have eaten duck, rabbit, crab and eel, with the occasional boar or deer. Along with fragments of fourteenth-century pottery, the midden also contained a bronze pin and two spindle whorls. At the time, clothing included tunics, shirts, cloaks and hats woven from rough wool or flax. In Forvie, they would have been dyed the colours of the landscape: crowberry and heather for purples and yellows, lichen and seaweed for browns and greens.

Today, all that remains of the medieval village lies buried in dunes at the far end of the shore. Heading that way now, we followed a wrack line littered with brittle, barnacled crab shells and the bones of seabirds: gulls and a razorbill, the scoured-white domes of skulls, a hollow ribcage with archangel wings. And as we made our way along the sand, David told fragments of the stories that grew up in the centuries after Forvie's inundation by sand.

The earliest describes how after the death of the Laird of Forvie, his lands were inherited by his three young daughters. But either deceived by a wicked uncle, or driven from their home by a mob of villagers, the women were cast adrift in a leaky boat. And from the sea, they lay a curse on Forvie.

> If ever maidens' malison
> did licht upon dry land
> Let nocht be fund in Forvie's glebes
> Bot thistle, bent and sand

Malison is a medieval word for a curse: if the women were ever to reach dry land (and they did), nothing would be found in Forvie but thistle, bent and sand. Their curse raised the nine-day storm, and to this day Forvie continues to 'dree its weird' or suffer its fate.

Another story of its loss involves an incomer priest, which David described first reading as an epic poem. In the Gothic version he tells today, the old priest dies and is replaced by an outsider. The new priest, though, is only seen at mass and confession. And when confessional sins and secrets are whispered to neighbours, the villagers become suspicious. Children start to go missing. One night, as locals take turns to watch the kirk, the priest is seen carrying a body inside. Hidden behind the altar, a passage leads down to a sea cave, where the villagers find the bodies of the missing children. Confronted, the priest reveals himself as a practitioner of the Dark Arts and raises the storm.

I'd hear the full story the following evening, returning to Forvie's ruined kirk with my daughter as the light began to fade. Out of the wind inside the stone walls, I lay my phone between us on the grass. With a touch of the screen, David began telling

'The Priest of Forvie', recorded here in the kirk a few years earlier for *Haunted Voices: An Anthology of Gothic Storytelling from Scotland* (2019). Sitting back against the old stone wall in the half-light, lulled by the rhythm of the words, we slipped under that oldest of spells, spoken story.

> Some say it went on for nine days and nights. But when the wind finally fell, dawn could be seen in the east. Forvie strand lay storm-shocked and wind-wrecked. Strange and new: great hills of sand distorted beyond recognition what should have been familiar to the fishermen sailing north later that day past Forvie Ness.

In the centuries following the loss of Forvie, Britain and Europe would experience what became known as the Little Ice Age, which for many brought longer winters and colder summers, heavy rains and crop-destroying thunderstorms. This change in climate appears to have coincided with a rise in the belief in weather magic (which had long drawn sailors to the wind-sellers), along with a search for scapegoats. As accusations of witchcraft began to escalate, control of the weather would go on to become a feature of the witch trials that swept across Europe.

Parting company with David at the Old Kirk Burn, I'd followed a sandy path that led off through marram grass to the ruined church. On a high point among stabilised dunes, its four walls had been partially rebuilt from fallen stone. Passing through the door-opening, I crossed to the far corner of a grassy rectangular space. Inside, the sound of the wind died away. Sheltered by four walls, the undulating turf grew thick over medieval rubble and the old kirk floor. Tired from walking through dune sand, I looked around for a spot to rest, choosy as a dog as I found a place where grassy indents fit the shape of a body. I then lay back to watch the sky's shifting greys, feeling the zing of worked muscles and blood through veins. Along the tops of the walls, late summer grasses bowed feathery seed heads to the wind.

Woodcut of witches conjuring a storm, 1489

Built in the 1100s, at what is thought to have been the highest point of the village, Forvie Kirk was dedicated to the eighth-century Irish saint St Adamnan. While little is known of Scotland's pre-Christian Pictish religion, it is thought to have resembled Celtic polytheism. Later influences included Norse paganism (kirk is from the Old Norse *kirkja*, meaning church) and also the Cult of Saints: a form of Roman Catholicism brought to Scotland from the sixth century on, mainly by Irish missionaries. By the time of the 1413 sandstorm, in common with most of Scotland and Europe, the church and people of Forvie were predominantly Catholic. A century and a half later, the Protestant preacher Reverend Masson had no doubt as to the cause of the storm. 'This judgement came about,' he wrote in 1570, 'because the folk of Forvie were papists and grossly ignorant.'

By then, what had begun in Germany as the spiritual doubts of a monk named Luther had grown into the religious movement known as Protestantism. At the time, the rise of the printing press was accelerating the spread of ideas, and printed pamphlets now fanned the flames of religious conflict across Europe. The result was a split within the Christian Church. By 1560, the once Catholic Church of Scotland – The Kirk – had broken with Rome and Scotland was a Protestant country. Mass was outlawed, and the Kirk took over existing chapels; as a result, throughout much of Scotland, Catholicism became an underground faith practised in private houses. In a cleansing of the 'glitter and rich hangings' of the old Church, chapel interiors were whitewashed to conceal murals and colourful paintwork. Shrines, icons and high altars were removed, and replaced with pulpits and plain tables for communion. Both pagan and Catholic 'profane pastimes' were forbidden, among them well-dressing and penny weddings, the 'singing of carols, or other profane songs, guising, piping and dancing'. There were also campaigns against 'popish feasting' and the celebration of Easter, May Day, Midsummer, saints' days and Yule or Christmas (often said to be the reason for Scotland's famously hedonistic New Year's Hogmanay). Together, it would contribute to the common depiction of Scottish Protestantism as grim and joyless.

At chapel, a new emphasis on discipline and godly behaviour brought sermons that could last three hours. There were also 'kirk sessions': local church 'courts' concerned with social control. With sixty per cent of Scottish cases involving sex (compared to five per cent in France), many accused women of fornication, promiscuity or adultery. Punishments included excommunication and public rebuke, sometimes with the accused sat by the pulpit on a raised 'repentance stool'. Increasingly, these kirk sessions were also used to identify witches in the local community.

I'd come across Isobel Gowdie's confessions while reading of the seventeenth-century Great Sand Drift at Culbin Sands, eighty miles from Forvie. Accused of witchcraft in 1662, Gowdie gave a famously detailed account of her pact with the Devil – who at their first meeting foretold that a farm at Culbin would be buried in sand by a storm the next day. 'He was a big, dark, hairy man, very cold,' she described at her trial, 'his feet were always forked and cloven. Sometimes he would be with us as a deer.'

This image of the Devil had complex origins, heavily influenced by the gods of pagan religions opposed by Christianity. Often, they were deities associated with sex, fertility and the wild, with drinking, dancing and merriment. As well as goat horns and cloven feet like the Greek god Pan, the Christian Satan often had a tail like the ancient Egyptian god Bes, was horned like the Celtic deity Cernunnos, and took the name of the Philistine god Beelzebub, 'Lord of the Flies'. While in medieval plays the Devil could be little more than a comic nuisance, with the Reformation he grew darker and more bestial: a figure of otherness to be feared and despised. In Scotland, as well as being known as Black Duncan, Black Donald, Auld Hangie and Auld Clootie, he was also Auld Mahoun, from a medieval name for the prophet Muhammad.

At the pulpit, continuing the long tradition of identifying the Devil with both religious and political enemies, he became a constant adversary. As an outside threat, it provided a common enemy to rally around (although now, with two competing routes to Christian salvation, both Catholics and Protestants accused each other of being in league with the Devil). Increasingly, across Europe, this took the form of flushing out witches from within a local community.

Causes of the moral panic that erupted in the European witch craze were varied and complex. With the continent still recovering from crises including plague and wars, the stormy, unsettled climate of the Little Ice Age brought hardship and poor harvests, increasing tensions and instability. While belief in witchcraft was nothing new, in the past it had often been dismissed as little more than pagan superstition. Yet now, in a climate of religious intolerance stoked by a political elite, a heightened fear of the Devil grew into the idea of a diabolical conspiracy.

More than thirty years after the invention of the printing press, the prosecution of witches gained intellectual clout following the publication of *Malleus Maleficarum* (1487), 'Hammer of Witches'. A German clergyman's treatise on witchcraft, this was a guide on how to identify, hunt and interrogate witches – and for two centuries would sell more copies than any other book except the Bible. Women, the text claimed, were far more susceptible to the temptations of the Devil, due mainly to their insatiable lust. Passions made them weak-willed, inclining them to turn to witchcraft to satisfy carnal desires. In recommending torture to obtain confessions for heresy, *Malleus Maleficarum* led to witch trials and prosecutions becoming more brutal. This was necessary, the text claimed, as witches were in league with the Devil, and so not only responsible for local harm. They were also a threat to Christianity itself.

Scotland was particularly fierce in its prosecution of witches, with more than 2,500 people, mainly women, tortured and executed by the Kirk and state. (This compares to about 500 put to death in England with its much larger population, and was around four times the European average.) One reason was the personal involvement of King James VI of Scotland in the trials. With witches widely thought to have control over the weather, he believed they were to blame when in 1589 the arrival of his new wife, Ann of Denmark, was delayed by a series of violent storms. After heading there himself and waiting out the weather in Scandinavia, he became convinced it was part of a wider witchcraft conspiracy, with the storms conjured to keep his fourteen-year-old Queen from the Scottish throne.

By 1597, he too had published a compendium on demonology and witchcraft. Titled *Daemonologie*, it was intended to educate a 'misinformed populace' on the reasons for persecuting a witch in a Christian society. The book drew on his experience as a judge at Scotland's infamous North Berwick witch trials, in which the King helped interrogate those accused of raising the storms that had delayed his wife (and sunk a ship loaded with wedding gifts). This Scottish trial was preceded by the Copenhagen witch trials, which were instigated by the Danish finance minister after he was accused of failing to properly equip the fleet delivering Ann to the King. Instead, the minister blamed the fiasco on witchcraft, which led to the torture, confession and execution of a number of Danish women accused of raising the storm.

On returning home, King James also set up his own tribunal, and a similar witch hunt began in Scotland. Here too, confessions were extracted by torture. Along with sleep deprivation (also a feature of the kirk sessions), fingernails were removed using pliers, thumbscrews applied – 'pilliwinks' in Scotland – and the 'iron boot', which crushed the victim's shin bones. At some trials, the accused were also forced to watch the torture of family members. In the North Berwick trials, Agnes Sampson was accused of raising the storm that delayed the Queen, with the King personally involved in extracting her confession. A widow and folk healer, Agnes was known locally as the Wise Wife of Keith, and initially 'stood stiffly in denial'. Later, she was subjected to sleep deprivation, pinned painfully to her cell wall in a 'witch's bridle', and had her head 'thrawen' (constricted) with a rope. Finally, when her head and body were shaved and 'the Devil's mark was found upon her privates', Agnes confessed. She and other women, she told the King, had raised the 'contrary wind' by tying a dead man's hand to a baptised cat they cast into the sea. In the winter of 1591, Agnes Sampson was taken to Edinburgh's Royal Mile, garrotted and burnt at the stake.

With torture also used to extract the names of accomplices, over the two years of the Berwick trials around seventy people were tried for witchcraft. This helped fuel a wider panic, with communities – and suspicious neighbours – encouraged to seek out the witches in their midst. In Scotland, as elsewhere in Europe and America, the accused were often older unmarried women, and others marginalised from mainstream society.

At Scottish witch trials in particular, it was common for the accused to confess to having made a pact with the Devil. Seventy years after the death of Agnes Sampson, a Satanic pact featured heavily in the trial of Isobel Gowdie, in which she claimed to have conjured the Culbin sandstorm. Her confession is widely considered the most extraordinary on record in Britain. As well as naming the thirteen members of her coven, Gowdie also provided a wealth of vivid detail, which as well as Christian demonology drew on older shamanic and folkloric 'fairy' traditions. She described spells and curses to raise the winds and spoil crops, clay effigies used to inflict illness on the sons of the laird, and her ability to shapeshift as a hare or jackdaw. She also gave lurid accounts of murder, human sacrifice and sex with the Devil in the local kirk.

Theories on what lay behind her remarkable account range from psychosis and attention-seeking to ergotism (which causes hallucinations and was proposed as a cause of the Salem witch trials). Others suggest Gowdie was a talented and creative storyteller, skilled in the oral tradition and responding to her audience. Perhaps seeking leniency, she appears to have been encouraged by the rapt attention and 'itchingly curious' questioning of investigating ministers. Whatever the reasons for the elaborate nature of Gowdie's confession, most experts believe that after conviction she was burned to death. Later, elements of her story – such as a coven of thirteen witches – would go on to influence Wicca, a modern interpretation of pre-Christian traditions.

The sand blow described in Gowdie's confession was at Culbin, which three decades later would suffer a more catastrophic inundation. This time, in October 1694, the Laird of Culbin is said to have been made a pauper in a matter of hours – although in reality it would have taken longer. 'The wind comes rushing down through the openings between the hills,' wrote John Martin of Elgin at the time, 'carrying with it immense torrents of sand, with a force and violence almost overpowering . . . Nothing can be seen but sand above, sand below and sand everywhere'.

Afterwards, as the gales also changed the course of the River Findhorn, it was almost impossible to find the site of the Barony of Culbin. With some exaggeration, the estate is said to have included sixteen farms, a chapel, a forge and a mansion, with rolling lawns and a famously fruitful orchard. And while in truth Culbin's destruction was accelerated by the stripping of turf and marram grass, the laird blamed the loss of his estate on a local witch's curse.

Others, though, believed he'd brought disaster on himself by disregarding the Sabbath. In time, this became the story told today, of the Laird of Culbin and the Devil. Playing cards late one Saturday night, the laird insisted on playing past midnight. When he boasted that he'd play on even against Satan, the Devil himself appeared and challenged the laird to three games. The first would be for his land, the second his life, and the third his immortal soul. As the storm blew up, the two played on, while the estate was lost to drifting sand. To this day, they continue their card game in the buried mansion. And when the sands shift to expose the chimney, the Devil's laughter can be heard from deep inside.

In the centuries following the Great Sand Drift, sightings and stories of Culbin abounded, as the shifting sands revealed traces of the estate. Following a visit in the 1890s, the Scottish artist George Bain described the tradition:

> A portion of the old mansion house, a hundred years ago, appeared like a ghostly spectre amidst the sand, and became an object of superstitious interest to the people of the neighbourhood, especially as one man who had bawled down the chimney heard a voice distinctly respond to his cry.

Postcard of Culbin Sands

Yet in time it was reburied in sand 'as suddenly as it came on the scene, and has not been seen for eighty years.' As well as parts of the mansion, the old dovecote was said to have appeared, along with the upper branches of the laird's famous orchard. Having blossomed and borne fruit, wrote Bain, the trees were again swallowed up.

Surviving records suggest origins for some of the legend's details: the sixteen farmhouses were perhaps sixteen tenants (in five or six houses), and the dovecote from a standard phrase of legalese. Yet an eternal card game with the Devil features in many a Scottish tale, a legacy of the Kirk's belief that playing cards were the *De'il's buiks*: 'the first books in the Devil's library'.

Today, there is no sign of the Barony of Culbin, or even the dunes, as from the 1920s a pine forest was planted to stabilise the sands. Just before that, sandstone blocks were found, showing part of the laird's family coat of arms. A decade later, while the pines were still being planted, the shifting sands also exposed an outline of foundation stones: briefly, with no record made of the site.

I lay back in the grassy quiet of Forvie Kirk, far from the sound of the wind in the dunes. It lent a feeling of sanctuary, as if the ruined church might offer protection from what lay outside. I thought of those who'd gathered within its walls in the past, perhaps during a nine-day sandstorm. Today, like the bones of their ancestors, traces of those lives still lie undisturbed beneath the sand. Yet one day those sands would shift again, and storm waves carve into the dunes. After all, these were places of revelation as much as concealment. It was no wonder their stories lingered. And by now, I should have guessed just how many would tell of retribution: of sandstorm as Flood, whether conjured by witchcraft or curses, God or the Devil. I stood up and at the doorway glanced back. By the north wall – long associated with the Devil – flattened grasses showed the imprint of my body still fitting the kirk's uneven floor.

The Pennystone, Blackpool

9

Singleton Thorpe, Kilgrimol & Waddum Thorpe

Blackpool, Lancashire

'Change here for the Las Vegas of the North,' came the announcement as the train pulled into Preston. Reaching Blackpool late on a Sunday afternoon, I headed straight for the seafront tram. It was September and away from the promenade, the wide main streets were quiet. Many of the shops were shuttered and twice I passed the spiderweb glitter of smashed plate glass. Nearer the seafront several bars were open, piping music out into the street, where smokers stood outside on plastic grass. As the softest of rain began to fall, the town felt exhausted after a hard weekend.

By the time I reached the North Pier tram stop, the smell of candyfloss and hot doughnuts mingled with newly wet tarmac. Below, out on empty watercolour sands, the iron legs of the pier were exposed. I'd come to Blackpool because, according to tradition, in the sixteenth century a 'sudden irruption of the sea' had swept away three local villages: Singleton Thorpe, Kilgrimol and Waddum Thorpe. Inevitably, these places had their stories. The ghosts of villagers wandered the dunes, and church bells tolled beneath the sand or sea: as a portent of storms, on New Year's Eve or the winter solstice. Close to one of the legendary villages, there was also the chanting of monks. Appropriately enough, though, any bells heard off Blackpool's promenade were accompanied by the ghostly drunken laughter of revellers at the Penny O'Pint. And for more than two centuries, locals had told of those who'd glimpsed a last trace of the pub out at the Pennystone rock. So I'd come to see what lay behind the stories.

For this trip, unusually, I'd booked a room in a seafront hotel – at the northern end of the Blackpool Illuminations. And I soon saw why my sea view had cost little more than a pitch at some campsites. Beyond the tram's rain-streaked glass, hotel after hotel slid by, from the Victorian splendour of the Imperial to conference blocks, budget glamour and tired bed and breakfasts. Here and there, an elegant terrace or seafront facade was boarded against squatters. Outside one, the forecourt parking bays were empty but for a skip filled with a gutted interior: splintered bedside tables, net curtains, floral armchairs. Only a week after the end of the summer holidays, Blackpool appeared to have many more rooms than visitors.

In 1788, the poet and historian William Hutton made this same journey on foot, during a three-month health stay with his wife and daughter. The following year he published *A Description of Blackpool in Lancashire Frequented for Sea Bathing*, the earliest known account of Blackpool. It is also the first record of the tradition of the Pennystone, which would later be said to mark the site of lost Singleton Thorpe. Describing a settlement of around fifty houses, Hutton felt Blackpool 'does not merit the name of a village, because they are scattered to the extent of a mile'. Sea bathing had begun there several decades earlier, with a wealthy, fashionable Georgian crowd drawn by the health-giving properties of seawater. Increasingly, both drinking and bathing in seawater were seen to cure everything from melancholia and nervous tics to fevers, jaundice and leprosy. By that time, a private road and stage-coach service linked Blackpool to the outside world, with about six of its houses 'remarkable as presenting a more respectable and modern exterior'. It also boasted an alehouse, a barn that served as a theatre and bathing machines wheeled out into the sea to preserve the bathers' modesty. Yet most of its houses remained 'ill-lit' thatched cobble cottages, home to farmers and fishermen who worked off what was then a shingle beach.

Today, Blackpool's promenade is one of the longest in the world, defended against the Irish Sea by massive concrete sea walls. Yet in Hutton's time, this was a narrow dirt track above a sixty-foot slope to the beach. Divided from fields by banks of earth, the cliff-top path was wide enough, Hutton thought, for only a foot traveller to pass in safety. So he was surprised to be passed by a wagon, 'with no more than six inches between its wheels and the edge'. Fifty years earlier, a local told Hutton, the farmer had built his field bank the width of four roads from the edge. Yet 'his four roads were, long ago, washed away.' From up on the cliff, the man pointed to a rock in the sea, at least a half mile from shore. He described how some ages back, a public house had stood beside the rock, on land 'as firm and high' as where they stood now. Iron hooks were fixed in the stone, where travellers once tethered their horses while they drank their penny pots of ale. It was, the man said, how the Pennystone got its name.

Getting out at the Bispham tram stop, I crossed Pennystone Road and headed up to my single room with its view of the sea. Beyond a flat roof and promenade shelter, the tide was way out, exposing miles of wet sand and meandering gullies. In front of the hotel, the foreshore was dominated by a monumental rock. On maritime charts, this was Carlin Rock, with the Pennystone shown further from shore. Yet it was perhaps not as simple as that. So far, I'd been told variously that this legendary rock stood half a mile, a mile or half an hour from shore; that it could be reached only on very low spring tides; that no one had seen it in generations.

Out there now – still hours off low tide – there was no sign of any Pennystone. Yet my stay would coincide with the lowest tide of the year. So my intention was at least to try to find it. How many others, I wondered, had gone looking before me: for iron tether-rings set into rock, for the legendary cobble road that led on to Singleton Thorpe.

From the window, I could just make out a distant shape in the sea. If that was the Pennystone, it was way, way out. I couldn't imagine the tide would go out that far, even on a big spring low. I felt a flicker of unease. This wasn't a shore I knew well. Also, the infamous Morecambe Bay sands were only a few miles north. It was there that twenty-one trafficked Chinese cockle pickers lost their lives in 2004, after a gangmaster was said to have misread tide times. Like so many others – and perhaps from growing up beside the Sheppey mudflats – I'd been haunted by descriptions of how the cockle pickers were cut off by the rising tide. Out on Morecambe Bay sands, locals said, the flood tide came in 'faster than a man could run'. Water surged up gullies like those I could see from my window, rising from all directions as channels flowed together to form shrinking sandbanks.

I checked the tide table again on my phone. I would be timing any attempts to see the Pennystone with care.

As well as the Pennystone, I would also be looking for Kilgrimol. The most likely-sounding site lay on the far side of Blackpool, so a couple of days later I took the tram south to Starr Gate at the end of the line. Starr was an old name for the marram grass that stabilised the dunes, which once extended north into Blackpool. Before the sea wall, in the early days of double-decker tramcars, the South Blackpool dunes were so high they obscured a sea view from the tram's upper deck.

Starr Gate has long marked the boundary between Blackpool and neighbouring St Annes, which as half of Lytham St Annes has been described as 'a northern byword for posh'. And as I made my way down onto the beach, I found the division was abrupt. Blackpool's miles of concrete sea walls came to an end at a slope of tyre-like hexagons (known as 'sea bees', they trap sand to help dissipate wave energy). Yet to the south lay miles of golden dunes and sandflats, with people walking their dogs in hazy sunshine. It was in striking contrast to the Golden Mile I'd just passed through on the tram: the heart of what J. B. Priestley described in the 1930s as 'the great roaring spangled beast' of Blackpool.

From what I'd read, the likely site of Kilgrimol lay a mile or so south-south-east of the sea bees. So I set off along a strandline at the base of the dunes, distracted as ever by the peculiar bounty of the sea. Entangled with seaweed I found all the usual plastic forks and lighters, along with toy sand moulds in the shape of a lobster, a starfish, a shark. Scattered among them were also the fragile tests of heart urchins, dislodged when foreshore sands were last disturbed by heavy seas. Although brittle and hollow now, some had retained their spines, and lay among the weed like tiny heads with neatly parted hair. Gentler, more recent waves had left impossibly delicate drifts: worm tubes built from grains of sand, mussels and razor shells thin as babies' fingernails – and in among them a bouncy translucent bloodshot eyeball.

Of the Fylde's three 'lost villages', only Kilgrimol appeared in medieval records. This was due to its proximity to an ancient boundary of the Priory of Lytham, which extended down to the shore near the concrete sea bees. Still known today as Division Lane, the boundary was once a twelfth-century cart track. By the sixteenth century, it separated the 'sandgrown'uns' this side from the 'mossogs' or 'moss-dwellers' on what is now the Blackpool side. For local author Kathleen Eyre, writing of the two sides of Division Lane in the 1960s, there remained 'a lingering coolness'. Today, the sixteenth-century 'sandgrown 'un' has largely been replaced by the local word 'sandgrownian'. And while some Blackpudlians also now use it to describe themselves, others claim it applies only to those conceived beneath a pier.

In the days after arriving in Blackpool, I'd met several people with a keen interest in local history, from both the mossog and sandgrown sides of Division Lane. All had been very generous with their time and knowledge. They were also patient with my outsider's attempts to tease fact – or at least record – from the welter of fiction and conjecture surrounding the lost settlements (which at times felt like struggling through the Fylde's impenetrable sixteenth-century boglands). The previous day, I'd sheltered from the rain beneath a coffee shop overhang with Michelle, who'd grown up in Blackpool and drew Ordnance Survey maps from her shopping bag. Later, I met local historian Peter and his wife Maureen in the conservatory of their immaculate St Annes bungalow, where they gave me tea and copies of charter grants and the 1741 Starr and Bent Act. Blackpudlian Juliette sent photographs to help me recognise particular rocks. And David brought typewritten folktales from the local archive, before dropping me back at the bus stop in a black BMW.

Of the three legendary villages, the existence of Kilgrimol was the least controversial. It was first recorded in the 1190s, when the heirless Richard FitzRoger granted his lands to the monks of Durham Priory. In a document drawn up by FitzRoger, he described the boundary extending 'From the ditch on the western side of the churchyard of Kilgrimol, above which I have erected a cross, as far as the sea.'

With little to go on, clues were inevitably sought in the name. As with Ireland's enchanted Kilstifeen, the prefix Kil- is thought to derive from an early form of Christian chapel known as a *keeill*. Often established by seafaring monks between the fifth and eleventh century, these simple churches were founded not just in Ireland but also Scotland, the Isle of Man, Cornwall and the north of England (with an appealing idea that the word *keeill* reflected how some were roofed with a keel: perhaps even the upturned boat of the missionary monk). Kilgrimol, then, was thought to mean the church of Grim. Here on the Lancashire coast, many Norse incomers are thought to have arrived in a wave of Viking migration around AD 902, following their expulsion from Dublin by the Irish. So the name Grim may well have been locally common. Constructed of wood, mud and stone, these early *keeill*s rarely survived, although churches were often rebuilt on the sites. The ending '-ol' may be from *meol*, an old word for sand dune, making Kilgrimol 'the church of Grim in the sand dunes'. Alternatively, some records have the spelling Kilgrimhow, with '-how' perhaps deriving from the Old Norse *haugr* meaning hill or mound, and also used for a burial ground.

Kilgrimol is next mentioned in the sixteenth century, when Division Lane became a focal point of ongoing clashes between the 'mossogs' and 'sandgrown'uns'. These centred on ownership of the cart track, along with rights to grazing and shipwreck that washed up on shore (in 1338, for instance, Widow Sybil Butler was accused of dragging an anchor over to the mossog side of the boundary). By 1530, tensions appear to have come to a head when 'riotous bands' destroyed their neighbours' buildings and drainage ditches, and pulled up the starr grass – in what became known as the Battle of Mad Nook. In the ensuing court case, one witness described how since his father's time, two miles of pasture had been 'worn into by the sea'. And another described the similar erosion of 'Kelgrymoles Churchyard'.

Later, in another court case, a tenant described Kilgrimol as 'flooded and washed into the sea'. At the time, an old stone cross – perhaps FitzRoger's – still marked the site. Known then as Churchyard Slack, the area later became known as Cross Slack (as with the Scottish dunes, 'slack' was from the Old Norse *slakki*, meaning a shallow depression). While the tiny hamlet of Cross Slack is long gone today, the ruins of its last cottages remain in living memory.

'A curious tradition has existed for ages,' wrote the antiquarian Reverend Bulpit in the early 1900s, 'that at special times anyone putting his ear to the ground at Churchyard Slack, the bells could be heard ringing!' Here in St Annes, they are said to be accompanied not by drunks but by monks chanting vespers. Yet as I made my way up into the dunes, the sound of waves and the wind through marram grass was drowned out by traffic noise, leaving little chance of hearing monks or the bells of Kilgrimol.

Climbing sandy paths to the top of the tallest dune, I looked out over lower-lying ground inland. On the far side of the road were the gentle hillocks of grassy, long-stabilised dunes. Once common land, it was now a strip of nature reserve between the road and the railway line; beyond that lay Blackpool Airport and St Annes Old Links Golf Course. It was somewhere out there – beneath the even gentler undulations of roughs and fairways – that many believed Kilgrimol lay. For while the burial ground was said to have been eroded by the sea, this stretch of the Fylde coast has a long history of its advance and retreat.

In *The Battle of Land and Sea* (1909), William Ashton describes how after storms, peat beds were sometimes exposed beneath the sandbanks off St Annes. He also writes of trenches cut into the sand hills between the railway and the sea road, which revealed a series of 'stanners': shingle beds marking earlier coastlines. The oldest maps, he suggests, show that in the fourteenth century this part of the coastline lay half a mile further inland (contrary to the Blackpool coast further north). By 1610, he says, John Speed's map of Lancashire shows it a mile inland.

This coast's mutability is supported by records of floods and 'rages of sand' that periodically overwhelmed farmland. In 1549, blown sand left tenant farmers unable to pay their rents. As channels and sandbanks shift in the nearby Ribble estuary, more or less sand is exposed at low tide, and blown inland during onshore gales. Homes and farmland, then, remained dependent on the protection of the sand dunes. In turn, the dunes relied on the binding roots of the starr grass. By 1667, this led to a manorial court order that 'no person or persons shall Cutt or get any Starr to give or sell'. Later, two Starr Lookers were appointed, and given powers to fine any locals neglecting to plant starr grass on an appointed day 'for the good of the Common'.

But marram grass was a useful material, for everything from brushes and rush matting to thatch in place of straw. So, two decades after the Great Flood of 1720, when 'forty dwelling houses' were washed away here, the Starr and Bent Act of 1741 strengthened the power of the Starr Lookers. 'Many idle and disorderly persons residing near the said coasts,' it stated, 'do unlawfully and maliciously in the night time as well as by day, cut, pull up, and carry away the starr or bent . . . instead of working in an honest manner.' The fine was a steep twenty shillings, half of which went to the informer.

From up on the dune, I could also see an innovative modern version of the work policed by the Starr Lookers. Below, along the top of the shore, lines of dead Christmas trees poked from the sand. This was part of the local dune regeneration scheme. Donated by residents to the Fylde Sand Dunes Project, the browning branches and dry needles of the buried trees trap sand, which in time allows the starr to take hold and form embryo dunes. Along the Fylde coast, say the group, urban expansion has reduced the extent of the dunes by over eighty per cent – increasing the risk of both floods and sand blow. Here, the planting has continued for more than a decade, and similar successful schemes are now found on dune coasts from Scotland to Cornwall.

Having waited for a gap in traffic, I crossed to the old common land, where its low hind dunes were the colour of summer slipping into autumn. Here the sand was bound by pale grasses, heather and low bramble: the matted vegetation of a dune system that crept seawards long ago. Heading for the railway line, I followed paths worn by dog walkers, treading above long-buried shores. Somewhere beneath the dune soil lay the 'stanners' of old storm beaches, so perhaps remnants of ancient strandlines.

Close to the fenced-off railway, I climbed an abandoned concrete structure to see out over the golf course. According to older Ordnance Survey maps, the tiny hamlet of Cross Slack – once Churchyard Slack – was somewhere in the rough just south of a copse of wind-huddled trees. In the 1960s, the last of its derelict cottages could still be seen from the train. In their time, they were the traditional cobble and thatch cottages described by William Hutton on his sea-bathing visit in 1788. Home to subsistence farmers and fishers, and allegedly the odd wrecker, their low-ceilinged rooms were lit by oil lamps and the light of turf and driftwood fires.

One of the last remaining was known as Granny Fisher's, once the crowded home of a farming family of eleven. Back then, one regular visitor to Cross Slack was Reverend William Bulpit. A vicar in nearby Southport, he was born in 1841 and is described in Ashton's *The Battle of Land and Sea* as a 'painstaking antiquarian' (and elsewhere as 'short in stature' and 'rather autocratic'). Throughout the Victorian era, antiquarianism had become an increasingly popular and fashionable pastime, not least among the clergy – who often had time on their hands. Like many, Bulpit's interests ranged from collecting artefacts and watching excavations to recording local history, folklore and traditions. He came to Cross Slack in search of relics of Kilgrimol. Through repeated visits, he came to believe that the threshold stone at Granny Fisher's was once the base of the twelfth-century boundary cross described by FitzRoger. With so large a family in the cottage at the time, the stone remained where it was. Years later, though, the wife of the farmer Ned Fisher recalled her husband ploughing up masonry close to the cottage. She remembered certain stones having 'curious markings and inscriptions', and Bulpit helping move them to a safe place in the cottage garden, pending further investigation. Years later, though, the forgotten stones – perhaps remnants of a Kilgrimol church – were discarded down a disused well.

Alongside his other antiquarian interests, Reverend Bulpit also collected local folktales. In *Historical Notes on the Fylde* (1913), he records a story of Blackpool's Marton Mere, in which the spirit of Kilgrimol's priest helped banish 'the serpent of paganism':

> In the days before the missionaries came there were evil spirits in the water marshes around Marton Mere, who were propitiated by the Britons. When Grim, the priest from Kilgrimol, came teaching the people, he cast the chief spirit into the mere and it took the form of a great worm or conga eel. In the bad days of the Danes the eel was loosed and came out to the dwellings of those who took refuge on the shore, and ate sheep and even children. Their priest could not lay the spirit, and so he went to Cross Slack, where Grim's oratory had stood, and hoped Grim would aid him by a vision.

Soon after dawn the phantom bell rang, and a voice told the priest to bait the eel with a cross cake disguised with bacon. 'The cross cake stuck in his throat and caused agonies of suffocation', writes Bulpit. 'He could not leave the Mere, and even yet, on a moonlit night, a swell on the water marks where he rolls in agony.'

Jumping down, I landed with a sandy thud. From the ground, this scrap of old common land was a precious remnant hemmed in by sprawling rooftops that peaked over grasses. To the sand-grown south lay suburban Kilgrimol Gardens, while to the north, the ever-present roller coaster and Blackpool Tower were faint above new builds.

Writing in 1909, five years before his death, Bulpit described a dark peaty layer some nine feet below these dunes. This was, he said, 'the surface of the old days'. In 1893, at a similar depth, excavations had also revealed a stone roadway running near parallel to the railway. For Bulpit, this was 'probably the old Kilgrimol road'. By then, he believed Kilgrimol was likely to have been a small Christian settlement founded by missionaries, perhaps plundered by the Danes. The old name Churchyard Slack implied a church had once accompanied the burial ground, with the early dates suggesting a 'clump-clad, raddle and daub' building. Suggesting the site would originally have been chosen for its access to the sea, Bulpit imagined a channel that later silted up, which allowed sand to overblow the peat. Maybe that was when Kilgrim – the church of Grim – became Kilgrimol in the sand hills. At least that's what the few traces in the dunes and records suggested to Bulpit. Out there now, where the ruins of Granny Fisher's were reputedly demolished to make way for a new sixteenth tee, the grassy carpet of the Old Links keeps its secrets.

I'd made my first attempt to reach the Pennystone soon after arriving in Blackpool. Crossing tramlines to the promenade in gentle rain, I descended paths and steps to a concrete slope that was green with weed. There was no longer a shingle beach at its foot, just wide-open sandflats and a chip fork afloat in a tide-pool. Otherwise, presumably due to the weather, the shore was deserted. Heading out onto reassuringly firm wet sand, I made first for the rock that dominated the foreshore. As I drew closer, it was increasingly imposing, rising from pool-shine like a two-humped beast.

I'd seen photographs of it already on the internet, usually captioned Carlin Rock or Carling Stone, although sometimes Mussel Rock or Pennystone. My favourite was taken roughly a century ago. A black-and-white group portrait, it was perhaps an extended family, with the women posed in summer hats and long white dresses against the dark of mussels. Sitting in spotless white, they appear to have forded the tide-pool and scaled a rock two or three times their height. Today, though, I didn't stop at Carlin. Instead, I headed out to the distant rock I'd watched break the surface from my window (after my initial unease at seeing the Pennystone so far out, I'd rooted binoculars from my rucksack to find it was a boat). More predictably, the rock had emerged later on, exactly where it was shown on the chart. Encouragingly, while still a long way out, it wasn't nearly as far as the boat.

The lowest tide of the year was early the next morning. Tide tables showed it thirty-four centimetres lower than tonight, which on sands this flat could make quite a difference. So I saw this evening as something of a recce: to check the route was safe and gauge my chances of reaching the Pennystone in the morning. I'd also headed out too early. This was keenness in part, but also because the rain meant I'd soon lose the light.

Out beyond ribbed sandflats, the distant rock dipped below the waves like a sea monster. Now, walking out into the shallows, I could get no closer than fifty or sixty feet. I had no idea of the depth of the surrounding scour pit and how much of the rock lay beneath the surface. I checked the time. Low tide was in fifty minutes. Yet there seemed little chance of reaching it tonight. I passed the time walking along the water's edge, which meandered around the gentle undulations of sandbanks. In the distance, the skeletal North Pier and Blackpool Tower were veiled by gentle rain. Further still, the pale sweep of the roller coaster hung in the air like a stilled murmuration.

Soon I returned to stare out at the Pennystone. Dark and bristling with mussels, it was now a magnet for herring gulls. Youngsters squabbled for space in the water, while adults dropped feet-first to the summit, displacing rivals. When I'd arrived, gulls were poking around Carlin nearer shore. Now, most were out here. All around me, reflected in wet sand, they advanced on thin legs in silence. In fading light, the scene was drained of colour until a gull lifted off, weighed down by the fleshy, splayed arms of an orange starfish. Abruptly, from behind me in this curious waiting place, the squabbling of gulls rose to a cry that was unnervingly human.

Again I checked the time. Low tide was in fifteen minutes. Nothing much would change, then. I waded out anyway as far as I could, shin-deep in the tea-colour sea. Still at least forty feet from the Pennystone, I retreated as a series of waves filled my boots.

Back on shore, I emerged onto a very different promenade. Now that daylight had slipped away, the wet road shone with the neon reds and blues of 'AMUSEMENTS'. Inside the hotel, I passed the door to the small, dimly lit bar, intensely conscious of the sound of my wet socks in rubber boots. When I'd first arrived there was no one about, so I'd gone into the bar to find a haggard-looking man sat alone at the counter. Nursing a flat pint early on a Sunday evening, he looked almost beaten by his weekend.

'You'll want Alan,' he said, and pointed to a bell on the bar top. 'He does everything. The bar, breakfast, the rooms.' Turning slowly back to his pint, he shook his head as if in disbelief, and said how much I was going to enjoy Blackpool. Alan was bald and big as a bouncer, a Geordie running the hotel in his mother-in-law's absence. As he checked me in, I asked about the Pennystone. 'Nope, never heard of it,' he said, and handed me the room keys with a look that was hard to read. 'You've come to see a rock on the beach?'

Now, as I climbed the stairs, there were more people in the bar and, sadly, curling my toes didn't lessen the regular squelch. In the room, I emptied my boots in the spotless toilet and stood them upside down in the shower. Throughout the evening, periodically I stood and stared out to sea. Beyond the glitter of street lights on rain-beaded glass, the Pennystone and eventually Carlin slipped beneath the surface. Soon they were also swallowed by darkness. Later still, waking in the small hours, I looked out to the moon-drawn sea pressing up against concrete.

Unlike Kilgrimol, the existence of Waddum Thorpe and Singleton Thorpe remains controversial. Neither appear on maps, in Domesday or monastic records. Instead, they are first mentioned in the 1830s, at the very end of the Georgian era. The earliest reference to Singleton Thorpe is in Peter Whittle's *Marina: An Historical and Descriptive Account of Southport, Lytham and Blackpool* (1831). '1554,' he writes, 'a sudden irruption of the sea took place near Rossal Grange, and a whole village called Singleton Thorpe was washed away by its fury – the inhabitants were obliged to flee from the ancient spot and erected their tents at a place called Singleton to this day.'

Singleton Thorpe is mentioned again six years later in *The History of Blackpool and its Neighbourhood* (1837), by the local antiquarian Reverend William Thornber. Often known as 'Blackpool's first historian', Thornber repeats the tradition of the Pennystone told to William Hutton in 1788. He describes a local story 'handed down from father to son', of an inn near the Pennystone, with penny pints and iron hitch rings in the rock.

Fishermen had seen these rings, he says, although they may well have been 'placed there by some merry wag'. Yet Thornber goes on to describe how eighty or ninety years earlier, a violent storm had stripped away the sand that ordinarily half-buried the Pennystone. Witnessed by 'a gentleman who lived in the neighbourhood,' the scouring had revealed 'walls evidently encircling an enclosure'. This alone was enough to convince Thornber that a large tract of land had been lost to the sea here, 'were it not a matter of history that Singleton Thorpe once stood in the vicinity'.

At the time of the book's publication, the vicar was popular with his parishioners, and a striking figure in the local community. A 'fine, gigantic looking man', Thornber was described by friends as 'exceedingly gentle and kind-hearted . . . when unruffled'. For the vicar also made enemies. 'Woe to him who gave offence to Mr Thornber,' wrote another friend later, as the clergyman was 'sure to punish the offender.'

Reverend William Thornber

Still frequently quoted today, the Blackpool vicar has been variously described as erudite, brilliant, erratic, restless, frustrating and furiously energetic. In the blogs and forums of today's equivalent of the Victorian antiquarians, Thornber was also eccentric, flawed, a brawler, a bare-knuckle fighter, a drunk and a fantasist. Yet in the years after his book came out, the Reverend was widely seen as a reliable source of local history. He'd become a Church of England vicar in 1829, in a golden age of the English vicar. With Blackpool's population small at the time, Thornber's ministry left him plenty of time to pursue other interests. Half a century before Reverend Bulpit, Thornber was using his leisure time to record a Blackpool that would soon be lost. This included local folklore, customs and superstitions: beliefs previously so common they were considered unremarkable.

Many historians, though, were dismissive of this antiquarian interest in the 'humdrum' detail of everyday lives. True historical writing, they claimed, was about ideas and interpretation. It should seek to analyse, understand and explain the past – not merely record observations. Yet the antiquarians strongly disagreed, priding themselves on avoiding the historians' tendency to fancy, conjecture and distortion. Their work was a science, they said, based on scrupulous observation and attention to detail.

Being both local and a clergyman no doubt helped Thornber's antiquarian cause, allowing him to form 'the acquaintance of every old native living in or near the town', from the 'old dames' to the 'hardy fishermen' who were 'always proud to relate to him the traditions . . . and the folk lore they had heard in their youthful days'. Thornber felt such beliefs had lingered in Blackpool due to its historic isolation; in the past, access to the mosslands had been difficult for much of the year, with the dirt roads often dangerous and liable to flooding. Another reason for local credulity, Thornber felt, was 'the effect of the magnificent grandeur of the ocean on unenlightened man'. Yet Blackpool's isolation was increasingly a thing of the past. Now it had roads and a stagecoach service, Thornber noted, such customs and superstitions were dying away.

Times were also changing for Thornber. Having worked as the local vicar for fourteen years, in 1843 he was suspended for drunkenness. By then, the clergyman had already gained a reputation for drinking and fighting in a fast-changing Blackpool. Within three years – by which time Thornber had resigned from the Church – the railway had also reached this 'scarcely prepared' town. From then on, the Victorian working classes began arriving in droves, released from factories and mills for a week in summer. With extended families and entire streets of people decamping for a week by the sea, the Blackpool of Thornber's childhood had changed beyond all recognition.

Thornber's second book, *Penny Stone*, was a slim work of fiction. A retelling of the tradition of the Pennystone, it made creative use of his local antiquarian research. More controversially, Thornber also merges the tradition of the Pennystone with that of Singleton Thorpe, placing the village close to the legendary rock.

Protected by sand hills, the book's Elizabethan Penny Stone inn stood in a vale where 'age and storms had destroyed most of the groves of oak trees'. As a well-known frequenter of Blackpool's inns – and later a pub landlord himself – Thornber describes the Penny Stone in loving detail, from its porch 'clothed with creepers and ivy' to the hallway shaped 'like the hull of a ship inverted'. Inside was an open fireplace and three-legged stools, beneath rafters hung with dried bacon and beef. Outside, the Pennystone 'reared its misshapen block near the porch'.

Thornber's story builds to the cause of the storm that will destroy the village. First there is an attempted murder by a group of 'Popish plotters' who frequent the Penny Stone (among them ranty and feckless Bess, who is 'continually brooding over the rapid decay of Popery'). Afterwards, the landlord Jock is tried for witchcraft, as not only has the witchfinder seen his imp-teats, but his customers are also happy to give evidence against him. Among them is Bill o' th' Cow-gap, who 'swears he knew he were bewitched, or he wod not hev bin sic'.

At this point, as well as moving Singleton Thorpe to the Pennystone, Thornber also changes the date the village was lost. From the traditional 1554, he moves it to 29 July 1588, to coincide with the English defeat of the Spanish Armada in the Channel: an unlikely and momentous Protestant victory. (With Spanish ships blown off-course by a change in wind direction – that became known as 'The Protestant Wind' – it was seen in England as proof of God's support for the Protestant cause.) So in Thornber's retelling of the loss of Singleton Thorpe, on that same day 'the firmament suddenly darkened' over the inn's Catholic plotters. As the storm thundered in, 'at one sweep the protecting barrier of sand hills disappeared before it . . . Trees were uprooted, prostrated, or snapped asunder, then one by one, the mud wattled huts of the villagers were undermined, til not a single building reared its head.'

'Nothing', he wrote 'resisted the force of the sea except the Pennystone'.

More than a decade after the publication of *Penny Stone*, the Lancashire dialect poet Edwin Waugh met Thornber out at the rock by chance. The poet's visit to Blackpool coincided with a spring tide 'foretold as higher than any for a century previous'. Finding crowds already in town to witness a flood, Waugh got drinking in the local pub with a fisherman in his seventies. Laughing at visitors not understanding the effect of the wind on tides, he told Waugh:

> There'll be no tide warth speykin' on – silly divuls, but 'iv ye want to see summat warth rememberin', ye mun go to low water. It'll be a rare seet . . . here'll be skeers [cockle beds] an' rocks eawt as hesn't bin sin ov a hundred year.

So approaching the big low tide, Waugh was guided out across the sands by the fisherman. Collecting whelks along the way, the man pointed out particular rocks: Old Woman's Head, Mussel Rock, Carlin and Colt. Finally, out near the water's edge rose the 'gloomy mass' of the Pennystone. 'As we drew near it,' wrote Waugh, 'we saw five persons come over the shining sands towards the same spot.' This included a local friend of Waugh's 'accompanied by three "brethren of the mystic tie", one of whom was Mr Thornber'. Together, the group forded 'a little moat of salt water, nearly knee deep' and climbed the Pennystone, 'clinging to its Triton locks of seaweed'. Sat on the rock looking out, the group celebrated with what is said to have been a bottle of whisky.

'I took the opportunity of inquiring where he found the materials for his tradition,' wrote Waugh of Thornber. 'He answered that there was no doubt of its fundamental truth; "but, as to the details wrought in to the story," said he, pointing to his forehead, with a laugh, "I found them in a cellar, in the rock there."'

Already, many no longer considered Thornber a factual writer to be trusted. One problem was that later writers often repeated elements of his novel as historical fact, leading to some of its changes being absorbed into the local tradition of the Pennystone. This was a rewriting of local history that would become increasingly common among late Victorian collectors of folklore. And for Thornber, it led many to question the reliability of much else he'd written.

In the decades after he left the Church, Thornber remained well known for his local campaigning, alongside the boxing, drinking and occasional brawling. By the 1860s, he was landlord of the Beach Hotel – which in time would be pulled down to make way for the Blackpool Tower. Later, after Thornber's behaviour grew increasingly erratic, some alluded to 'darker rumours'. Eventually, after knocking down a policeman for placing a hand on his shoulder, the ex-Reverend was taken to a mental institution, where he lived until his death in 1885. Long before that, writing of the transformation of Blackpool around him, Thornber had noted how 'the landscape suggested in a moment the sobering fact of my own weakness . . . I too might change'.

By the time of Thornber's death, the Blackpool 'village' he'd known as a child was unrecognisable. Its population of around

500 was now over 35,000, with the town able to accommodate an estimated three million visitors a year (this would rise to around seventeen million by the First World War). Along with England's first electric tramway, the town also now boasted two pleasure piers, which exemplified local tensions around the types of visitor Blackpool wanted to attract. Like other piers springing up around Britain at the time, the first – now the North Pier – offered more space for the Victorian upper and middle classes to promenade in the invigorating sea air. Out over the water, they could take in the sea views away from the more 'vulgar distractions' of Blackpool's seafront. Entertainments on this first pier were seen as 'improving': symphonies and recitals, with Sundays reserved for a local church parade. This all proved a huge success, although a problem for those keen to keep the pier select – with the tuppence entrance fee not enough to deter the lower-class 'trippers' arriving by train.

So Blackpool soon had a People's Pier too. With dancing every day from dawn until dusk, it was the start of an ongoing pier rivalry that reflected the concerns around class. Those promoting the health-giving benefits of Blackpool wanted wealthy, respectable visitors who would exercise restraint – not the 'bawdy' working classes with their 'drunkenness and questionable morality', and their states of undress at the beach.

By this time, the promenade between the piers had evolved into the Golden Mile, with the gardens of its hotels and boarding houses increasingly let to 'vulgar and assertive' stallholders. In the past, everyone from fortune tellers to pedlars and showmen had operated on Blackpool's beach, but complaints brought new regulations. Along with the 'donkey wallopers', those allowed to remain on the sands included ventriloquists and the Punch and Judy shows; among those excluded were the palm readers, phrenologists and 'quack doctors'. In time, Blackpool's seafront showmen would display Living Skeletons and Two Tonne Alice, the Tattooed Man, Siamese Twins and the Leicester Fat Boy. Later came the Starving Brides: a fasting woman in a wedding dress, displayed in a barrel or glass-topped 'coffin'. Another popular variation was the ex-Rector of Stiffkey, who had recently been defrocked for associating with prostitutes. (Initially shown 'starving and freezing' in a glass-fronted barrel on Blackpool seafront, he would later be 'roasted alive' as he protested his innocence, while a mechanical devil prodded his buttocks with a pitchfork.)

A regular on the seafront tram now, I looked at the North Pier as we came to a halt. More than Blackpool's other two piers – with their arcades and white-knuckle rides – this one had retained its Victorian architecture: its ornamental cast iron and minaret roofs, if not the Indian Pavilion. Inspired by empire, Britain's Victorian pleasure piers were a fairly eccentric demonstration of engineering prowess and mastery over the sea. Yet those that have survived – just over half of the hundred built – remain uniquely vulnerable to fires, storms and rising seas. Out there now, unlike at my first glimpse, the Irish Sea surged against the pier's iron legs.

In *The Battle of Land and Sea* Ashton describes 'a man still living' who remembered cattle grazing where the North Pier stands today. Another recalled visiting his grandparents in a row of cottages there in the 1850s, before their end wall was lost to the sea. There is no doubt that in the centuries before Blackpool's first concrete sea wall, this stretch of coast had lost fields, cottages and farms. The most well-documented loss was Uncle Tom's Cabin, Blackpool's first entertainment venue, which stood on the cliff a mile north of the pier. Having begun as a stall selling ginger beer in the 1850s – with fortunes told by Gipsy Sarah – it evolved into a bar, tea room and dance hall, with sideshows alongside the fortune telling.

'No lawns, gardens or bowling green,' one visitor commented in the 1870s. 'Is it because there is no sense of permanence with

Postcard of Uncle Tom's Cabin,
Blackpool's first entertainment venue, *c.*1900

the sea encroaching year by year?' By the late 1890s, postcards show Uncle Tom's collection of wooden buildings teetering at the edge of the cliff. By then, it was losing four to eight feet a year. Over previous decades, erosion had increased significantly, as Blackpool's shingle was removed for use as ballast on the railways. This left no beach to protect the foot of the cliff, with contractors also dredging the 'scars' or shingle banks offshore – which previously had reduced the force of waves reaching shore. In 1901, the smoking room at Uncle Tom's Cabin was the first to go over.

The tram doors closed and we pulled away from the Golden Mile. By now, I'd passed through that stretch many times, glimpsing its past through the kaleidoscope of entertainments on offer today. Along with the opulence of the Tower Ballroom, there were still seafront fortune tellers, arcades and carousels, Crystals on the Prom and Ripley's Believe It or Not! (shrunken heads, the Human Unicorn, a two-headed calf). With the town having reinvented itself as a party destination through the 1980s – after cheap flights and package holidays decimated visitor numbers – the 'main stag and hen strip' still had its karaoke bars, lap-dancing and strip clubs with 'regular pole routines'. Once again Blackpool was in the process of reinvention, this time proposing Las Vegas-style casinos to fill its empty hotel rooms.

On the day of the lowest tide of the year, I woke to the sound of tyres in the wet. The wind had picked up in the night, but it was too dark yet for any sign of the Pennystone. In still-damp boots, I closed the hotel's front door and breathed the salt air. Out over the sea, scudding cloud gave glimpses of the near-full moon.

Down on the foreshore, I followed the same route across the sand as before, half expecting to see others on their way to the rock (if not a small group of vicars). But apart from a distant dog walker, headed in the opposite direction, I was the only one. When I reached the water's edge, the same amount of the Pennystone was exposed as when I'd left the night before. I paddled out as far as I could, but the rock remained deep in its scour pit, with the choppy brown sea still flowing in. By the time I checked my phone, the tide had already turned. While it *had* dropped lower than last night, the chop meant I'd barely got closer. It brought to mind Waugh's elderly fisherman, laughing at the naivety of tourists expecting floods on the highest tide of the year. Disappointed, I wandered back to shore, as rain again moved in from the west to shroud the Tower and pier.

On a similar tide in 1893, Alfred Halstead – editor of the *Blackpool Times* – led an expedition in search of the ruins of Singleton Thorpe. A photograph taken that year shows crowds on Blackpool beach wearing dark formal dress. In the background the People's Pier is spectral in mist, with Blackpool

Tower half built on the seafront (soon to house a menagerie, ballroom and circus with performing polar bears). The group set out from the shore at Rossall, several miles north of where I was now – and mentioned in Whittle's first reference to Singleton Thorpe. 'In the year 1792,' he wrote in *Marina*, 'at low water mark, a number of trunks of trees lay in various directions upon the sands of the sea, which proved that there had been a village near Rossal'. As at Borth, the peat-preserved trees actually date back to prehistoric times (before the steep Mesolithic rise, sea levels were low enough that it was possible to walk the ninety miles from Blackpool to the Isle of Man). Given the extraordinary degree of preservation of the trees, though, it's easy to see how people would assume they were contemporary with Singleton Thorpe.

Yet it wasn't just the trees and the claims of Whittle and Thornber that inspired Halstead's expedition. Fifteen years earlier, the geologist Charles Eugene De Rance had also gone out on a big low tide, and described finding horse troughs and ruined 'shippons' (barns) filled with seawater. So that day, on one of the lowest tides of the year, Halstead and a 'small party of adventurous spirits' set out from somewhere near Rossal. Armed with pickaxes and spades, they began following the exposed roots and trunks of the forest.

Out near the water's edge they reached 'what looked like a log tree . . . quite different in shape from other trees half buried in the sand. Digging and shovelling the sand from it laid it all bare, and we found it to be a straight and square piece of timber.' Finding marks where other timbers had been fastened to it, Halstead suspected it was the rafter of a large room of a house. The group also found what appeared to be the foundations of a cottage, and another rubble-wall foundation – 'but it was too near the waves to follow it to the end'.

Their findings – so briefly exposed – were typical of the timber longhouses common in Lancashire from medieval times until the seventeenth century (with the roofing joist reminiscent of Thornber's smoky rafters hung with dried meats in *Penny Stone*). As in other submerged locations, it's quite possible that the sediments would preserve timbers over such long periods of time.

Several years later, Halstead returned on another spring low tide, this time with labourers and carts to ferry artefacts home. On this second visit, the group are said to have retrieved door posts and tree branches, and what appeared to be part of a lintel. Later, though – like the masonry ploughed up near Granny Fisher's – the relics were lost. Halstead, however, was convinced they'd found Singleton Thorpe. 'That we were on the site of the ruined and wave-swept village there could be no doubt.'

More recent searches have proved inconclusive. On a big low tide in 2016, members of the local Wyre Archaeology group searched an area similar to Halstead. In the brief window allowed by the tide, the group did find – and photograph – 'wood and stone features' part buried in the sand. And they did appear to have once been part of a building. Yet nothing was retrieved, or radiocarbon-dated, and a subsequent return to the spot found only the submerged forest.

Even so, remnants of sixteenth-century buildings are no proof that Singleton Thorpe existed. Thornber first described the village in his 1837 history of Blackpool, years before *Penny Stone*. Yet, as mentioned, the first record of the name Singleton Thorpe had come six years earlier in Peter Whittle's *Marina*. Some suspect Thornber simply repeated Whittle, who may be unreliable. On the publication of *Marina*, for example, a letter to the *Preston Chronicle* described it as 'a scrap-book of shreds and patches of fine poetry and sentiments . . . and scraps collected chiefly from your paper'.

On Singleton Thorpe, Whittle quotes as his source the seventeenth-century antiquary Roger Dodsworth. All records of the loss of the village lead back to him, where things become opaque. In general, Dodsworth is a credible source. He was born in 1585, only thirty years after the 'irruption of the sea' was said to have taken place. As his father was registrar of York Minster, he was also granted special access to records held there, and for a time lived relatively locally.

In his history of Blackpool, Thornber too refers to the Dodsworth manuscripts. Yet in *The Battle of Land and Sea*, Ashton complains the Reverend 'gives neither chapter nor page' and says his own thorough searches of the 'voluminous mass of documents now in the Bodleian Library of Oxford' found no mention of either Singleton Thorpe or Waddum Thorpe. Others since have said the same thing. On the other hand, less than a quarter of the Bodleian's 161 volumes are said to be indexed, with other Dodsworth manuscripts also held elsewhere. And no one appears to have checked them all.

So this is where the trail to Singleton Thorpe peters out. Although Waddum Thorpe has inspired no stories, unlike Singleton Thorpe it *was* mentioned in an earlier record. It is often said to have been a mile offshore of the dunes south of Blackpool, so seaward of Kilgrimol. In the first version of the tradition I heard, Waddum Thorpe was lost in 1554, in the same 'mighty inundation' as Singleton Thorpe. Others, though, have claimed the village washed away in 1532, in another great flood that swept two miles inland. Several quote Charles Leigh: a physician born in 1662 in the nearby village of Singleton (mentioned in Domesday and where Whittle claimed survivors from Singleton Thorpe had erected their tents). Interestingly, there is no record of Leigh ever mentioning a Singleton Thorpe, although he is quoted as saying Waddum Thorpe was still in existence in 1601. But once again, there is no record of this in any surviving documents.

In all, then, there is no reliable evidence that either of the two villages ever existed. Yet settlements have no doubt been lost to the sea along this stretch of coast. It's also quite possible some were lost in the sixteenth century as tradition claims – whether to floods or more gradual erosion. Given the lack of records, it's more likely they were smaller than villages: isolated farmsteads, perhaps, or hamlets. The *Thorpe* does appear to be a Georgian invention. But might the names have deeper roots? Perhaps a lost farmstead north of Blackpool was once part of the Singleton Estate. Or another to the south was known as Waddum or Waddam (in Old English, this is an appropriately watery and flood-prone name). Unfortunately, due to rising seas, we're unlikely to ever learn more, with any last traces becoming increasingly inaccessible or already lost to erosion.

Having failed to reach the Pennystone on the lowest tide of the year, I woke the next morning with other plans. Yet on the way to fill the small plastic kettle, I looked out to a clear, still day. With the sun just risen, the cliff cast long shadows out across the foreshore. I found binoculars and returned to the window. Today, beyond a distant strip of flushed sand, the Pennystone broke the surface of a calm blue sea. According to the tide table, tomorrow's low would be considerably higher than today's, with the rest of the week higher still. I slipped the teabag back into its sachet. If I wanted one last try, it would have to be now.

Once again, I crossed the tram rails and headed down to the shore, past dated concrete walls shaped to look like rocks. Later, I learned Bispham's sea defences had been built in the 1980s and were now considered 'life expired'. Blackpool's 'Hold the Line' policy meant their replacement would begin next year – at a cost of £61.2 million for this mile-and-a-half stretch (two decades earlier, Blackpool's central sea wall and promenade had been replaced at a cost of £73 million). With one of the longest promenades in the world, the ongoing project of defending Blackpool against the sea would remain a vast undertaking.

Glancing back towards shore from out on the sands, the scale of the task felt inhuman.

Beneath a washed-clean sky, the Pennystone remained surrounded by sea. Today, though, without the chop, I could wade a little closer. Again, in search of a shallow approach, I tried from various directions, and each altered the shape and character of the Pennystone (with the serpentine sea monster first turning lumpen and squat, before dividing into misshapen flukes). This time, the closest I could get was twenty feet. But that was all, and it was already almost low tide. Today, though, in the stillness, the water felt more like a pool. So I took a few, ever more tentative steps, feeling ahead with my toes for seabed sand. With the water at the very top of my boots I stopped again, and stood staring at the rock I'd read so much about. From this side it rose deep in shadow, holding on against south-westerly storms with a gnarled and stubborn resistance. Dark with mussels and dripping from overhangs, it appeared entirely of the sea.

Only now, I was no longer sure it was the Pennystone. Or at least not the Pennystone that originally inspired the tradition. Everyone writing in the 1800s located the Pennystone north of Blackpool. Reverend Bulpit describes it roughly where I stood now, 'half-a-mile west of Bispham station'. Thornber, though, appears to place it further north. And others describe it closer to Rossall or Cleveleys, where Halstead went in search of Singleton Thorpe. The lack of detail is perhaps unsurprising, given few landmarks in the nineteenth century. But it's possible that some earlier Pennystone has already slipped from view, even on the lowest spring tides. Since the early 1800s, sea levels have risen by around eight inches, a significant change on such flat, open sands. In Roman times, the coast lay perhaps a mile further west. So, many great rocks that once dominated the foreshore – relics of those earlier coastlines – have long since been lost to the sea.

When I'd met Michelle at the coffee shop, she was sure no one had seen the Pennystone in more than a century. Brian, a friend of hers, thought that by the time Victorian authors came to write of it, an earlier Pennystone had long since disappeared. Sounding a bit like Reverend Thornber, he described its location as 'the cause of many a good punch-up in the past'.

The day before, as I'd sat in the promenade shelter, a local woman said her family always called the rock nearest shore the Pennystone (after all, Carlin stood opposite Pennystone Road and dominated the shore). This made me wonder if, as an earlier Pennystone slipped from view, the name and tradition might be shifting again, to a more prominent feature on the foreshore. Perhaps in a way – long before penny pots of ale – that's what the name really meant. In Charles Hampson's article 'Place Names of the Fylde' (1944), it simply reflects the eroding coastline.

> The name PENNYSTONE is derived from pen 'point', naess 'headland', stan, 'stone', i.e. 'the stone at the point of the headland', indicating both the physical character of the coast line and its bounds in an earlier day.

Today, low tide was at 8.13 a.m. and by the time I checked it was 8.08. Opaque with suspended sediment, the water now barely rose and fell. As sand continued to settle, the water cleared just enough that I glimpsed the rippled sea floor and could see its depth. So I took one more step, and then another.

I was so close now I could almost reach out and touch it.

'Fuck it,' I thought. I stepped out, almost at the moment of low tide, and seawater surged inside my boots. Gingerly, I waded on. With the water now above my knees, I finally leaned out and touched two fingertips to the Pennystone – or at least to the nearest of its tight-lipped mussels. Seeing no sign of any iron ring,

I waded straight back out, with a surge of exhilaration that caught me by surprise.

'I TOUCHED THE PENNYSTONE' I texted to my family as I headed back to shore, to a fairly underwhelmed response.

Ruins of a cottage at Old Hallsands

10

Old Hallsands

Devon

I'd seen the ruins of Hallsands twice before, although only from a wooden platform at the top of the cliff. The first time, some fifteen years ago, the old village road still led down to two holiday homes. But on returning a decade later, the road had collapsed in a landslide and one house looked abandoned. Behind the other, a series of long ladders were tied together, allowing precarious access down the near-vertical face of the cliff. Beyond there, all that remained of Old Hallsands were a few ruined walls, clinging to rocky ledges high above the sea. It was hard to believe that as recently as the early 1900s this was a thriving fishing village, with thirty-seven cottages, a shop and bakery, a post office and a pub.

Given the loss of the only road in, I was keen to see the ruins from the sea. Hallsands is little more than an hour-and-a-half's drive from where I live, so I'd initially sounded out a few friends and neighbours who kayaked. No, they'd said, they wouldn't take me. Much of the reason was their unfamiliarity with Start Bay, with Start Point notorious for its currents and tide races. Eventually, though, I was put in touch with James. Not only was he a kayaker local to that stretch of the South Devon coast, but he was also a climber. My initial hope was that a low spring tide might reveal enough of a beach to land – if only for a while. But once James mentioned he was a climber, I'd begun wondering if it might also be possible to get up to the level of the old village.

I set off on a Wednesday after the school run, although it wasn't the lowest tide of the month – or even that week. The previous two days had been windy, with today's forecast a brief lull before the winds picked up again tomorrow. After that, we would slip into October and I might miss my chance. So I felt warily hopeful as I drove into Devon, where the weather was as capricious as it was leaving Cornwall. By the time I reached the narrow lanes that led to the sea, I'd seen everything from mist, blue skies and breezy sunshine to ominous cloud and heavy downpours. Far from any main roads, Hallsands already felt out on a limb, long before I reached lush grass growing down the middle of the road.

In a white Transit with a red kayak on the roof, James was easy to spot – not least as he was the only one parked by the beach. Emerging from the cab, he had a grey ponytail beneath a faded cap, and sun-browned skin from spending much of the summer on the water. This was the first time we'd met, so I had plenty of questions as we slid the kayak from the roof and carried it down to the water.

In a soft Devon accent, he said he often passed the old ruined village, usually taking kayakers out to Start Point. But he hadn't ever tried to land there, and had no idea what to expect today.

'You realise we might not be able to land?'

I did, I said. All week I'd been trying not to get my hopes up.

As we ferried gear from the van to the kayak, he told me that as a kid – when there was still a road down to the ruins – they'd often walked out there. Later, on still days, he'd sometimes kayaked into inlets below the cottages, and looked up between their roofless walls to the sky. For years, though, he'd only glimpsed them in passing from the sea.

As James packed the kayak, I mostly stood watching, reassured by the unhurried way he did things. Each task, however small, appeared to have his full attention. He placed spare clothes and two-way radios into dry bags and folded them shut, slipped spare paddles in beside our seats. Opening waterproof hatches, he stowed climbing ropes and harnesses, carabiners, hard hats. 'Just in case,' he said, sealing the circular rubber cover on the hatch with care.

From out on the water, what remained of the old Hallsands' access road sagged like a concrete hammock. Directly beneath, a sea-gouged chasm slanted into inky darkness deep inside the cliff. On the village side, a sea wall ended in old ragged stone patched with mortar, before a shuttered and seemingly abandoned Sea View: the only house to survive the storm that destroyed the village in 1917.

Below the looming cliff, the last of the ruined cottages perched on a wave-cut platform thirty feet above the sea. Previously about forty foot wide, the terrace was originally carved thousands of years ago, when sea levels were higher. Yet through the past century and a quarter, storms and high tides had reduced it to spurs of bare rock that reached out into the sea. Today, it seemed a strange and ill-advised place to build a village. Yet by the late 1800s, rich fishing grounds offshore at Skerries Bank meant the ledge was crowded with stone and whitewashed cottages.

This 'Hole below the cliff' – later Hallsands – was settled by the early 1600s, although fishermen watched for shoals of mullet there from at least the fourteenth century. Tucked into the lee of the cliff, the cottages were sheltered from prevailing south-westerly winds – and protected from storm waves by a wide shingle beach. The older houses were built close to the face of the cliff, with a few even built *into* the rock. At the northernmost end of the beach, a few hewn steps led up to a thatched cottage where the front door seemed to open into the cliff itself.

By the 1850s, the population of this narrow fishing village was over a hundred, with the same family names recurring again and again: Trout, Steer, Prettejohn, Lynn, Stone, Login, Patey, Mingo. In *A Londoner's Walk to the Land's End* (1855) the writer Walter White described a rugged cliff path to a wild, lonely part of

Devon. Below were 'about a dozen rude little cottages, some close to the shingle, others . . . on ledges and recesses of the cliff.' Entering Hallsands in deepening afternoon shadow, he doubted finding lodgings for the night, with the houses 'so out of proportion to the large families inhabiting them'. Yet at the corner of one large cottage hung 'a swinging sign, ambitiously inscribed *The London Inn*.' Inside, he found old and young fishermen sat drinking cider, while the 'ancient hostess' darned stockings by the window. Yet when asked about a bed for the night, she said no: she wouldn't 'take a gentleman in unless she could make him comfortable'.

There wasn't room enough upstairs for the family, she told White, let alone a stranger. Sometime later, after he suggested four chairs and a blanket in the parlour, she relented. So after cider in the 'kitchen' with the men, he found 'his bed ready, spread on a double rank of chairs.' And there he slept like a log, lulled by 'the solemn plunge of the surge upon the beach, not forty feet from the window'.

Today, the kayak slipped above the green of deeper water, sheltered by the cliff from the westerly breeze. Although almost two hours off low tide, ebb sand was already emerging near what was once the centre of the village. I was delighted, as it meant not only would we be able to land, but we'd also have plenty of time.

Our plan, then, was first to paddle out to the end of the village. In places, eroded inlets reached right back to the base of the cliff, leaving the southern ruins isolated on spurs of rock. So the stone had never been dismantled for reuse as was common elsewhere. Instead, as the whitewash and render weathered away, it left stone the colour of the cliff. Sometimes, it took a while for man-made angles to emerge from the rock: the unnatural straight line of a wall, a door jamb, perhaps, or a window ledge. Now and then we shipped paddles to drift closer, lulled by the rise and fall of the kayak, peering for remnants of what were once people's homes.

'Look,' said James, pointing towards shore. At the far end of the village, above the narrowest of ledges, were the very last traces of a building lost long ago. Squared holes were cut into the rock-face, presumably sockets for rafters or joists. From there on, it was nothing but cliff. Looking back as we turned at Long Rock, it gave a sense of the village fading from view, as it slipped further from the first- and second-hand stories of those who lived there.

By the late 1800s, the Hallsands population was over 150, with houses on both sides of a single narrow street. Almost everyone in the village made their living from the sea, either directly or indirectly, although a few also supplemented the fishing with trades such as blacksmith or carpenter. There was a shop and bakery known after the owners as Mingo's, with supplies brought in by pony and trap. The steep access road meant much came by sea, although the butcher brought his horse-drawn van across the beach.

Old Hallsands, *c.*1900

Old photographs show hens in the street, and a mix of thatched and slate-roofed cottages huddled behind low stone walls known as 'quays'. Crab pots are stacked on a wide, gently shelving shingle beach, with wooden rowboats pulled up out of reach of high tide; back then, they could be left on the shingle all year round. In rough weather, though, bringing boats in to shore could be difficult. So strong Newfoundland dogs – with their webbed feet and oily coats – were trained to swim out and retrieve a rope tied to a piece of wood. Until motorisation from the 1930s, the dogs were said to have been as essential to the Start Bay fishermen 'as the sheep-dog is to the farmer'. One of the Hallsanders' Newfoundlands was also famed locally for having dragged a drowning child from the sea before going to a cottage for help.

In some early photographs, washing is strung out to dry on the beach. On other days, pole frames on shore were hung with drying fish. When I checked one grainy photograph with a fisherman friend, he said they were 'ray backs'. Like other low-value fish, the Hallsanders used them as crab bait (since Victorian times, only the 'wings' of a skate or ray could be sold at the fishmongers, as the pale, creamy underside had a 'face' with lips too voluptuous and genitalia that looked 'too human'). Decades earlier, before his night at the London Inn, Walter White had been struck by the sight of rays hung to dry on the beach. 'The children', he wrote, 'were carrying piles of them from place to place on their heads.'

At the time, only the men went out fishing and setting crab pots, although the whole village turned out for the seine netting. At certain times of year, a hill-man or spotter kept watch from the cliff for shoals of mullet or mackerel. At the spotter's signal – a whistle or movement of an arm – a cry of 'Aye boat!' would pass through the village. With this, the women ran from cottages and 'the pub would empty out'. When the hill-man removed his bowler hat, the rowboats headed out to surround the fish. By that point everyone was quiet so as not to spook the fish. Eventually, when the slippery, heaving mass was pulled ashore, most of the village pitched in, including the women in their ankle-length skirts and white bonnets. A harsh living in an isolated spot, it made for a close-knit community.

'We all felt in those days one big happy family,' said Edith Patey of her childhood in the village, speaking in later life. 'When everyone was "in the same boat" so to speak. We were all humble and poor people. Sharing was uppermost in village life.'

As we approached the inlet, the kayak cut through shallows the colour of aqua glass. In places rocks broke the surface; elsewhere they were submerged and dark with drifting weed. Soon, the kayak grounded on sand.

Unrolling a dry bag, I found the maps I'd copied that week, which showed the cliff-line and high-water marks either side of the dredging: 1884, 1894, 1904 and 1915. Various buildings and other village features were also marked, along with the occupancy of houses two years before the storm that destroyed them. From the maps, we'd landed close to the village centre, by the slipway below the London Inn. As far as I could see, though, there was no longer any trace in the sea-worn rock. Instead, the eroded platform loomed above the low-tide sands, higher than a two-storey building. Wave scour, and tar lichens way above head height, showed most of the time it rose straight from the sea.

Once, this barren ledge was the heart of the village. By the end of the 1800s, the London Inn had been extended to include extra rooms, a piggery and stabling for the visiting packhorse men. In the summer months, pleasure steamers from Torquay and Dartmouth also stopped off with visitors, with the inn well known for its local white ale. Opposite the pub was Mingo's shop, as well as the Mission Room, which was used for religious meetings until a Bible Christian Chapel was built on the cliff in the 1850s. After that, it was a community reading room, used for sing-songs and shanty nights that drew friends and family from neighbouring villages. It was a tradition of 'making your own entertainment' that continued here long after Old Hallsands was lost. For the oral history project 'Guardians of the Reef', Jim Trout recalled similar evenings decades later at the nearby Hallsands Hotel, where the local fishermen sang and played mouth organs, with one Start Point lighthouse keeper on the spoons and another playing the bones (traditionally a pair of cattle ribs).

With the tide still falling for over an hour, we had plenty of time. Given my lack of climbing experience, James suggested he go off on a recce to check for routes up. With several ruins isolated out on rocky spurs, this would involve a number of climbs. 'I'll try this way first,' he said, heading out around rocks below the site of the old London Inn. And then he was gone.

Intensified by the wall of cliff, all the sounds of the sea seeped in. The tide was just low enough now to get out around promontories to inlets further south, where the first houses were lost more than a decade before the rest of the village. As I made my way round, I put a hand to rock. Exposed for more than a century, it was scoured a clean grey veined with quartz. More resistant, those dense white ridges flowed like water: faults and folds created by the unimaginable force of tectonic collision. Denuded of sand and shingle, it was these that weakened the rock: clefts and fissures, eventually hollowed out to the sea caves we'd seen from the kayak, that in time undermined the cliff. Yet it also made for beautifully sculptural rocks. Below the tide-line, some were studded with yellow limpets. Huddled in drifts between ridges of quartz, the molluscs sat tight on lifelong home scars they return to each low tide (having headed out to graze when the tide was in). The scars are worn by rotations of their shell. And here and there, the rock was marked with the circular grooves of those that had never returned.

Our first climb was to the southernmost houses of the village, up on an isolated promontory. From down on shore, the most striking wall was two storeys of stone, rising from the very edge of the rock. Its four window holes faced Start Point, but the lack of first-floor lintels gave it the look of turrets. Dramatic against fast-changing skies, it was like the Hallsanders' battlements confronting the sea. Either side, the wave-cut platform had eroded right back to the cliff, leaving inlets filled with fallen boulders. Of the two climbs we'd settled on earlier, this was the easiest, with James offering me a helmet but no harness or rope (although we'd need those for the second climb, he said).

Then he was off up the rocks like a goat. To begin with I was close behind, careful to watch exactly where he placed each foot – not least as I was faintly obsessed with his shoes. More like gloves, their soft black soles had five toes that moulded themselves to the rock. There was a spare precision in the way James moved from rock to rock, which again I found reassuring (all the while we weren't far from the ground). With no experience beyond scrambling over rocks at the beach, I began to enjoy the climb: the care in selecting a hold or ledge, the sensation of transferring my weight. Then I came to a halt.

Ahead, great boulders were wedged in a chasm. Over on the far side now, James had crossed with little more than a big, fluid step. But the gap was wide. An unwitting glance also confirmed it was heart-stoppingly deep. *Crevasse*, I thought, but didn't say. I couldn't imagine why he thought I'd be able to cross it. Serious doubts began to sidle in.

On hearing my noises of dissent, James goat-footed his way back down. From a casual lean, he recommended exact positions for hands and feet, places I should press my weight against rock – in an easy, unconcerned tone that I imagined worked well with children. Minutes later, on the boulders above, the flood of relief soon passed. I'd only have to cross it again coming down.

Eventually, though, I hauled myself up onto the promontory with concealed delight.

Our way was blocked by the turret wall, but a gap by the cliff led through to a small, room-like space hewn from the rock (similar places described by Walter White were fishermen's stores). Inside the main room, the floor was buried beneath the stone of fallen walls. Despite the exposure, in the lee of walls, stone lay among grassy carpets and cushions of thrift. It was far less barren than it looked from below. In the adjoining cottage, the walls were barely waist-high, and stonecrop and samphire flourished among rubble like an artfully planted rockery. This wasn't the whole room, though, as one side fell abruptly away to the shore. Treading with care, I reached a narrow doorway facing the sea, the threshold slate broken where generations of boot soles had worn it thin.

From there I stepped down to bare rock. High above the sea, I walked out as far as I dared. At the edge, all that grew were stunted succulents in gaps between several flagstones still laid roughly square. Against the odds, through a century of gales and storm waves, their weight appeared to have kept them in place. As far as I could tell – from the maps, old photographs and family descriptions – this small windswept plateau was once the home of William Trout, his wife Eliza Ann and their four young daughters.

I knew the layout of their cottage from reading *Sisters Against the Sea* (2005) by Ruth and Frank Milton: William Trout's only grandchild and his wife. The book goes on to tell the story of the daughters after the loss of Old Hallsands, but for me the early family detail had brought the village to life. William Trout was born in 1860, one of seven children who – as was common at the time – slept three or four to a bed, head to toe. A fisherman like his father and grandfather, William went on to marry a neighbour, Eliza Ann. Described by the family as quiet, prudent and God-fearing, she was descended from another branch of the

Trout family (with both her husband and fisherman father named William Trout). The couple's small, inherited cottage was second from the southern end of the village: two-up, two-down with a slate roof that had previously been thatched. Like many of the Hallsands cottages, it had limewashed walls, flagstone floors and a scullery out back. In the yard outside, not far from the door, was the privy with a bucket.

At home, life revolved around the cast-iron range, known as a Lidstone after the local company that made them. Beside a small black oven was an open grate, where a big, blackened kettle and crock pot hung from an iron bar. (As well as fish or rabbit stew with potatoes or 'dough boy' dumplings, Eliza Ann made 'composite pasties' – sweet one end and savoury the other – and 'seaweed pudding'). Before the Lidstone, back when the cottage was thatched, William's father 'could well remember the old open hearth which sent the smoke down the chimney, fogging their rooms, "smutting" everything'. Now, though, the range had pride of place, and was thoroughly cleaned and blackleaded every Friday. 'Living under the cliffs meant that even in midsummer, the sun had left the village by the late afternoon, and so the stove was lit practically all year round'.

Another reason it was kept lit were the wet clothes so common in fishing families (in Devon, as in Cornwall, nothing dries when the mizzle sets in). So the Trouts' clothes horse often steamed gently by the fire. Like the old Spurn lifeboatmen, the Start Bay fishermen wore no life preservers out at sea, although most couldn't swim. Instead, they wore heavy leather overtrousers, a cloth cap and hobnailed boots. There was also one 'buxom woman who carried her man on her back to the boat so that he would start the day dry' (after the village was lost, this was often said to have been the custom of all the Hallsands fishwives).

As for most of the villagers, money was tight for the Trout family. Through long winters, in rough weather or when fog hung over the village, the fishermen were sometimes unable to go to sea for weeks or even months. To make ends meet, William also laboured on local farms, sometimes paid in turnips, or allowed to catch rabbits to be stewed on the Lidstone. Another of the Hallsanders' winter jobs was making crab pots from willow withies. And while much of this was done outside, the fishermen also spent winter evenings by the fire making 'skippers': sharpened hazel sticks used to mend pots and keep the bait in place.

Then one spring morning in 1897, a noisy and unusual boat rounded Start Point and headed their way. At the time, some of the fishermen gathered on the beach, unsure if the boat was in trouble and prepared to go out to its aid. Soon enough, though, they learned it was a dredger from Plymouth, come to remove shingle just offshore of their village. This would be used for concrete to expand the naval dockyard, a contract won by the engineering firm Sir John Jackson Ltd. Alongside his engineering and shipping businesses, Sir John Jackson also had political ambitions, and would later be elected Conservative MP for Devonport in Plymouth. Initially, he'd applied to dredge the nearby Exe estuary. Yet there the main landowner (a major Conservative Party donor) had objected, claiming the scale of the proposal could seriously damage the Exmouth waterfront.

So instead, Sir John applied to the Board of Trade for a licence to dredge off Hallsands and neighbouring Beesands. A well-connected negotiator, he was granted the licence on very favourable terms, without the knowledge or consent of the villagers. Although the agreement allowed dredging below the low-water mark, a clause said the licence would be revoked 'if any damage was caused to the foreshore or district'.

By late spring, suction-pump dredgers and shuttle barges were removing 1,600 tons of shingle a day from the seabed off Hallsands. Already, the angle of the beach had changed, with both high- and low-water marks shifting inland. Alarmed, the villagers lodged complaints through their Liberal MP, Frank Mildmay. An inspection and inquiry followed that June, with the fishermen meeting representatives of Sir John Jackson Ltd. As well as describing how the disruption was affecting catches, the fishermen warned that a lowered beach would leave their houses at risk during storms.

This was countered by Sir John Jackson's men, who said holes in the seabed would simply refill with sand from offshore. The fishermen disagreed: shingle would also be dragged from their beach, until their homes were destroyed. Yet to bitter local disappointment, the inspector decided in favour of Sir John Jackson Ltd. The dredging, he said, was unlikely to pose any significant threat to the village. While accepting no liability for damage to the shoreline, Sir John Jackson Ltd paid the fishermen £4 each for disturbance to the fishing (plus a joint £20 'Christmas gratuity'). The licence was not revoked, and dredging continued as before. Again without the knowledge of locals, the company also obtained a further licence, this time to dredge *between* high- and low-water marks – so from the Hallsands foreshore itself.

By 1901, the villagers had lived with the dredgers outside their windows for four years. Directly in front of the village, the shingle beach had now fallen by up to twelve feet, leaving a sizeable gap beneath the quay steps and the shore. As a yardstick, the fishermen used Wilson's Rock near the London Inn, which before the dredging had barely protruded from the beach. Now, it was a fourteen-foot stack. Across the shore, other large rocks were also exposed, many of which had never previously been seen by the villagers. Speaking to a reporter from a local newspaper, the landlord of the London Inn pointed to a sea wall where 'people used to play capers with a donkey and make him jump it'. On the seaward side was a drop of some fifteen feet, 'enough to kill any donkey who took the wall now'.

During storms and high tides, waves now lashed the walls of the cottages. They'd also begun to scour out foundations, undermining the old sea walls and the London Inn. Sir John Jackson continued to deny responsibility, claiming storm damage was unrelated to the dredging. Yet with the plight of the village drawing the attention of local press, he offered a concession. The company would make good any damage caused by 'ordinary gales or tides' while extraction continued and for six months afterwards. By then, the Hallsanders had come to dread an easterly or south-easterly gale. Though far less common than prevailing south-westerlies, the lack of shingle had left the east-facing village dangerously exposed.

At particular risk was the southern end of the village. The Trouts' cottage stood forward of its neighbours, and spring high tides now came within three feet of their home – in the past, it had been more than seventy feet. The protective pebble ridge they'd looked out on was gone, with Sir John required to replace the footings of their failing sea wall with concrete. Without the wall they could lose this end of the road: their only access to the rest of the village. By now, cracks had also begun to appear in the yard outside the Trouts' door. But as fast as William filled them, new cracks opened up. All the while, outside their window, the noise and dredging continued apace.

As winter approached, a new Board of Trade inspector warned a severe storm could now cause major damage to the village. With the local fishermen increasingly desperate, there were confrontations on the beach with Sir John's dredger men. In neighbouring Beesands, this culminated in fishermen hauling the dredging buoys ashore, which led to the retreat of the dredgers. So Hallsands fishermen threatened to do the same. By then, though, unbeknown to the villagers, the Board of Trade had decided to halt the dredging. After almost five years, Sir John Jackson's licence was revoked, and by 8 January 1902 the dredgers were gone.

To begin with, there were celebrations at the London Inn. The Hallsanders continued to have fears and misgivings, but through spring their beach began to reform. By late summer, the increase in sand and shingle meant Wilson's Rock had reduced in height by almost half. Throughout the disruption to fishing that came with the dredging, families like the Trouts had struggled to make ends meet. But as life returned to something like normal, there were hopes that the worst may have passed.

That winter, though, the first easterly storms soon scoured away the sand and shingle that had returned over summer. In the new year, gale after gale saw the Trouts staying up all night, huddled around the fire behind battened windows. With three young daughters now, Eliza Ann would pray for their safety and for the wind to subside. At times now, the force of waves flung open the front door, flooding the kitchen and filling it with shingle. One wild night, shovelling away stones so the door could be closed, William's hurricane lantern blew out and he was almost blown over in the dark. Again and again that winter, the family swept out water and William trowelled mortar into cracks and holes.

With the Trouts' cottage second from the end, the only house more exposed than their own was Aunt Ann's next door. So early that February, with another easterly gale on its way, Ann Trout took her furniture and moved in with her niece up the road. By morning her cottage was in ruins. With the foundations washed out, the seaward wall had collapsed overnight, taking part of the upstairs and downstairs rooms. 'Quite one third of the house has disappeared,' wrote a reporter for the *Western Morning News*.

Within days, parts of the sea wall and road had also collapsed, leaving the Trouts' cottage protected only by 'planks and furze [gorse]'. By then, their other neighbours – John Gillard, his wife and two children – had also taken their furniture and moved in with a neighbour up the street. Yet outside that house, the sea wall also showed signs of subsidence, and within a day they'd all had to move again.

The storm damage wasn't limited to the southern end of the village. At the London Inn, the sea wall had also slipped, allowing waves to wash out the compacted ground behind. At high tide, the sea now surged into what had been a small courtyard. Nearby, the inn's glass 'teahouse' was shored up with planks and the entrance porch undermined. Undeterred, customers began to enter through the cellar instead. The only reason one sea wall had survived the gale, locals told a reporter, was because a fisherman and his son had spent Sunday morning up to their waists in freezing water, holding stones in place as the sea washed them out. 'Surveying the cottages from the sand,' wrote the journalist, 'gives one the impression that the whole place is crumbling and sinking down, and so fragile does it appear that one wonders why the place is not evacuated'.

Postcard of the London Inn after storm damage, 1903

Campaigning for compensation on behalf of the villagers, their MP Frank Mildmay tabled parliamentary questions, organised meetings in the Mission Room and secured the services of the engineer and geologist Richard Hansford Worth. A 'gentleman' with a long white beard, he was described by friends as 'the last of that vanished race of Victorian antiquaries' and would go on to act for the villagers unpaid. His reports showed Hallsands' beach shingle was not of local origin, and he concluded that its loss through dredging would be permanent. Emphasising the stability of Hallsands beach through previous centuries – albeit with fluctuations – the engineer was in no doubt that the 'dredging had contributed on no small degree to the disaster'. We know now that Start Bay is a 'closed system', with the cliffs at either end preventing the loss or replenishment of shingle by long-shore drift. So while beach levels vary naturally as shingle shifts from one part of the bay to another, the overall quantity had been roughly constant for thousands of years. As the fishermen had predicted, holes left by the dredgers appeared to have been filled by shingle dragged offshore from Hallsands beach.

Later that year, as a result of campaigning, an offer of £1,000 compensation was made to the villagers. With half from Sir John Jackson Ltd and half from the government, it was to pay for new sea defences, along with the repair and replacement of houses lost or damaged in the storms. Yet quotes supplied to Hansford Worth showed the cost of sea walls alone would be more than was offered. As not everyone in the village was willing to sign, the offer was rejected. But the Hallsanders now faced a dilemma. Holding out for more money would delay the work, leaving the village at risk through the coming winter. Eventually, with negotiations dragging on, Frank Mildmay personally guaranteed a further £1,500 so work could begin.

Given the location, this was beset with problems. By the first autumn storms, the only wall finished was the southern sea wall in front of the Trouts' cottage. With winter approaching, the rest was now a rushed battle against time and tide. 'Not one wall', said Hansford Worth, 'has been constructed that has not within a very few days of its completion received the full brunt of a heavy sea long before the concrete could acquire anything approaching its ultimate solidity'.

That December, it was the northern end of the village that took the brunt of a severe south-easterly gale. With the storm raging over a weekend, a reporter for the *Western Morning News* reached the village on the Monday morning. By then, the northern stone quay had been lost, and he found William Login salvaging furniture from his ruined home. The gale had blown hard all Saturday, William said, with the tide coming in that afternoon 'shaking everything to pieces'. Instead of abating, the wind rose. As large stones battered their quay, William and his father 'soon saw that our cottages would come down.' While the old stone sea wall withstood the onslaught for a couple of hours, by midnight the quay gave way. 'In about half an hour,' William told the reporter 'all that stood on it was sucked away like feathers, and the front of our houses fell out'.

William's wife and seven children had spent the night in the Mission Room. Next door, his father's house was near destroyed. 'The front walls are entirely gone, leaving the whole of the interior visible; the roof has partially collapsed, and the ground floor overhangs the chasm in front, held together by joists'. Yet 'Strangely enough, the back of Robert [Login's] house is still considered habitable, and his family are still occupying the kitchen and one bedroom'.

Another neighbour, Mr Barber, was equally unwilling to leave. Only when the sea surged over his house did he finally agree to be hauled up the cliff by rope (today, that beach is known as Barber Cove). In the past, before the loss of the beach, the Hallsanders said they'd known worse storms that had caused no damage. But on Saturday night 'the village itself seemed part of the sea'.

That winter saw the Trouts paddling around in their yard almost to their knees, and the kitchen regularly flooded. Their cottage was now exposed on the end, and the only reason it wasn't lost like Ann Trout's was the protection of Hansford Worth's sea wall. Yet unnervingly, the seaward wall of their cottage was showing signs of instability, with scouring of the stonework dislodging the lintels. William could only fill the cracks for so long. Eventually, before the rest of the cottage went with it, the failing wall was taken down and replaced.

By February, another of the village's central sea walls had collapsed. As the ground washed out from behind, it left a chasm right across the street. Until a temporary plank footbridge was built, the Trouts' end of the village was cut off from the rest – along with the piped spring water supply. By then, there was also no longer access to Barber Cove in the north: the only way to reach the cottages now was via a thirty-foot ladder from the beach at low tide.

Later, searching eBay idly for old postcards of Hallsands, I came across a striking photograph of the plank bridge over the chasm (known locally as a 'chang'). A hen had wandered out onto the planks, above a gaping ravine that spanned the street and disappeared into one of the cottages. Although its thatched roof remained intact, a great slice of the front wall had collapsed into the hole, exposing floorboards and the patterned wallpaper of an upstairs bedroom. Even in faded sepia, the dark gash in the cottage is shocking. Postmarked Hallsands Nov 1904, it suggests not only was the post office open as usual, but also the crumbling village was attracting tourists.

Increasingly, Hallsands houses were being lost in this way. To begin with, the early cottages had been built on platforms of rock. Yet as the village expanded, houses were also built in between. This ground appeared solid: infilled with compacted blown sand and shingle, and the surface bound with the roots of salt-loving plants. But when sea walls failed, waves swept away this softer ground, and buildings were swallowed by the changs.

Other houses were simply battered by the sea and stones. That March, Aunt Ann Trout, now seventy-five, was washed out yet again. Her nephew and his wife had prepared for the storm by moving beds away from windows nailed over with boards. But by 4.30 a.m., waves had torn them away and smashed the glass. Soon,

Plank bridge over a chasm, 1901

the sea had ripped off the thatch and was pouring into rooms from above. Aunt Ann's nephew described how they'd had to 'bore holes in the bedroom floor to let it down into the kitchen' and then another hole in the kitchen wall for the water to escape.

Since the early failure of its own sea wall, the London Inn had suffered repeated damage. After the season's first gale, the landlord told a reporter how when the glasshouse collapsed, two fishermen and two coastguards helped retrieve his bedroom furniture.

> The roof came down on us and we had a narrow escape . . . Then the gable gave way, tearing down the stove and nearly blinding us with dust. It was with the greatest difficulty that we grasped things to prevent us falling into the surf . . . We had just got out the last of the furniture when the whole pile went like a pack of cards. I heard the bystanders shout, 'What has become of the men?'

Earlier in the day, men employed to build Hansford Worth's sea walls had helped make a temporary bridge so customers could still enter the pub. Yet before long that too was swept out to sea. When the gale subsided, as well as the 'teahouse' and makeshift bridge, the inn had lost its kitchen, a bedroom and the beer cellar. The cider kegs had been saved, though, and for a time a makeshift bar was set up in a building opposite. By late spring, the chasm had widened and the London Inn was in ruins.

That year, Hansford Worth produced a map of Hallsands showing the high-water marks of 1894 and 1904. They are shown as almost a hundred feet apart. Above his signature is written:

HOUSES SHADED BLACK, DESTROYED
HOUSES HATCHED, DAMAGED AND SOME DOOMED

'The general opinion at Hallsands,' noted Hansford Worth, 'appears to be that it's time enough to leave when the house leaves you.' In *Hallsands: A Village Betrayed* (2002), Steve Melia suggests one reason for the reluctance to leave was that most Hallsanders owned their own homes, which was unusual at the time (additionally, the absence of a single powerful landlord may have weakened opposition to the dredging and claims for compensation). Unsurprisingly, the tenacity and stoicism of the villagers often featured in local press reports. 'The Hallsander is a study for the psychologist at the moment', wrote one *Western Daily Mercury* journalist. 'Perhaps it is because the inherent fortitude of their race and calling come to their aid, and cause them to observe this outwards show of remarkable calmness.'

With negotiations for compensation ongoing, the *Western Morning News* began a relief fund. Shocked by reports and photographs of storm damage, readers donated a total of £631 – worth more than £50,000 today – which would be used to build four houses at the top of the cliff. Officially Mildmay

Cottages, they would become known as the Western Morning News houses.

Given the extent of the damage over winter, the official offer of compensation for the village as a whole was raised to £3,500. This still involved no acceptance of liability, and was conditional on every householder agreeing the settlement would be final. Later, locals would also learn that revoking the licence had not actually ended the dredging. Instead, Sir John Jackson Ltd had begun removing sand and shingle from the Skerries Bank further offshore, unchallenged and without permission. This continued for another two years, while Hallsands homes were being lost to the sea.

With insufficient money to rebuild the village inland, the Hallsanders chose to use the compensation to fund repairs to damaged cottages and build stronger sea walls. By 1906 Hansford Worth's new concrete walls were in place, defending a village now reduced to twenty-five houses.

Over the next decade, with the fishing no longer disrupted, life in the village returned to some kind of normality. Like others, the Trout family felt more secure behind their new sea wall. One day in 1908, though, the three eldest daughters came home from school to find their father ill after a soaking at sea. William struggled to return to fishing, and it was soon clear he no longer had the strength to haul pots. Following a diagnosis of what the family called 'split lung', they were told he would never go back to sea. With no son to take on his two-man fishing partnership, the family feared destitution: already, the doctor was sometimes paid with a crab. So eventually, with her mother's fearful and grudging consent, the eldest daughter Patience left school and took her father's place in the boat with her uncle. Aged thirteen but gawky and strong, she was partnered the following season by her younger sister Ella. With Eliza Ann always at the window watching for their safe return, the pair became known – and respected – by the fishermen as 'the maidens' (later, during the First World War, Ella would receive an OBE for rowing out a mile to rescue a crewman clinging to the wreckage of a bombed ship). In 1910, less than a year after his daughters had been fishing full-time, William died of his lung condition at home. That same year, Sir John Jackson was elected Conservative MP for Devonport.

In *Sisters Against the Sea*, William Trout's grandson describes the family's recollection of the autumn storms of 1916. Over the previous decade, despite the exposure of their now end cottage, the seafaring sisters had grown confident in the concrete defences outside their kitchen window. 'So when a strong easterly wind whipped the sea over their sea wall . . . Patience and Ella complacently swept the water out of their kitchen. Eliza Ann, though, grew increasingly uneasy.' Following further gales in October, the telltale signs of undermining began to appear. Repeatedly, as they'd seen their father do before, Patience and Ella filled gaping cracks in the walls with mortar. Soon, though, material was also washing out from inside the sea wall – and once again they had to walk on planks across a chasm to their home. 'Eliza Ann was petrified,' say the family. In 1904, the waves had swept right over their house. 'In those days she had had a husband to lean on. Now she was alone with her children.' Days later, after Uncle Jack deemed their cottage unsafe, Eliza Ann and her four daughters moved up the street to a room at Uncle Bob's house. By next morning, high tide had already washed out the plank bridge and caused further damage to the cottage. Having fought so hard to remain, the Trout family would not return to their sea-battered home.

From the ruined doorway up on the platform, I looked out at the remains of the flagstone floor. It was likely their scullery or kitchen, where William and his family swept out shingle and seawater after gales. Now at the edge of barren rock, splashed with white, the last slates were a lookout for gulls.

*

Back down on shore – by way of the gaping crevasse – James and I headed back to the kayak for the climbing gear. The tide was now close to its lowest ebb, and I made my way out around smooth remnants of Hansford Worth's sea walls. In old photographs, the new concrete was angular: sharp-edged above a narrow beach. Today, the fallen, sea-worn boulders were embedded in the sand. Elsewhere, the concrete had been poured directly onto rock at the base of the wave-cut platform. Beneath slippery fringes of wrack, the scoured cement surfaces were pimpled with local shingle used in the mix. Very gradually, it was washing free to return to the shore.

While James sorted ropes at the kayak, I waited below an isolated wall high on a spur of rock. This was the other place I hoped to reach. On my first visit to Hallsands many years earlier, the wall looked much as it had for decades: the gable end of a two-storey cottage, with a central stone chimney-breast and windows that looked out to Start Point. Once the viewing platform was built on the cliff, the wall had become a central and resonant feature in long-lens photographs of the ruined village. Now, though, the window lintels and triangle of the gable were gone. Piece by piece, it was losing its *houseness*.

From below, I watched James toe his way up rock that was close to vertical. This time I wore a harness clipped to a rope, which he secured to hidden anchor rocks above. Down near shore, the rock was smooth and worn, and that first stretch like placing hands to an elephant's flank. Yet up out of reach of ordinary tides, the sheared ledges were sharp beneath my fingers. Placing one hand or one angled foot at a time, I was unused to such considered movement – although secure, this time, in a harness. Nevertheless, once again I scrambled up onto the top with relief. James's route had brought us up behind the gable end. Against the cliff-face, samphire flourished from stonework around once-plastered rock, where another Hallsands family had made use of every nook on their wave-cut ledge. Out beyond the narrow promontory, beneath indigo cloud, the changeling sea was now a milky turquoise. Glimpsing 'inside' the cottage through a ragged gap in the wall, I made my way round over fallen stone and thin fragments of roofing slate.

Despite a relatively settled decade, records seen by Steve Melia show that two years before Hallsands was lost, villagers clearly had concerns. Following a cliff fall in 1915, Mr T. Barber – of Barber Cove and a former chartered engineer – had written to several public bodies. 'It is evident,' he told the District Council, 'that unless steps are taken during the ensuing summer to provide an adequate sea wall right along the front, the village will become untenable.'

This was mid First World War and no action was taken. The following year, when the Trout family were finally forced to leave their cottage, a civil servant at the Board of Trade wrote the following note: 'Mr Barber is evidently an old man. He has known Hallsands intimately for 62 years and does not like being told what to do. If there was anything in this surely we would have heard from the District Council or Mr Mildmay.'

On Thursday, 25 January 1917, as the Barber family had feared, one of the houses in their cove suffered storm damage. The following day, rather than abating, the south-easterly gale intensified. With a high spring tide due at 8 p.m., the Hallsands fishermen began hauling boats up into the street before dark. As this was wartime, there were fewer younger men in the village than usual. As the tide rose and conditions continued to deteriorate, some families evacuated their children to the Western Morning News houses up on the cliff.

Aged seventeen at the time, Edith Patey recalled that night towards the end of her life. Their cottage was one of a row facing Wilson's Rock, and by the time her father returned from shifting boats, the windows were shuttered and battened against the wind and rising tide. 'Dad came in the back door,' she told a reporter in 1970. 'So Mum got his tea ready.'

With the sea roaring outside the battened windows, her father went through to the scullery to wash his hands. At that moment the walls came toppling down, and he grabbed the door frame as the floor opened up. 'We felt like being right in the sea,' Edith said. 'The roaring waves bouncing over us, the rafters all breaking in. We could see the white waves foaming underneath the floors. The sea came down the chimney'.

'Well Dad calmly knew the safest place we could huddle together,' she said. He moved furniture and slung up a sail to protect them. 'To this very day that safe place is still there, where we were all saved.'

With the waves reaching roof height, some houses were destroyed from above. Trapped inside, families ripped up floor-boards so seawater could pour downstairs, as they tried to prevent collapse. All through the hours of high tide, it remained too dangerous for people to leave. Forty-foot waves hurled shingle and exploded against cottage walls, as Hallsanders hunkered by lamplight against the roar and tremor of the sea. Slate roofs were torn off, and fires extinguished as seawater poured down chimneys. Although Hansford Worth's sea walls would survive the onslaught, overtopping waves washed out the ground behind. Cavities opened up beneath houses and the sea seethed in, flushing out foundations until walls built on sand collapsed. One fisherman, James Lynn, described seeing 'two huge waves crash against his house and knock most of the front of it clean in. The lamp was extinguished, and the people were in utter darkness'.

By midnight, four houses had been destroyed and all were damaged. But although the storm continued to rage, the respite of low tide now allowed people trapped in their homes to escape. In the cold hours before dawn, they made their way to safety up the flooded village street, avoiding the wreckage of neighbours' homes and gaping chasms where the ground had opened up. Well aware they had no more than the brief reprieve of low tide, people salvaged what little they could carry. The last baby to be born in the village – seven-day-old Jack Lynn – was carried up the cliff in a fisherman's mawn: a willow basket used to hold fish.

As feared, the village was lost on the following high tide, as waves surged back in against weakened buildings. When local journalists arrived, it was to utter devastation. Along the narrow, torn-up street, fallen walls were like gaping wounds in the cottages. Bare rafters were exposed like bones. There were shattered slates and sodden heaps of thatch. Like the scene of a shipwreck, splintered timber, fishing gear and broken furniture was strewn across the shore and drifted at sea.

Incredibly, all seventy-nine villagers survived without serious injury. Yet twenty-four families were now left homeless, some having lost their livelihoods. By the time the Trout sisters scrambled over rocks to see what had become of their cottage, all that remained was the rebuilt seaward wall. The rest had collapsed under the weight of the sea. A photograph shows twenty-year-old Ella in a long coat and woollen hat, staring straight at the camera outside a cottage reduced to matchwood and rubble. Over the following days, the sisters would arrange for someone to dig the Lidstone from the debris.

'What are we going to do?' one fisherman asked a reporter, looking out at the devastated village. 'We have spent the whole of our lives here fishing. We know no other trade, and we are useless. We have no homes, much of our furniture is lost. I tell it's hard, very hard, for our wives and families. It's all gone.'

Up on the narrow promontory, I walked out onto what was once the floor of a living room. A fragment of back wall stood tucked against the cliff, where a row of misshapen joist holes showed the low height of the ceiling. Side-on to the sea, the remnant of gable end was strengthened by the stone of a chimney and hearth. Crouching before the hearth's worm-eaten lintel, I caught an incongruous glimpse of cobwebs thick with dust up the chimney. It was here that generations sat before the fire, thawing wet feet and cutting skipper sticks, filling the dragged-in bathtub on a Saturday night with another kettle of hot between each of the bathers. At least until that last January night, when so many huddled against the sound and fury of the sea.

Now, the floor before the fireplace was barren rock: scoured by a century of wind and waves and driving rain, darkened by a passing shower.

A year after the storm's devastation, an independent report received by the Treasury recommended compensation of £10,500. 'If we offer at once,' responded the Assistant Secretary to the Treasury, 'we shall only be pressed for more – the Hallsands fishermen, as past history shows, are past masters in squeezing. One sympathises with them in the disaster which has overtaken them, but a year or more has now elapsed, and it is probable that by now they have managed to get homes and a livelihood.'

In truth, many were still overcrowding the homes of family and friends. While they fought for compensation, some had rented rooms in neighbouring Beesands; in summer, others returned to live in their derelict cottages or camp among the ruins. Another branch of the Trout family reroofed the old Mingo shop, where they lived until once again the sea washed them out and they moved into the loft above the chapel.

Eventually, a lower payment of £6,000 was made in 'full and final settlement' of the villagers' claim. Although twenty-five cottages had been lost, delays and inflation left enough money for only ten new houses to be built: Fordsworth Cottages, in what is now North Hallsands. Those who'd previously owned their own homes were also shocked to learn they'd have to pay rent for the rest of their lives. By the time the houses were built, a separate inquiry found Sir John Jackson guilty of overcharging the nation on war contracts. After resigning from Parliament in disgrace in 1918, he died a year later.

Ruins of Hallsands' Bible Christian Chapel

With or without the dredging, the village of Hallsands would in time have been lost to the sea. More recent research suggests the dredging was followed by three decades when shingle was anyway shifting north in Start Bay (due to the effect of the North Atlantic Oscillation on the position and intensity of the jet stream). So the beach at Hallsands is also likely to have been narrowing naturally. Yet there is little doubt that the dredging hastened the loss of its beach. If the fishermen's early warnings had been heeded, who knows how long the village would have survived. As beach levels have never recovered, many locals believe the effects of the dredging are still felt today.

During the notorious storms of 2014, both Beesands and North Hallsands suffered considerable damage, including the loss of roads. In Beesands, the concrete sea wall was soon repaired.

Yet in contrast, despite 'sympathetic noises', the policy for the thirty-odd houses of North Hallsands is 'No active intervention' (one reason given is the now high concentration of second homes and holiday lets). So while residents have raised money for their own boulder defences, in future no public money will be spent defending the village. For those with ancestors who lost homes in Old Hallsands, it is considered a second betrayal.

Up on the cliff-top today, the old chapel teeters at the edge in ruins. Fordsworth Cottages are set further back. But up near the chapel, the colourful Western Morning News houses stand only feet from the edge; although scheduled for demolition in 1986, residents overturned the order and continue to live there.

A few days earlier, I'd come across some old British Pathé newsreel footage, the kind once shown in cinemas before the main film. Shot in 1960, four decades after the loss of the village, it featured Elizabeth Prettejohn, the last resident of Old Hallsands.

While every cottage was damaged or destroyed in the storm, the highest house survived, and was habitable once its roof was repaired. This belonged to the Prettejohn family, former owners of the London Inn – which they'd sold before the first storm damage. Born at the inn in 1884, Elizabeth was the youngest of seven. Aged thirty-three when the village was lost, she would return to the family home within a year, and for decades looked after her brother there, while he made nets and sails for local fishermen. After his death in 1952, Elizabeth stayed on alone. By then she was a self-appointed guide for the summer 'trippers' who came to look around the Hallsands ruins, with 'GUIDE' painted on the wall of her cottage.

In honeyed colour, the newsreel shows a very different place to the ruins I looked out on now. Filmed more than sixty years ago, the village is caught midway between now and the years before the dredging. The grassy wave-cut platform is scattered with gaunt house-shaped ruins. Behind eroding sea walls, there are still remnants of window frames and chimney pots, stone hearths with tufts of grass in place of a mantelpiece. Somewhere there was also the safe place where Edith Patey's family had crouched beneath her father's sail.

'The once proud fishing village of Old Hallsands,' intones the narrator, much like the one describing bones at Dunwich. 'Today it is deserted but for one person, the last inhabitant and keeper of memories . . . Nearly eighty and refusing to give way to the irresistible advance of the sea, Miss Elizabeth Prettejohn continues to live her strange but full life.' In a brown belted coat and headscarf, she clambers among the ruins collecting firewood, and feeds hens that range free among the ruins and in her cottage with the cats. Several times, tugging on a crab line or wandering among the ruins, she pauses to look out to sea and tilts her lined and weathered face to the sun.

By then, her only remaining neighbour was the youngest of the Trout sisters, up on the cliff. Equally unwilling to leave where she'd grown up, Edith was now a recluse, in what would become an increasingly dilapidated Trout's Hotel. The sisters' story, though, had been one of success. The idea for the hotel had come to Ella – outgoing, single-minded and now with an OBE – while out fishing with Patience. Part-built by the sisters themselves (they even made the concrete blocks), the hotel was paid for using the family's compensation alongside money from fishing and a bank loan. After opening in 1925, the sisters ran it as a thriving, fashionable and unusual business alongside the fishing – until Patience and Ella's deaths in 1949 and 1952. As the fourth Trout sister had married, this left Edith as sole proprietor, which led to the hotel's closure in 1959.

Over the next sixteen years, its uncut lawns were overgrown with brambles, dock and giant hogweed. In *Sisters Against the Sea*, Edith's relatives describe their fortnightly trips to bring groceries. By then, visitors to the ruined village were also curious about the seemingly abandoned Trout's Hotel, with some wandering into the garden to peer through windows. So Edith began to keep the curtains drawn. With the electricity cut off, she moved about by candlelight, heating tins of soup on a driftwood fire. In time, swollen with damp, the back door stuck fast, and for the next twelve years the family – like Edith herself – had to enter through the downstairs toilet window. Inevitably, both Edith and Trout's Hotel drew gossip and speculation, with one local newspaper headlining a piece 'The strange story of the hotel that never has any guests . . . or vacancies.'

To the family, Edith seemed content with her own company, whether shut up inside the hotel, beachcombing down at Barber Cove, or wandering the ruined village. In time, though, even Elizabeth Prettejohn became reluctant to approach her. Sometimes, on their visits, the family tried to get Edith to move out of the hotel. 'No,' she'd reply. 'Got to stay here and see to this place.' Eventually, in 1975, she died of hypothermia and self-neglect. When the family came to clear out the hotel, they found the few rooms she'd used crammed with driftwood. Beneath makeshift clothes lines every surface was cluttered with tins and milk bottles, hundreds of stale and mouldy loaves, bags of sugar 'like blocks of concrete'. Yet the rest of the hotel was as it was when it closed. In the sunroom were still glass-topped tables and Lloyd Loom wicker chairs. Snow-white linen lay neatly folded in the sideboard, and the hotel silver shone as it had when cleared away in September 1959. Even the kitchen calendar remained on that date.

Eleven years after the death of Elizabeth Prettejohn at the age of eighty, it was the end of another last link to Old Hallsands.

From up on the rock by the hearth, I could see across the inlet to where the old heart of the village had now slipped into afternoon shadow. On that barren platform was once Mingo's shop, a quay and slipway, the Mission Room, rows of cottages, the old London Inn. Yet none of it would reach the end of the First World War.

It was a sense of stopped time I'd felt repeatedly in these places lost to the sea. Hallsands' old fishing cottages would never move

Ruins of a cottage at Old Hallsands

on. They would not be connected to mains water or electricity. They would never be converted to holiday lets or second homes with stunning sea views. There would be no Farrow and Ball painted hearths, no sea-life motifs, no staged photographs with cut flowers and croissants.

Instead, there were just sloping ribs of rock. Levelled in places for a cottage floor, and grooved – like the limpets' home scars – with channels to drain seawater and rain. There was a ruined corner where two walls once met, an edge of stone where a century ago older Hallsanders would wait for someone to stop and pass the time. In the place where Eliza Ann often hesitated before crossing the plank bridge over the chang, there was nothing but air. A century on, very little remained but rock. How long would it be – how many easterly gales – before there was no longer any trace that people lived here?

Afterword

Some months after my visit to the Isle of Sheppey, another house was lost to the sea. With little warning, the villa-style bungalow went over the cliff at the end of Surf Crescent. The owner, Emma, was in her forties, and had bought the house two years earlier for herself and her children – under the impression it would last forty years. But arriving home from work one Friday in June, she noticed bricks in the driveway had begun to separate. Later that evening, sat on her sofa with a glass of wine, she heard a disturbing 'crackling and crunching' and the blinds fell off the wall. Well aware of the dangers, the family picked up their phones and ran, the children without any shoes.

Later that night, their driveway, car and front garden fell part-way down the cliff, to lie in a landslide lake. Over the weekend, as news crews sent up drones for photographs, part of the house hung out over the edge. Then overnight the cliff subsided and the house went over, although nobody heard it go. In that week's newspapers, aerial photographs were stamped 'YESTERDAY' and 'TODAY'. The second shows the bungalow's timber walls, windows and furniture scattered down the cliff like matchstick smithereens. Two years on, when I checked Google Maps, the end of Surf Crescent was now a ghost road leading out over the cliff.

Over the coming century, the rate of loss there is expected to double at least. On some parts of the British coast, that rate will be even faster; in Yorkshire, of course, the soft Holderness cliffs are already retreating by more than two metres a year. Much of that predicted increase will be due to climate change and rising seas. After thousands of years of stable sea level, it's now rising by over four millimetres a year. Over coming decades, that rate is expected to accelerate, to levels not seen since the Mesolithic. Depending on future greenhouse gas emissions, current models suggest a possible global sea-level rise of one metre by the end of the century. The heating climate will also increase storminess in many regions, raising wave heights and the power of storm surges. In other parts of the world, particularly Asia, the impacts will be far greater and more immediate. Human settlements have always concentrated along coasts and estuaries, and this century, as vast swathes of land fall below the high-tide line, hundreds of millions of people will be forced from their homes. In the Pacific, a one-metre rise will leave some currently inhabited islands entirely submerged.

As I was nearing the end of the book, a chance conversation led me to the history slider on Google Earth Pro. This allowed me to revisit fast-eroding coastlines like those at Happisburgh, Blackgang Chine and Skipsea, and travel back through earlier decades. Of course, it became an obsession. Slipping back and forth through time in aerial photographs, I was able to control the sea's advance or retreat: watch houses appear on cliff-tops and vanish, caravan parks rise and fall, the retreat of fibreglass dinosaurs. As so often in the two years I'd wandered the eroding edges of Britain and Ireland, I was struck by the contrast of human history against the vast sweep of geological time. Again and again I was reminded that the familiar outline of these islands – that we might draw if asked – is no more than a moment in time.

Yet in so many ways we have always tried to hold back the tide, from ritual and prayer, and the clanging of church bells, to artificial reefs and concrete sea walls. Both here and across the world, this coming century will require increasingly difficult and contentious decisions around what to protect and for how long.

Looking out over what was once a prehistoric forest

Acknowledgements

I am grateful to my agent Clare Alexander for wise guidance from the start, and my excellent editor Abi Scruby, who has taught me so much. My thanks also to Judy Spours for copy-editing, Lydia Blagden for the cover, and Caroline Westmore and all involved at John Murray. Thanks once again to Tracy Watts for her work on the maps, and to Pete Watson for permission to use his beautiful opening photograph of the Goodwin Sands (taken five miles from shore with a drone sent up from the Dover Sea Safari boat, with me just out of shot on the sands). I am also grateful for the financial support of a Society of Authors grant, and to Mark Richards for his early faith in me.

For generosity with their time and knowledge I would like to thank David Brown, Stuart Bacon, Juliette Gregson, Jane Hamilton, Michelle Harris, David Hoyle, Colin Johnson, Anthony Morris, Peter and Maureen Shakeshaft, and Aindrias de Staic. My appreciation also to Annabel Drysdale at Forvie National Nature Reserve, Abigail Fraeman at NASA, Sue and Julian Perry, Adrian Rundle, Katharine Sawyer, Professor David Sear, Steve Simmons, and David Waterhouse at Norfolk Museums.

As ever, I am indebted to friends and family who read or listened to early drafts and chapters, and offered their thoughts and encouragement: Pamela Dearing, Tony Harcup, Sue Lord, Lois Wakeman, Mandy Walker, Amelia Wise, Saan, Joe and my mum. Thanks also to friends for everything from insightful conversations, contacts and local knowledge to a bed for the night or a spot to park the van: Jo Atherton, Ashley Bussell, Dave Atkin, Laurie Harpum, Tessa Jackson, Jo Jolly, Nigel Judge, Sarah McCartney, Carl Sayer, Gillian and Tricia Scott, Derek Spooner and Mandy Walker.

Gratitude also to those who helped me reach places that at times seemed inaccessible: James in Devon, Brian, Anthony and Finbar in County Clare, and my friend Carl Thorne – for the lost-wallet loan that got me home from Spurn. Time and again, I also benefitted from the kindness of strangers.

Most of all I am grateful to my family. To my mum and dad for their support in so many ways, and to my husband and children: for their love, curiosity and humour, and for coming along for the ride.

Note on Images

Page xii: Photograph of Goodwin Sands by Pete Watson, 2022.
Page 20: Map from Clement Reid, *Submerged Forests*, 1913.
Page 40: Engraving of Blackgang, Isle of Wight, by George Brannon, 1857.
Page 56: Etching of Maud from Worthington G. Smith, *Man, the Primeval Savage* (Edward Stanford, 1894).
Page 93: Figurative map of St Brendan's legendary voyage, 1621.
Page 107: Map from Thomas Johnson Westropp, *Brasil and the Legendary Islands of the North Atlantic: Their History and Fable. A Contribution to the 'Atlantis' Problem* (Royal Irish Academy, 1912/1913).
Page 118: Engraving of Kilnsea Church by Henry Gastineau, 1829.
Page 133: Chart showing Spurn and the Den, from Greenville Collins, *Great Britain's Coasting Pilot. Being a New and Exact Survey of the Sea-Coast of England* (Freeman Collins, 1693).
Page 143: Borth's old palisade sea defences, early 1900s. Postcard from private collection.
Page 159: News pamphlet on the Great Flood of 1607. Frontispiece from William A. Jaggard, *A true report of certaine wonderfull ouerflowings of Waters, now lately in Summerset-shire, Norfolke and other places of England*, 1607 (Cardiff University Special Collections, GW4 Treasures).
Pages 168–9: Postcards showing the loss of All Saints, *c.*1905–19.
Page 175: Illustration from Olaus Magnus, *Historia de Gentibus Septentrionalibus (Description of the Northern People)*, 1555.
Page 207: Illustration from Ulrich Molitoris, *De Laniss et phitonicis mulieribus* (*Concerning Witches and Sorceresses*), 1489.
Page 214: Culbin Sands, contemporary postcard, date unknown.
Page 232: Reverend William Thornber, nineteenth-century photo, photographer unknown.
Page 239: Uncle Tom's Cabin, *c.*1900, contemporary postcard.
Page 253: Hallsands, *c.*1900, contemporary postcard.
Page 264: London Inn after storm damage, 1903, contemporary postcard.

Page 268: Hallsands main street looking south showing storm damage, *c.*1901, contemporary postcard.

Further Reading

Aldhouse-Green, Miranda, *The Celtic Myths* (Thames & Hudson, 2015)

Arnold, John H. and Goodson, Caroline, 'Resounding Community: The History and Meaning of Medieval Church Bells, *Viator*, 43 (2012)

Amkreutz, Luc and van der Vaart-Verschoof, Sasja, *Doggerland: Lost World Under the North Sea* (Sidestone Press, 2022)

Ashton, William, *The Battle of Land and Sea* (W. M. Ashton & Sons, 1909)

——, *The Evolution of a Coast-Line: Barrow to Aberystwyth, and the Isle of Man, With Notes on Lost Towns, Submarine Discoveries, &c.* (E. Stanford, 1920)

Bacon, Jean and Bacon, Stuart, *The Search for Dunwich City Under the Sea* (Segment Publications, 1979)

——, *Dunwich Suffolk* (Segment Publications, 1988)

Bailey, Geoff and others, *The Archaeology of Europe's Drowned Landscapes* (Springer Open, 2020)

Bain, George, 'The Culbin Sands: The Story of a Buried Estate', *Nairnshire Telegraph* (1900)

Blackburn, Julia, *Time Song: Searching for Doggerland* (Jonathan Cape, 2019)

Blass, Tom, *The Naked Shore* (Bloomsbury, 2016)

Borlase, William, *Observations on the Ancient and Present State of the Islands of Scilly* (W. Jackson, 1756)

Bulpit, Rev. W. T., *Historical Notes on the Fylde* (Spring Bros, 1913)

de Burton, Thomas, *Chronicle of Meaux Abbey* (1396)

Canton, William, *A Child's Book of Saints* (J. M. Dent, 1906)

Carew, Richard, *The Survey of Cornwall* (Tor Mark Press, 2000; first published 1602)

Charman, Dan and others, *The Lyonesse Project: A Study of the Coastal and Marine Environment of the Isles of Scilly* (Cornwall Archaeological Unit, 2016)

Comfort, Nicholas, *The Lost City of Dunwich* (Terrance Dalton, 1994)
Cracknell, Basil, *Outrageous Waves* (Phillimore, 2005)
Crawford, O. S. G., 'Lyonesse', *Antiquity* (1927)
Crowther, Jan, *The People Along the Sand – The Spurn Peninsula & Kilnsea: A History, 1800–2000* (Phillimore, 2010)
Daniel, Glyn E., *The Prehistoric Chamber Tombs of England and Wales* (Cambridge University Press, 2013; first published 1950)
Egberts, Linde & Schroor, Meindert (eds), *Waddenland Outstanding* (Amsterdam University Press, 2018)
Eyre, Kathleen, *Sand Grown: The Lytham St Annes Story* (Landy Publishing, 1999)
Finkel, Irving, *The Ark Before Noah* (Hodder & Stoughton, 2014)
Frietag, Barbara, *Hy Brasil: The Metamorphosis of an Island – From Cartographic Error to Celtic Elysium* (Rodopi, Amsterdam, 2013)
Gaffney, Vincent and Fitch, Simon, *Europe's Lost Frontiers* (Archaeopress, 2022)
Gaffney, Vincent, Fitch, Simon and Thomson, Kenneth, *Mapping Doggerland: The Mesolithic Landscapes of the Southern North Sea* (Archaeopress, 2007)
Gardner, Thomas, *An Historical Account of Dunwich* (digitised, Gale ECCO, 2018; first published 1754)
Gattie, George Byng, *Memorials of the Goodwin Sands, and Their Surroundings, Legendary and Historical* (W. H. Allen, 1880)
Goldsmith Carter, George, *The Goodwin Sands* (Constable and Company, 1955)
Gottschall, Jonathan, *The Storytelling Animal* (Mariner Books, 2013)
Green, Matthew, *Shadowlands: A Journey Through Lost Britain* (Faber & Faber, 2022)
Haslett, Simon K. and Willis, David, 'The 'Lost' Islands of Cardigan Bay, Wales, UK', in *Atlantic Geoscience Vol. 58* (2022)
Head, George, *A Home Tour Through the Manufacturing Districts of England, in the Summer of 1835* (John Murray, 1836)
Heaney, Seamus, *Field Work* (Farrar, Straus and Giroux, 1981)
Hutton, William, *A Description of Blackpool in Lancashire Frequented for Sea Bathing* (Pearson and Rollason, 1789)
James, Henry, *English Hours: A Portrait of a Country* (Heinemann, 1905)
James VI of Scotland, *Daemonologie* (digitised, British Library; first published 1597)
Kavanagh, K. E. and Bates, M. R., 'Semantics of the Sea – Stories and Science Along the Celtic Seaboard', *Internet Archaeology Journal*, 53 (2019)

Kingshill, Sophia and Westwood, Jennifer Beatrice, *The Fabled Coast: Legends & Traditions from Around the Shores of Britain & Ireland* (Arrow, 2014)
Kramer, Heinrich, *Malleus Maleficarum* (1487)
Lambarde, William, *A Perambulation of Kent* (1576)
Leary, Jim, *The Remembered Land* (Bloomsbury Academic, 2015)
Lewis, John (Vicar of Minster), *The History and Antiquities Ecclesiastical and Civil of the Isle of Tenet in Kent* (London, 1723)
Lyell, Charles, *Principles of Geology* (John Murray, 1830)
Lyons, Imogen, 'Rising Sea Levels, Fact and Folklore' (MSc dissertation, Lancaster University, 2019)
Magalotti, Conte Lorenzo, *The Travels of Cosmo the Third, Grand Duke of Tuscany* (digitised University College, Cork; first published 1669)
Marsden, Philip, *The Summer Isles* (Granta, 2019)
McNamara, Kenneth J., *The Star-Crossed Stone* (University of Chicago Press, 2011)
Melia, Steve, *Hallsands: A Village Betrayed* (Forest Publishing, 2002)
Milton, Ruth and Milton, Frank, *Sisters Against the Sea* (Halsgrove, 2005)
Norden, John, *A Topographical and Historical Description of Cornwall* (Frank Grahan, 1966; first published 1584)
North, F. J., *Sunken Cities* (Cardiff University Press, 1957)
Nunn, Patrick, *The Edge of Memory: Ancient Stories, Oral Tradition and the Post-Glacial World* (Bloomsbury Sigma, 2018)
——, *Worlds in Shadow: Submerged Lands in Science, Memory and Myth* (Bloomsbury Sigma, 2018)
Ó Floinn, Bairbre, 'The Lore of the Sea in County Clare', *Dal gCais*, 9 (1988)
Parker, Rowland, *Men of Dunwich: The Story of a Vanished Town* (Granada, 1980)
Pethick, John and Lee, Mark, *Spurn: Geomorphological Assessment* (Natural England, 2018)
Pitcairn, Robert, *Ancient Criminal Trials in Scotland* (Bannatyne Club, 1833)
Plath, Sylvia, *Lyonesse* (Rainbow Press, 1971)
Pollington, Stephen, *Leechcraft: Early English Charms, Plantlore and Healing* (Anglo-Saxon Books, 2000)
Reid, Clement, *Submerged Forests* (Adamant Media, 2006; first published 1913)
Roberts, Alice, *The Celts: Search for a Civilisation* (Heron Books, 2016)
Sawyer, Katherine, *Isles of the Dead?* (Archaeopress, 2015)
Sear, David, Bacon, Stuart and others, *Dunwich 2008 Project Report* (Esmée Fairbairn Foundation, English Heritage and Dunwich Museum, 2009)

Sear, David, Murdock, Andy and others, *Dunwich Project Final Report* (English Heritage and others, 2012)

Sear, D. A., Scaife, R. G. and Langdon C., *Touching the Tide* (Southampton University Press, 2014)

Shakeshaft, Peter, *St Annes on the Sea: A History* (Carnegie Publishing, 2008)

Sheppard, Thomas, *The Lost Towns of the Yorkshire Coast* (Mr Pye Books, 1986; first published 1912)

Speight, Sarah, *A Gentlemanly Pastime: Antiquarianism, Adult Education and the Clergy in England,* c.*1750–1960* (University of Nottingham Press, 2011)

Sturluson, Snorri, *Prose Edda* (*c.*1220)

Tanner, Kathy and Walsh, Peter, *Hallsands: A Pictorial History* (Tanner & Walsh, 1984)

Thomas, Charles, *Exploration of a Drowned Landscape* (B. T. Batsford, 1985)

Thomas, R. S., *Collected Poems 1945–1990* (J. M. Dent, 1993)

Thornber, William, *The History of Blackpool and Its Neighbourhood* (Blackpool and Fylde Historical Society, 1985; first published 1845)

——, *Penny Stone; Or, a Tradition of the Spanish Armada* (digitised, British Library, 2016; first published 1886)

Troutbeck, John, *A Survey of the Ancient and Present State of the Scilly Islands* (Goadby and Lerpiniere, 1794)

Walters, H. B., *Church Bells of England* (Oxford University Press, 1912)

Waugh, Edwin, *Rambles in the Lake Country and its Borders* (Whittaker & Co., 1861)

Westropp, Thomas J., *A Folklore Survey of County Clare* (Transactions of the Folk-Lore Society, 1912)

White, Walter, *A Londoner's Walk to the Land's End: and A Trip to the Scilly Isles* (Chapman & Hall, 1855)

Whittle, Peter, *Marina: an historical and descriptive account of Southport, Lytham and Blackpool, situate on the western coast of Lancashire* (Peter and Henry Whittle, 1831)

Wilby, Emma, *Visions of Isobel Gowdie: Magic, Witchcraft and Dark Shamanism in Seventeenth-Century Scotland* (Liverpool University Press, 2010)

Wojturska, Rebecca (ed.), *Haunted Voices: An Anthology of Gothic Storytelling from Scotland* (Haunt Publishing, 2019)

Index

Page numbers in *italics* denote images.